Democratic Reform in
JAPAN

Democratic Reform in JAPAN

Assessing the Impact

edited by
Sherry L. Martin
Gill Steel

LYNNE
RIENNER
PUBLISHERS

BOULDER
LONDON

Published in the United States of America in 2008 by
Lynne Rienner Publishers, Inc.
1800 30th Street, Boulder, Colorado 80301
www.rienner.com

and in the United Kingdom by
Lynne Rienner Publishers, Inc.
3 Henrietta Street, Covent Garden, London WC2E 8LU

© 2008 by Lynne Rienner Publishers, Inc. All rights reserved

Library of Congress Cataloging-in-Publication Data
Democratic reform in Japan : assessing the impact / edited by Sherry L. Martin and Gill Steel.
   p. cm.
  Includes bibliographical references and index.
  ISBN 978-1-58826-581-4 (hardcover : alk. paper)
  1. Democracy—Japan. 2. Japan—Politics and government—1989– 3. Political culture—Japan.
4. Political participation—Japan. I. Martin, Sherry L., 1971– II. Steel, Gill, 1965–
  JQ1681.D46 2008
  320.952—dc22

2007043332

British Cataloguing in Publication Data
A Cataloguing in Publication record for this book
is available from the British Library.

Printed and bound in the United States of America

The paper used in this publication meets the requirements
of the American National Standard for Permanence of
Paper for Printed Library Materials Z39.48-1992.

5 4 3 2 1

Contents

List of Tables and Figures	vii
Foreword, Ikuo Kabashima	xi

1 Introduction
   Gill Steel and Sherry L. Martin — 1

Part 1 The National Level

2 Reforming the Liberal Democratic Party
   Ellis S. Krauss and Robert Pekkanen — 11

3 Campaign Behavior: The Limits to Change
   Dyron Dabney — 39

4 Diet Members and Seat Inheritance:
   Keeping It in the Family
   Naoko Taniguchi — 65

5 Policy Preferences and Party Platforms:
   What Voters Want vs. What Voters Get
   Gill Steel — 81

6 Reforming the Bureaucracy
   Eiji Kawabata — 101

Part 2 The Local Level

7 Keeping Women in Their Place:
   Penetrating Male-dominated Urban and Rural Assemblies
   Sherry L. Martin — 125

8	Prefectural Politics: Party and Electoral Stagnation *Robert J. Weiner*	151
9	The Potential and Limits of Antiparty Electoral Movements in Local Politics *Robin M. LeBlanc*	175
10	Civil Society and Democracy: Reforming Nonprofit Organization Law *Yuko Kawato and Robert Pekkanen*	193

Part 3 Conclusion

11	Contemporary Japanese Democracy *Sherry L. Martin and Gill Steel*	213

List of Acronyms	221
References	223
The Contributors	239
Index	241
About the Book	253

Tables and Figures

Tables

4.1	Victory Rates for Hereditary vs. Nonhereditary Politicians, 1990–2003	70
4.2	Ministerial Experience and LDP Candidates' Performance in the 1996 Lower House Election	73
4.3	The Effect of First- and Second-generation Politicians on the Revenue of Local Governments	74
4.4	The Effect of Second-generation Politicians on the Growth Rate of Local Finances, 1997–1998	75
4.5	Measuring the Impact of Hereditary Seats	79
5.1	Influences on Voting, 1986, 1996, and 2003	98
7.1	Women's Representation on Subnational Assemblies, by Prefecture	136
7.2	Percentage of Seats Won by Opposition Parties vs. Women in the House of Representatives	140
7.3	Percentage of Seats Won by Opposition Parties vs. Women in the House of Councilors	141
8.1	Percentage of Uncompetitive and Competitive Districts, by Number of Viable Losers	155
8.2	DPJ and LDP Shares of Prefectural Assemblies After the April 2007 Elections	158

Figures

2.1	Percentage of Seats Gained in House of Representatives Elections, 1996, 2000, and 2003	18

2.2	Percentage of Total Seats Gained by Type of Seat in the 2003 Election	20
2.3a	Percentage of Seats Gained by Party in the 2005 Election, Single-member District vs. Proportional Representation	31
2.3b	Number of Seats Gained by Party in the 2005 Election, Single-member District vs. Proportional Representation	31
2.4	LDP vs. DPJ Votes Obtained in Tokyo Single-member Districts, Election Years 2000, 2003, and 2005	32
3.1	Politicians' Evolving Campaign Behavior, 1993, 1996, and 2000	56
3.2	Scale for Direct Mobilization Strategy and Indirect Mobilization Strategy	60
4.1	Proportional Changes of Second-generation Members of the House of Representatives Among Parties, 1958–2000	67
4.2	Victory Rates for Second-generation Candidates Running for the First Time	71
5.1	Voters' Perceptions of Parties' Ideologies vs. Position of Median Voter, 1967, 1983, and 1996	85
5.2	Lower House Diet Members' Ideological Self-placements, 1998–2005	86
5.3	Lower House Diet Members' Ideological Self-placements, 2005	87
5.4	Percentage of Citizens Who Consider Policy Issues in Their Vote Choice	90
5.5	LDP and DPJ Politicians' Policy Preferences, 2003	91
5.6	Coding and Sources of Variables	95
7.1	Women's Representation on Subnational Assemblies	126
7.2	Women Elected by Proportional Representation vs. Multimember Districts in the House of Councilors	143
7.3	Opposition Party Victories by Proportional Representation vs. Multimember Districts in the House of Councilors	144
8.1	Prefectural Assembly Election Closeness Ratios, by Election Cycle	154
8.2	Simulation: More Underdogs in a District Yield More Viable Candidates	161
8.3	Strongest Underdogs Given Random Distributions of Expected Votes	162
8.4	Simulated District Closeness Ratios	164
8.5	Simulated District Closeness Ratios Given One Sincere Entrant	165
8.6	Prefectural Assembly Election Closeness Ratios, by Seat Magnitude	168
8.7	Prefectural Election Closeness Ratios, by District Urbanness	169

10.1	The Number of Nonprofit Organizations After the NPO Law	199
10.2	The Number of Nonprofit Organizations, by Category	201
10.3	Breakdown of Activities of Civil Society Organizations in Ibaraki Prefecture, 1997	202
10.4	Amount of Policy-related Research Produced, by Group	206

Foreword

THIS WIDE-RANGING AND UP-TO-DATE PROJECT IS A SIGNIFI-cant contribution to the study of Japanese democracy. The authors question many of the clichéd assumptions about Japanese democracy and offer fascinating, sometimes divergent, interpretations that expand our understanding of democracy in the postwar years and offer valuable insights that can help us analyze changes in other mature democracies.

During the postwar period, Japan has maintained a democratic electoral system with free, fair, and regular elections that include a wide and unrestricted variety of competing political parties. And although money politics has been—and remains—a problem, Japan has some of the strictest election campaign laws in the world, intended to reduce the differences in financing among the candidates.

The stability of Japanese postwar democracy has rested on the farmers and small shopkeepers who overwhelmingly backed the Liberal Democratic Party (LDP) and gave it a crucial popular base. In return, the farmers and the middle class benefited from various kinds of patronage. This broad-based, supportive participation admittedly does not fit the citizen-based "town meeting" ideal of democracy. But it helped preserve the democratic system in the period shortly after World War II by softening the divisiveness and tensions among social groups and by moderating demands for radical change that accompanied rapid economic development.

Japan has not been an ideal democracy, and the LDP has generally managed to maintain power through a wide variety of means, both fair and questionable (since mid-1994, the LDP has maintained power as the dominant partner in coalition governments). The choice among candidates, however, is open, and voters have frequently used the ballot in strategic ways to achieve policy change. Even during its heyday, the LDP had to stay somewhat cautious about, and responsive to, public opinion, by enacting policies the public favored in order to win votes that might otherwise have gone to the opposition parties. This balance between single-party rule on one hand, and democratic accountability on the other, has been one of the defining characteristics of the postwar Japanese political system.

The end of the 1955 System and the wide-ranging reforms of the past few decades that culminated in sweeping and comprehensive reforms in the 1990s were intended to fundamentally alter the institutions and clientelist practices of politics in Japan. The answers to the question that drives this book—Have recent electoral, administrative, and fiscal reforms affected Japanese democracy?—are vital to augmenting our understanding of postreform political processes in Japan, and democratizing countries generally.

The chapters offer a wide range of perspectives on the influence of the reforms at various levels of government, ranging from macro discussions of electoral reform and the political process to micro case studies of campaigns and local nonparty and independent candidates. Most of the volume concentrates on electoral politics, but these chapters are supplemented by discussions of the reforms' impact on the bureaucracy, civil society, and women's participation in the political process, offering additional insight into the democratic implications of the reforms.

One of the great strengths of this project is that the authors do not attempt to provide a simple "one-size-fits-all" answer to the central, complex question of whether the reforms have deepened democratic practices in Japan. Instead, they provide nuanced arguments about how some aspects of democracy are strengthened by a particular change, while others are unaffected. We are left with a more realistic picture of the full range of democratic possibilities and how the crucial measures of reform on which the authors focus—representation, responsiveness, and accountability—demonstrate that democratic realities are more complex in practice than in theory.

—*Ikuo Kabashima*
Governor, Kumamoto Prefecture

Democratic Reform in **JAPAN**

CHAPTER 1

Introduction

Gill Steel and Sherry L. Martin

THE RECENT WAVE OF DEMOCRATIZATION WORLDWIDE HAS provoked a fresh round of theorizing about the importance of institutional arrangements in providing a foundation for democratic consolidation and long-term stability. To foster widespread citizen support and participation, democratic institutions must be responsive enough to citizens' demands to produce political and economic outcomes that are in line with their expectations (Pacek and Radcliff 1995; Rose, Shin, and Munro 1999; Levi 1998). Since most of the world's sovereign states are now democracies, there is a growing scholarly focus on identifying the institutional mechanisms that make democracy work better, and on how improvements can be encouraged and measured (Diamond and Morlino 2004, 128).

Within this context Japan serves as an important case in understanding how democracies in general, and more specifically democracies that are imposed from outside, evolve to achieve better democratic outcomes over time. In this project, we seek to contribute to a large and growing body of work on the role of institutions in deepening the quality of democracy and (re)engaging citizens—attitudinally and behaviorally—in the democratic process. The authors analyze whether the quality of Japanese democracy has changed, and if so for the better, as a result of the electoral and administrative reforms instituted over the course of the past two decades.

Proponents of reforms wanted to halt trends that indicated Japan, like other advanced industrialized democracies, was experiencing a "crisis of democracy" (Crozier et al. 1975). Over a thirty-year period, voting rates declined and collective feelings of trust in government fell even further in a polity where baseline trust was already comparatively low (Flanagan and Richardson 1977; Pharr 1997; Kabashima et al. 2000). Strong ties between

Liberal Democratic Party (LDP) politicians, business leaders, and bureaucrats, once lauded for generating the postwar economic miracle, entangled elites in a web of clientelism and corruption. Both LDP and opposition politicians were involved in a series of highly publicized scandals, highlighting the lack of accountability in the system (Pharr and Putnam 2000).

This took a toll on citizens' attitudes about and participation in the political system. From the early 1990s, Japanese citizens became further alienated from the political process amid a prolonged recession. In 1993, the year prior to electoral reform, only 23 percent of citizens claimed that they were satisfied with contemporary politics (ASSK Lower House Election Survey 1993). By the mid-1990s, monthly polls conducted by the *Yomiuri Shimbun* revealed that the percentage of voters unaffiliated with any party began to exceed 50 percent of the electorate. Voters, especially those in urban districts, were increasingly disengaged from the political process as it became abundantly clear that rural support helped to return the party to power even as its percentage of the overall national vote continued to decline (Tanaka 2003). The LDP translated less than a majority of votes into a majority of Diet seats. Lack of feasible alternatives at the poll sustained the view that parties had become less responsive to voters over time (Kabashima et al. 2000).

The LDP lost its overall majority in the July 1993 Lower House election following the scandals, and opposition parties managed to cobble together a coalition government (some LDP politicians left the party and formed new opposition parties). This government enacted a wide-ranging series of reforms that made the processes of government more accessible and transparent and armed citizens with the tools to hold officials accountable. In effect, the reforms were aimed at producing a freer, fairer, and more open political system.

Though reform of the Japanese electoral system in 1994 has attracted the bulk of academic attention as the "master key" to unlocking changes that would fundamentally alter the political terrain in coming years, electoral reform was only one of several pieces of legislation that profoundly altered the system of administration and changed the overall practice of governance. This shift began with reforms pursued by the administrations of Yasuhiro Nakasone (1982–1987), Ryutaro Hashimoto (1996–1998), and then Junichiro Koizumi (2001–2006). Recent work has focused more on government reforms after the economic bubble burst, but the Nakasone reform initiated efforts to strengthen the premiership, alter the balance of power between elected politicians and career bureaucrats, privatize public corporations, and delegate more responsibilities for social service provision to the private sphere.

Electoral reform was preceded by the Administrative Procedural Law (1993) that requires the government to open the process of administrative guidance—informal directives issued by government ministries to private sector actors—to the public, thus increasing transparency and accountability. It was followed by the Revised Political Funds Regulation Law (1994) to promote fairer and freer competition by reducing the influence of vested business elites. The Law to Promote Decentralization (1995) further devolves the administration of social policy to the local level, and has the potential to increase the value of representation through improving the responsiveness of policymaking at the local level. The Information Disclosure Law (1998) promotes increased accountability by stipulating that the government must disclose official documents that citizens can use in the evaluative process. One researcher has described the changes to information disclosure as having a "nearly revolutionary" impact in enabling citizens to gain access to information and monitor the processes of government (Noble 2005).

The Nonprofit Organization Law (1998) promotes citizens' participation by providing incentives to a growing third sector. The Revised National Administrative Law (1999) and the Revised Diet Law (1999) both increase accountability and representativeness by shifting the prerogative of policy proposal and formation to politicians, and away from bureaucrats. To this end, reforms to the government and to the Diet that the parties agreed on include creating new positions in the government, eliminating the government committee member system, and introducing a National Basic Policy Committee (see Takenaka 2002, 143). The reforms also strengthened the position of the prime minister and the Cabinet, and created four "super-*shingikai*" (deliberative consultation councils) within the Cabinet Office, the most important of which (the Council on Economic and Fiscal Policy) has the prerogative to set the direction of the budget and economic policy (Noble 2005, 142).

Japan provides a distinctive "natural experiment" for researchers interested in the changing quality of democratic representation and participation against the backdrop of institutional change. Japan scholars are in the enviable position of being able to examine the system before and after reforms to assess the extent to which the reforms have produced a qualitative change in institutional performance and voters' evaluations of the outcomes. This task is made more complex, however, by the difficulties inherent in "measuring" democracy. As Iris Marion Young observed, democracy cannot be measured in absolute terms, but is a matter of degree with tremendous variation observable across societies in the breadth and depth of commitment to democratic institutions and norms. However, the norm commonly invoked by those seeking to widen and deepen democratic practices is inclusion (Young 2002, 1355–1356). Legitimacy of democratic institutions and outcomes of policy processes are contingent on whether those impacted by policies are included in decisionmaking processes and are equipped with tools to influence policy outcomes. Some of the new reforms in Japan have the potential to bring citizens back into the political process.

The contributors to this volume use broad definitions of notoriously contested concepts such as representation, responsiveness, and accountability. As Bernard Manin, Adam Przeworski, and Susan C. Stokes note, the only thing theorists agree on is that "representation" implies acting in the interest of the represented (1999, 1312–1314). But clearly, as these authors go on to point out, "interest" is also an ambiguous concept, particularly when interests are in conflict. Our purpose here is not to reach a collective consensus on the meaning of these terms. Yet engagement with this debate is intrinsic to our exploration of changing institutional arrangements and the effects that they have on citizens' and representatives' attitudes and behavior.

The chapters in this volume focus on whether the reforms have improved the quality of democracy, by increasing the representativeness of the system, the accountability of representatives and officials, or by fostering the growth of citizens' grassroots participation. Contributors use different data and methods to evaluate how the reforms have altered the channels that connect citizens and elites at the national and subnational levels. In planning this project, we thought that it would be fruitful to frame individual contributions as a broad conversation about reforms that has not yet achieved a consensus. By encouraging variation in the definition and measurement of concepts central to assessing the quality of democracy, we increase the significance of the common points of convergence and divergence between individual chapters.

The first part of the book focuses on politics at the national level. In Chapter 2, Ellis S. Krauss and Robert Pekkanen situate readers, both newcomers to and long-time observers of Japan, by providing a broad overview of the questions and debates that animated Japanese politics under the so-called 1955 System, detailing the slow erosion of mass support and the consolidation of a new consensus around reform. They discuss elements of the prereform institutional framework that allowed elites to become increasingly insulated from voters over time, assess the extent to which old norms can be altered through the adoption of new rules, and offer insights on the long-term ramifications of electoral reform for democratic practice in Japan.

Krauss and Pekkanen set the course for the following chapters, and evaluate Japanese democracy along four dimensions—representation, accountability, pluralism, and competitiveness. All four dimensions reflect a deep concern with the inclusion of underrepresented interests in Japanese politics. A representative or responsive government adopts policies that are preferred by citizens, an accountable government is one that citizens can sanction on the judgment that officials are not adequately representing them, pluralism reflects the quality and quantity of access points available to different groups, and competitiveness measures change in the likelihood that political outsiders can successfully bring about an alteration in power. This concern with "inclusiveness" is echoed throughout the volume, even as individual authors stress one or more of these initial measures of democratic performance in the postreform period.

"Fairness," tilting the balance of political influence away from business and rural interests toward the average voter to establish a more even playing field, is fundamental to pluralist visions of democracy. In Chapter 3, Dyron Dabney describes how he conducted in-depth case studies of the campaign strategies of a small number of politicians before and after electoral reform to assess the impact of reform on candidates' choices about the balance of direct and indirect mobilization strategies. One candidate explains his reluctance to rely heavily on indirect mobilization strategies that use personal networks, saying that these traditional vote-gathering mechanisms produce a biased sample of the constituency with negative consequences for the quality of representation. If better democracy can be obtained through better campaign processes (i.e., enhanced responsiveness and communication among parties, candidates, and voters during the campaign phase), then the process is inherently less democratic if a broad array of views is not communicated, or views are weighed differently.

Naoko Taniguchi's concern with the large numbers of "hereditary politicians," or political dynasties, at all levels of Japanese politics is rooted in an ongoing debate about the trade-off between descriptive and substantive representation (Chapter 4). The overrepresentation of politicians who have "inherited" their seats—usually from fathers or fathers-in-law—suggests that Japanese democracy falls short on both accounts. Politicians come from backgrounds more privileged than the average citizen and the gap between the experiences of elites and those of citizens is increasing. This has important implications for the quality of the representation of a broad array of substantive interests. If the proportion of hereditary seats declines, this can be taken as a sign of the changing "face" of Japanese politics. In later chapters, Robin M. LeBlanc (Chapter 9) and Sherry L. Martin (Chapter 7) describe who the new entrants to Japanese politics are. Robert J. Weiner, however, suggests that institutional barriers ultimately disadvantage non-LDP candidates (Chapter 8).

Representation is also about "responsiveness," and our concern is whether reforms are altering the connection between citizens and politicians. A classic measure of government responsiveness to citizen interests is the distance between parties' positions on major issues and the position of the median voter. Using public opinion and elite surveys, Gill Steel measures how well voters' perceptions of the ideological positions of the parties, from the 1960s onward, match their own expressed positions to determine whether parties are responsive to the distance between themselves and voters (Chapter 5). Do parties seek to narrow the gap between themselves and voters? Most important, did electoral reforms deliver incentives for parties to more closely approximate the positions of voters? Steel's chapter, in examining both ideological distance between parties and voters and the policy preferences of politicians and voters, provides a comprehensive overview of changes in the nature of policy issues and ideological space over the course of the past forty years in Japanese politics. An important subtext here, and one that emerges in the second half of the book, is that "better" representation is about "choice," and the presence of viable choices reflects new incentives for parties to run more programmatic campaigns.

Despite a voluminous literature devoted to the bureaucracy generated by classic studies of Japan's developmental state (Johnson 1989a, 1995; Calder 1988), there has been a marked decrease in the proportion of work devoted to bureaucratic operations in the postreform period. This is the case even though specific reforms aimed to shift power from an unelected and entrenched bureaucratic elite to elected politicians. In Chapter 6, Eiji Kawabata outlines successive administrative reforms adopted in the periods before and after electoral reform to assess whether democratic change can be attributed to processes that were unleashed earlier, but gained momentum over the course of the 1990s and onward. In this ambitious chapter, Kawabata uses a case study of the Ministry of Posts and Telecommunications (MPT) to work beyond the prototypical question of whether politicians or bureaucrats exercise more power in the policymaking process. He takes us into the power struggle between politicians and bureaucrats to assess whether new norms of bureaucratic responsiveness, accountability, and capability (or effectiveness) have nonetheless emerged from this contentious relationship. Here too, readers are invited to grapple with how "better" democracy is defined and measured from a bureaucratic perspective. In agreement with Krauss and Pekkanen (Chapter 2), Kawabata also concedes that the pace and direction of the administrative reform effort owe much to individual prime ministers' agendas and the choices they make about how to change and wield the resources at their disposal.

The chapters in the second part of the book examine how reform has changed the nature of politics at the local and grassroots levels. An ongoing challenge to new parties and nontraditional actors seeking to influence national-level politics has been the barriers posed by the 1955 System to establishing a nationwide grassroots organization. Fiscal centralization demanded that local politicians rely heavily on the central government to deliver local goods and services that helped them to remain in office. Opposition parties have attained their greatest success where local tax bases are large enough to allow independence from the central government (Scheiner 2005). The LDP gained control of state resources during the early postwar period, and has since used democratic institutions to become further entrenched as the dominant party. Electoral reform, coupled with decentralization, the transfer of agency-delegated functions, and municipal amalgamation, offer new opportunities for previously excluded and underrepresented interests to break into Japanese politics on the ground level.

In Chapter 7, Martin examines the concept of representation in democracy through a close analysis of women's participation in national and subnational government. Women's descriptive representation is fundamental to pluralist notions of democratic practice; a large number of female officials is one measure of inclusiveness and fairness. Rising numbers of women elected to decisionmaking bodies in Japan indicate that voice is being given to women's interests, and that reforms have lowered the traditional barriers to entry that political outsiders faced under the 1955 System. Martin uses the experience of opposition parties in urban and rural Japan as a foil to dominant predictions about the impact of electoral and administrative reforms on the electoral success of political outsiders. Patterns of women's representation across the urban-rural divide and different levels of government suggest that strategies evolved by women in the prereform era put them in a position to maximize the opportunities afforded by institutional and socioeconomic change.

Analysts often associate competitiveness with alterations in power, or at least with a broadening of public appeals by parties in power in order to retain their electoral advantage. In this respect, competitiveness can facilitate greater responsiveness to voters and soften the impact of always supporting the losing team (Anderson and Tverdova 2001). Weiner examines competitiveness in local government elections and asks why they are so uncompetitive (Chapter 8). Why don't strong candidates emerge to challenge LDP dominance? Weiner examines the strategic behavior of opposition candidates to explain continued LDP dominance.

A deeper understanding of the potential for reforms to alter the top-down character of Japanese politics and to provide more access points for democratic participation from the bottom up requires renewed attention to politics at the subnational level. In Chapter 9, LeBlanc asks whether changes in the types of politics practiced and the types of people involved at the local level are enough to change Japanese democracy at the national level. Her participant observation and interviews with two grassroots organizations reveal local patterns of campaigning and elections that are at odds with Dabney's (Chapter 3) findings at the national level. LeBlanc uncovers local innovation in the forms of citizen movements that have emerged in response to perceived "democratic deficits." These new forms of citizen movements have developed organizational styles that reflect their commitment to autonomy and self-determination absent from political styles traditional to rural strongholds. LeBlanc finds that these "critical citizens" are deeply committed to democracy and deeply skeptical of established parties and politicians.

Some reforms have also encouraged the growth of civil society groups, groups that some see as the cornerstone of a healthy democracy. Civil society actors help to hold officials accountable, step in to provide services when the state is unable or unwilling to do so, and are the nuclei of pluralist versions of democracy in which interests compete in a free market. In Chapter 10, Yuko Kawato and Robert Pekkanen analyze whether introduction of the Nonprofit Organization Law (1998) has effectively lowered the barriers faced by nonprofit organizations (NPOs). They assess the extent to which NPOs have a greater impact at the local, rather than national, level. Even so, this law has contributed to the development of civil society in allowing NPOs to flourish. Short-term trends show a significant increase in a broad range of organizations immediately after the loosening of regulations that governed the third sector. Kawato and Pekkanen define the parameters within which we can expect further changes to evolve.

In sum, this volume is the product of a conversation between contributors about the impact of reform on the quality of Japanese democracy. What emerges from this conversation is that, to see change, we must look at the big picture. We cannot narrow our analysis to local or national politics, electoral politics or social movements, rural or urban politics, legislative politics or bureaucratic functions—each provides an important part of our understanding of Japanese democracy as a whole as it moves toward a new equilibrium.

Note

We thank the Society for the Humanities at Cornell University for a grant that made it possible for contributing authors to meet and discuss the issues that produced this volume. We also thank the contributors for their patience, perseverance, and valuable insights. It was our great pleasure to work with them.

PART 1
The National Level

CHAPTER 2

Reforming the Liberal Democratic Party

Ellis S. Krauss and Robert Pekkanen

ALMOST UNNOTICED BY THE FOREIGN MEDIA AND PUBLICS, A major change has occurred in Japanese politics during the past decade. The Liberal Democratic Party (LDP), Japan's ruling party for forty-nine out of the past fifty years, has undergone a profound transformation since the 1994 electoral reform of the House of Representatives and other reforms thereafter. Once a highly decentralized political party led by a comparatively weak leader (the prime minister), the LDP is now more centralized, led by an influential prime minister, and presiding over a transition in the way policymaking occurs (Machidori 2005) and citizens are represented. How did this transformation occur? Why? And what are the implications of this development for the quality of democratic life in Japan? These are the questions we will address in this chapter.

First, we will briefly describe the quality of democracy under the prereform electoral system from 1947 to 1993. Then, we will analyze how the electoral reform of 1994 was a catalyst, but not the sole cause, for this transformation and how the LDP changed, or did not change, as a result of it. Next, we will show how both the changes and constants culminated in the election of September 2005, an election that bodes well as being perhaps the most crucial in postwar Japanese political history. Finally, we will discuss how the results of that election seem to have ushered in a new era for the party, Japanese politics, and Japanese democracy, with attendant tradeoffs in the quality of democracy.

This chapter will primarily focus on four important qualities or dimensions of democracy: representation, accountability, pluralism, and competitiveness. By "representation," we mean how well and equally distributed representation is compared to the people represented. By "accountability," we mean how direct or distant the connections between a representative and his or her constituents are and whether those who represent them make policies responsive to those who elected them, as well as whether such policies respond generally to the preferences of all citizens or to narrow minorities. By "pluralism," we mean the extent to which power is concentrated or shared and divided and whether different interests and ideologies have at least the possibility of participating in government and policymaking. And by "competitiveness," we mean the extent to which those who are political minorities have the chance to bring about alternation in government and become a political majority, thus keeping the ruling party's or parties' "feet to the fire" with the fear of being turned out of office.

It should be noted that there are often trade-offs among and within these dimensions of democracy—no democracy can be perfectly representative, accountable, pluralist, and competitive simultaneously. For example, often a party system that is more accountable and responsive to a broad majority of the electorate can be less pluralist and provide less chance for alternation in government. More perfectly equal representation of political minorities can result in responsiveness to narrower segments of the population.

We focus on these dimensions of democracy because they are the ones most closely intertwined with the role and function of political parties like the LDP. Political parties organize and channel the votes needed for representation, make the policies that determine how well government responds and is accountable to which voters' preferences, and determine to a large extent how much power is concentrated and how likely it is that previously minority preferences will become majority preferences. Though no democracy is "perfect" on all dimensions and there are trade-offs both within each category and across them, these dimensions of democracy remain closely related to the functions of political parties and will enable us to systematically compare across time the changes in the LDP, and the effects of these changes on Japanese democracy in the postwar period.

Democracy, Japanese Style, 1947–1993

The 1955 System

By now, the nature and problems of Japanese politics under the 1955 System after the LDP was formed are fairly well known. A decentralized, but perennial, ruling party governed Japan from 1955 to 1993 with bottom-up policymaking; a weak prime minister; factional dominance in the selection of party and government personnel; specialized veteran Diet members who influenced policies in specific areas and provided lots of pork barrel benefits to their constituents; and attendant problems of corruption, over-represented rural districts, lack of attention to the "median voter," and weak political leadership.

The LDP both emerged out of the specific conditions of postwar Japanese democracy, and came to shape this democracy. The LDP was formed in 1955 by the merger of two smaller parliamentary conservative parties with rivalries among leaders between and within the two who jockeyed for power in the new majority governing party. To determine how the single new leader of the LDP would be chosen, they established a party convention and balloting for the first time. This made it necessary to ensure a loyal following among Diet members, who constituted the majority of votes at the convention, and party leaders began institutionalizing their followers into exclusive factions in the party, the major purpose of which was to help their leader become party president and thus prime minister (Thayer 1969, 16–24). In return, followers gained assistance in accessing party, legislative, and government posts and, because these became the objects of factional bargaining, help in gaining the party's endorsement to run in their election district and funding to mobilize votes.

The latter two advantages of belonging to a faction were not insignificant given the nature of the electoral system from 1947 to 1993. Japan had a relatively unusual single nontransferable vote (SNTV) system whereby three to five candidates (later two to six in select districts) were elected from each medium-sized electoral district. This meant a candidate's main rivals in gaining votes were not the opposition parties' candidates, but rather the endorsed rivals from within the LDP. Japan's Draconian election campaigning rules forbade virtually all contact with voters except during the short campaign period prior to the election and strongly limited advertising of all sorts, leaving candidates few ways to mobilize votes. Because the party could not aid any one of its multiple candidates more than any other in the district—indeed, it did not even have a party branch below the prefectural level—LDP politicians were on their own to find legal (and sometimes not-so-legal) ways to reach voters.

In the latter part of the 1950s, party politicians gradually developed a creative solution—the *koenkai* (candidate personal support organization). Through this private "club" of sorts, usually with several branches, the politician provided social and recreational opportunities for followers in the district, which also allowed him or her to reach them through "noncampaign" speeches and communications. In return, *koenkai* members were expected to turn out and vote at election time, and to mobilize their families, friends, relatives, and neighbors to do so as well. In effect, LDP politicians had created a nonparty, mass-membership political machine in their districts to mobilize a "personal vote" to address the intraparty, multiple-candidate rivalry problem created by the electoral system (Curtis 1971; Ramseyer and Rosenbluth 1993, 23–28; Otake 1998; Yamada 1998). Most likely, the prior existence of party leadership factions had also encouraged and financially supported the creation and expansion of *koenkai* because each faction leader had a vested interest in his faction's follower winning elections in the rivalry with other factions in the same district. In no district did more than one faction have a member.

The LDP politicians soon found other ways to differentiate themselves from the party rivals running in the same district. Some began to specialize in specific policy areas, joining and rising to executive positions within the party's Policy Affairs Research Council (PARC), the main policymaking organ within the party; Diet committees; sub-Cabinet posts; and eventually Cabinet posts in that area. Those who traversed this route and served in the main offices in that sector, especially in the PARC, came to be known as *seisaku zoku* (policy tribes) and had great influence on policymaking within the party, Diet, and government (Sato and Matsuzaki 1986, chaps. 7 and 8; Inoguchi and Iwai 1987; Ramseyer and Rosenbluth 1993, 31–34). An alternate route to differentiation pursued by other LDP politicians was to specialize in building their particular *koenkai* network by responding, often with pork barrel goods, primarily to constituents in one geographic area of the district. Given that it often required only 15–20 percent of the vote in the district to place in the top numbers of winners in that district, this geographic specialization was usually enough to ensure continued incumbency (Tatebayashi and McKean 2002).[1]

All this meant a very decentralized party in which party leaders, including the prime minister, exercised little influence over the key functions of a political party, that is, vote seeking, office seeking, and policy seeking (Strøm 1990). The *koenkai* were the prime means for vote mobilization. Negotiations among factions determined the party's leader, who became the prime minister, as well as Cabinet and other party, legislative, and government positions. The PARC and *zoku giin* (politicians belonging to a specific policy tribe) held great influence over specific sectors' policies. Indeed, despite the many ways that Japanese politics and policymaking formally resembled a "Westminster" parliamentary system of cabinet government, in practice they bore little resemblance to the British model. The prime minister was actually a weak political leader among the industrialized democracies. He was dependent on coalitions with other faction leaders and their chief followers, whom he had to appoint to his Cabinets, to stay in power. The LDP candidates had their own electoral base in their districts and neither party leader nor party image did much to determine their fates. Finally, an expert and influential national bureaucracy made up of the "best and the brightest" graduates of Japan's top universities initiated most policy and, along with the *zoku giin*, it controlled most of the information and expertise related to policymaking. So, aside from being able to put some energy behind selected policy proposals that were already on the agenda, the prime minister had little power (Hayao 1993). Prereform Japan could logically be labeled an "un-Westminster" parliamentary system (Mulgan 2003) with a "leadership deficit" (Mulgan 2000).

The system also provided great incentives for "structural corruption" (Johnson 1995) and "money politics" (Reed and Thies 2001, 382). The *koenkai* cost a fortune to maintain, and faction leaders and individual LDP Diet members were constantly attempting to raise money from business interests, both local and national, to fund these organizations and election campaigns. The decentralized policymaking in the PARC and the policy tribes also meant that politicians in each policy area developed close and mutually beneficial relationships with the interest groups and bureaucracies in their policy area.

Although corruption scandals occasionally became public, as Gill Steel and Sherry L. Martin describe in Chapter 1 of this volume, it was not until the late 1980s and early 1990s when a series of scandals involving top LDP faction leaders so shocked and alienated the public, exacerbated by the almost simultaneous bursting of the economic bubble of the 1980s which plunged Japan into a long structural recession, that pressure for "political reform" became overwhelming. In the pressure for reform, the electoral system, rightly or wrongly, had come to be the main target of attention and criticism. It was blamed for almost all the evils of postwar politics, ranging from the frequent corruption, through the noncompetitive election campaigns that rarely focused on issues and politics, to the dominance of the LDP and the lack of party alternation in government. In 1994, the non-LDP coalition government passed both electoral and campaign finance reform bills before itself breaking apart, allowing the LDP back into power again, although this time for a period in coalition with its former main rival—the Social Democratic Party of Japan (SDPJ), known until 1991 as the Japan Socialist Party (JSP) (Curtis 1999).

Democracy and the 1955 System

Democracy under the 1955 System provided trade-offs to the average voter and citizen. Representation was quite skewed in favor of rural voters because of the extreme malapportionment. Voters were not equal at all as it generally took up to three times as many voters to elect one representative in an urban area as it did in depopulated rural areas. It was diffuse in a formal sense because each voter in a district was ostensibly represented by several Diet members. In actuality, however, representation also was highly concentrated since each Diet member needed to cater to only a narrow portion of the district constituency, generally 15–20 percent, to be reelected (Reed and Thies 2001, 382). Given this actual small number of voters per representative and the mobilization of a personal vote via the *koenkai*, the accountability of representatives to their constituents in terms of constituents having a direct and often personal tie to the representative was quite high and responsiveness to a narrow stratum of voters in the district was also high. Because of the de facto concentration in representation, however, accountability to the voters was quite narrow. The LDP's and even other parties' Diet members responded not to the "median voter" but to narrow functionally and geographically segmented interests in their constituencies, especially to those who were members of their *koenkai* in the geographic part of the district in which they were strong, or to the interest groups in the district that supported them. Nationwide policy was much more responsive and accountable to rural areas than to the majority of the public who lived in urban areas. Corruption based on financial contributions also was common, thus reinforcing the tendency to respond only to narrow interests. Policymaking was segmented too through the LDP's PARC and *zoku giin* system. Broader public interests were often ignored because of this, and also because the main national leader and executive branch—the prime minister and Cabinet—were weak and not very influential in policymaking even within their own party.

In some respects, however, pluralism was fairly wide.[2] There generally were five or more political parties that represented different interests and ideologies. Thus, the LDP was a conservative party representing the largest plurality of voters—a majority in rural areas and a plurality in urban ones—chiefly consisting of agricultural, small business, and managerial interests. Its members represented ideologies that ranged from centrist to far right. The main opposition party, the Socialists, generally was equally divided between urban and rural representatives, but catered to the interests of one large leftist union federation. The support bases of the smaller opposition parties, such as the Komeito party, the Democratic Socialist Party, and the Communist Party, were all urban and represented more moderate leftist labor as well as the more marginal groups in society that the two major parties had ignored. Their ideologies were actually left of center, but often to the right of the most leftist Socialists. This pluralism, however, was quite segmented, as the descriptions above indicate, with each party representing somewhat different societal interests and ideologies and little cross-cutting commonalities across the parties (Muramatsu and Krauss 1987, 536–554). The intra-LDP pluralism of the powerful factions and *zoku* (policy tribes) also effectively served, to some extent, as a check on excessive concentration of power within a perennially ruling party with party discipline in Parliament (Thayer 1969, 55).

Finally, the system was not very competitive. The opposition Socialists could count on never taking power unless the LDP split because, even if they formed a coalition with all the other opposition parties (unlikely because of their ideological differences), they would not have a majority of seats given malapportionment and the advantages that the system gave to the largest party. The LDP therefore became the perennial ruling party and always had the option of taking a more moderate opposition party into coalition, further isolating the Socialists as a major opposition party in perpetual opposition (Curtis 1988, 117–156).

Democracy, Japanese Style, 1994–Present

The 1994 System:
Changing Representation and the Party System

The new 1994 electoral system, with its first election held in 1996, was a mixed-member district system (Curtis 1999). It provided for two separate types of voting and representation. One was a single-member district system similar to US congressional elections and British parliamentary elections in which the voter casts one ballot for individual candidates and only one representative is elected per local district, with "the first past the post" winning. Three hundred representatives were elected by this method. The other 200 (later reduced to 180) in the House of Representatives were elected by a proportional representation system somewhat similar to some European democracies. In the Japanese version, which was regionally based rather than nationally, the country was divided into eleven separate regions and voters in each region cast one ballot for a political party rather than a candidate. The parties prior to the election rank ordered their candidates in each region and the number of candidates from the list that went to the Diet reflected the proportion of votes for the parties in that region (Reed and Thies 2001, 383).

This type of mixed-member electoral system that combines the single-member district system with proportional representation has become one of the most popular in the world. Some countries such as Germany have had it for some time, but many other countries have recently moved to some variation of it, including New Zealand and Italy like Japan in the mid-1990s, as well as Venezuela, Lithuania, Russia, and, in the near future, Taiwan (Shugart and Wattenberg 2001a, 2001b).

The Japanese variety of the mixed-member system, however, had its own unique quirks. It was not a mixed-member proportional system such as in Germany and New Zealand where the total number of seats is adjusted to proportionally reflect the votes cast for each party in proportional representation, but rather the two parts were almost completely separate with no proportionality ensured. But more uniquely in Japan, candidates running in the single-member district portion could also be listed on their party's proportional representation list, and parties could rank several candidates equally at the same rank. Winners in single-member districts would take their seats from that portion of the system and have their names taken off their party's list. If the party received a smaller proportion of votes than that required to elect everyone at the same rank, in the LDP the double-listed losers in their single-member district but winners in proportional representation would be decided by whoever received the highest proportion of votes compared to the winner in their losing single-member district bid. In effect, this system allowed many proportional representation winners to "rise from the dead" after losing their single-member district race in their local district and become Diet members. Thus, they were called "zombie" representatives.

As noted above, the LDP came back into power in 1994 and during the next decade, four elections were held under the new system—in 1996, 2000, 2003, and 2005. As can be seen in the seat results by party of the 1996, 2000, and 2003 elections shown in Figure 2.1, although the LDP never attained a majority of seats in any period, it did come close and managed to retain its status as the largest and governing party by taking one of the smallest parties (since 2000 that party has been the New Komeito) into coalition with it.

Figure 2.1 also indicates other consequences of the electoral reform and

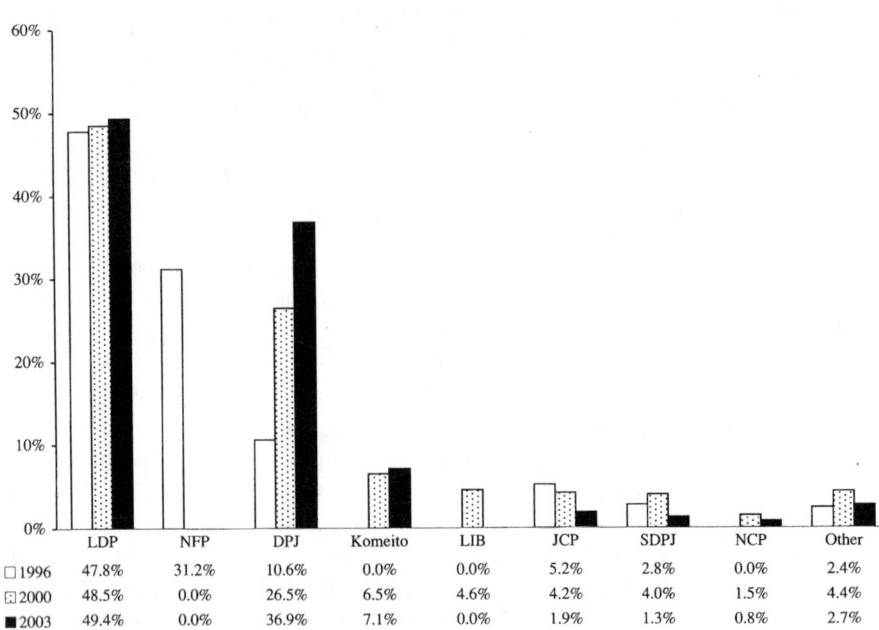

Figure 2.1 Percentage of Seats Gained in House of Representatives Elections, 1996, 2000, and 2003

	LDP	NFP	DPJ	Komeito	LIB	JCP	SDPJ	NCP	Other
□ 1996	47.8%	31.2%	10.6%	0.0%	0.0%	5.2%	2.8%	0.0%	2.4%
▨ 2000	48.5%	0.0%	26.5%	6.5%	4.6%	4.2%	4.0%	1.5%	4.4%
■ 2003	49.4%	0.0%	36.9%	7.1%	0.0%	1.9%	1.3%	0.8%	2.7%

Source: Scheiner (2006).

the nature of the new system. The hybrid electoral system provides both centripetal and centrifugal incentives for political parties. On the one hand, the single-member district portion with its need for a plurality of votes in a district to take the one seat makes it quite difficult for smaller parties to survive unless they merge to form a larger party, and thus encourages limited, perhaps even two-party, systems to emerge. On the other hand, proportional representation provides incentives to smaller parties to exist and gain representation, perhaps even a place in a governing cabinet if a coalition government is required, and with the proportional representation portion tacked on to the single-member district, a coalition government is actually likely. Thus, this portion of the system encourages parties to retain their independent identity and not to merge with others, tending to promote a multiparty system.

With these contrary incentives of the system, it is little wonder that periodically we find postreform smaller parties amalgamating (thus the New Frontier Party [NFP] and Democratic Party of Japan [DPJ] in Figure 2.1 were formed from mergers of other smaller parties), but also splitting off from larger parties (thus the New Komeito and Social Democratic Party of Japan [SDPJ], the former Socialists, were reformed after the New Frontier Party split up, and the Liberals [LIB] and New Conservative Party [NCP] were formed from party splits as well) (Scheiner 2006, 42–45; Reed and Thies 2001, 386–390).

Figure 2.1 also underscores the declining relevance of the left. Neither the SDPJ nor the Communists today remain viable forces in politics even though they cling to existence. This is to be expected given the fact that nearly two-thirds of the seats in the Diet are now single-member districts, which means smaller parties can survive only by winning a portion of the minority proportional representation seats. This is shown clearly in Figure 2.2, which gives the percentage of seats each party obtained in each of the two types of districts in the 2003 election. The two largest parties acquired between three-fifths (DPJ) and almost three-quarters (LDP) of their seats from single-member districts, but the smaller parties, with the exception of the NCP, attained over three-quarters of their seats from proportional representation. Previous elections since reform, in 1996 and 2000, showed similar patterns. The NCP was a microparty with only a handful of members who had broken off originally from the LDP and who continued to be dependent on the *koenkai* in their single-member districts for votes. The NCP has disbanded in the past few years.

The dual-listing provision of the new system combined with the choice of both parties to dual-list most of their candidates has added another interesting wrinkle to the consequences of electoral reform. Most candidates even in the LDP (over three-quarters) and DPJ (close to or over 90 percent) in the first three elections after reform who won a majority of seats in sin-

Figure 2.2 Percentage of Total Seats Gained by Type of Seat in the 2003 Election

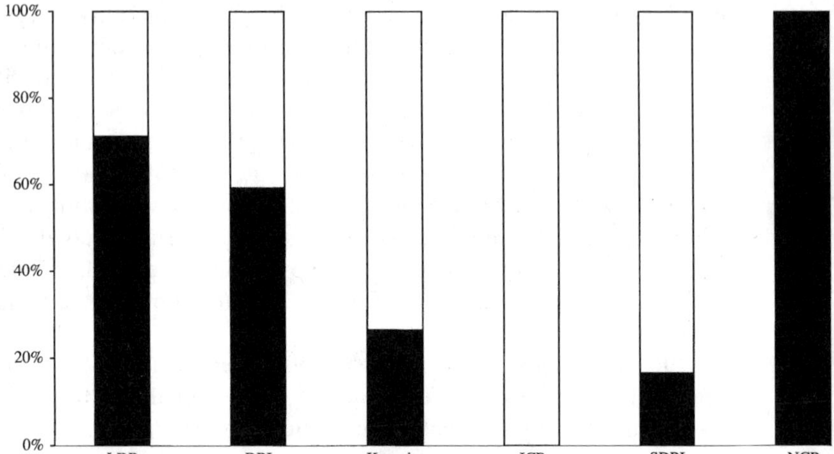

	LDP	DPJ	Komeito	JCP	SDPJ	NCP
☐ proportional representation	28.8%	40.7%	73.5%	100.0%	83.3%	0.0%
■ single-member district	71.3%	59.3%	26.5%	0.0%	16.7%	100.0%

Source: Various newspaper reports at the time of the election.

gle-member districts were dual-listed. This means that many of even the proportional representation representatives are failed single-member district candidates. In 1996 and 2000, a bit over two-fifths of all proportional representation representatives were "zombies," but in 2003 that component increased to almost two-thirds (63 percent) (McKean and Scheiner 2006).

Further, as Robert Pekkanen, Benjamin Nyblade, and Ellis S. Krauss (2006) have found in their study of how the LDP distributes party, parliamentary, and government posts after reform, such "zombie" representatives are given more than their share of pork barrel offices to facilitate a win in their single-member district constituency next time around. As predicted by Margaret A. McKean and Ethan Scheiner, the dual-listing provision, with its attendant large number of "zombie" winners, has transformed proportional representation candidates into single-member district candidates-in-waiting who are oriented to their constituents in local districts rather than fostering a transition toward a broader party that incorporates a wider range of interest groups and policy appeals as might be expected in a pure proportional representation system (2000, 447–477).

Also predicted by McKean and Scheiner, although nominally still a multiparty system, the new electoral system de facto is tending toward a two-party system due to the preponderance of single-member districts out of the total as well as the single-member district orientation of the "zombie" winners (2000, 447–477). The competition rate averages less than 3.0 candidates per district (2.4 or so in 2003) and is declining. If we exclude the Japan Communist Party's (JCP) single-member district candidates,[3] the candidate:seat ratio in 2003 was actually *less* than 2:1. Thus, as Maurice Duverger argued in his famous "law" (1954), single-member district electoral systems tend to promote two-party systems. But if the single-member district is tending toward a two-party system, it is one with a twist. Over one-third of single-member district constituencies in 2003 had both a single-member district winner and a "zombie" winner from that district, which means in effect that these are multimember districts (McKean and Scheiner 2000, 2006).

In terms of the ideological diversity of the party system, the largest opposition party is now the DPJ, a center party that on some issues—security and defense—is slightly left of the LDP but divided, and on some issues—deregulation and liberalization of the economy—slightly right of the LDP (Schoppa 2001). Therefore, as we have seen, larger parties like the LDP and DPJ are both centrist and gain most of their seats from single-member districts. The New Komeito is also centrist but, as shown in Figure 2.2, gets its seats from the regional proportional representation portion, mostly from urban areas. Thus, while the party system is now more representative of "the median voter" as the major parties are both in the center, far rightist voters' views are incorporated into the more "catchall" LDP and leftist voters' views are somewhat marginalized.

The type of appeals candidates and parties now make to mobilize the vote has changed because the "median voter" is now targeted more by the parties' mobilization efforts, and the sole representative in single-member districts now has to cater to a wider diversity of constituents than under the old SNTV system where only 15–20 percent of the vote was enough to ensure (re)election. Instead of only a personal vote mobilized mostly by some combination of constituent services, personal ties, and delivery of pork barrel goodies to the district, these continuing electoral techniques are now also joined by an emphasis on policy and issue appeals. In the 2003 election, the opposition DPJ appealed to voters by emphasizing its newly published "manifesto" or party platform in advance of the election, a gambit so popular that the LDP and other parties were forced to emulate it. This was one of the original aims of the reformers in the 1990s—to have election competition based more on parties and issues than on individual candidates' appeal, personal favors, and concrete benefits to a narrower portion of the district's voters. Whether these appeals have actually influenced voters' choices or not is another question, as Gill Steel shows in Chapter 5.

Malapportionment was reduced by the new electoral boundaries set for the smaller single-member district constituencies. Instead of voter:seat ratio approaching 3:1, the standard under the 1955 System, the disparity was reduced to 2:1. During the first few years after reform, it began to creep back up again until the Lower House disparity reached over 2.6:1.0. At that point, however, the Diet redistricted to bring it back down to 2.1:1.0 again in 2002 ("Package of Redistricting Bills Approved by Lower House" 2002). Japan's electoral system was now fairer to urban and suburban dwellers than previously, but still not equal in representation to rural residents.

Postreform: A More Influential Prime Minister

The new electoral system provided some of the resources that a skillful prime minister could use to enhance his previously weak power. First, because of the proportional representation portion of the system, voters now cast ballots for the party and not just individual candidates as in the single-member district portion. This meant that the image of the party leader acquired greater importance. And this was even true, if to a lesser extent, in the single-member district portion. With only one representative per district, the image of the individual candidate from each party became more entangled with the party that the candidate represented in the district. So, too, did the potential influence of the party leaders, including the prime minister, increase within the party. Proportional representation candidates now owed their ranking on the party list to the party leaders, and the electoral fortunes of both types of candidates were tied more than before to the party leader's image. Further, as described below, the electoral reform weakened, but did not destroy factions. This meant that one of the chief obstacles to more centralized leadership in the party had been lessened.

The new electoral system, however, was only one of several factors that were contributing by the turn of the century to a more influential role for the LDP prime minister and party leader. Another was administrative reforms that began to be implemented in 2001. These reforms were designed to enhance the power of politicians vis-à-vis bureaucrats, and the power of the prime minister and Cabinet in policymaking. Thus, the Cabinet staff was increased, Cabinet-level councils were established to advise the prime minister on important policy areas to lessen his dependence on the bureaucracy, and for the first time he was given the legal right to initiate policy proposals within the Cabinet (Shinoda 2000, 45–122; see also Kawabata's discussion in Chapter 6 this volume).

Finally, but of importance, there was one noninstitutional factor that had consequences for the party and its leader: the increasing influence of television over voters. The trend began in the early 1980s under the 1955 System. Prime Minister Yasuhiro Nakasone (1983–1987) was the first to recognize that television could be a means for the weak executive to offset the power of factions by appealing directly to the public via this mass medium. He used it to portray an image of an effective leader in domestic, and especially foreign affairs. He thus gained personal popularity among the public and, despite his weakness as the leader of one of the LDP's smaller factions, made himself indispensable to the party. Partly for this reason, Nakasone stayed in office five years, much longer than most of the prime ministers immediately preceding him or his successors, and even had the party give him a one-year extension on the limit of two two-year terms placed by the LDP on its president (Muramatsu 1987, 219–221).

Prime ministers for almost the next decade and a half varied greatly in both their ability and inclination to use the media. But gradually a pattern developed whereby the most successful leaders were those who could and did use the media, and those who couldn't or didn't did not last long. This was reinforced by the rise of a new brand of commercial television news that focused more on individual politicians than the bureaucracy and policy-making (Krauss 1998). Prime ministers like Noboru Takeshita (1987–1989), Kiichi Miyazawa (1991–1993), and Yoshiro Mori (2000–2001) were in the old-fashioned mold of backroom faction leaders, whereas those like Morihiro Hosokawa (1993–1994) and Keizo Obuchi (1998–2000) managed the media much better. Hosokawa, a young, popular, handsome former LDP politician from one of Japan's oldest political families, especially understood how the media worked from his days as a newspaper reporter. He used television to gain great popularity even as the leader of a disparate coalition of opposition parties who passed the electoral and campaign finance reform bills of 1994 during his brief ten months in office.

However successful or unsuccessful these prime ministers were, the growing importance of television separated the personal image of the prime minister from the party image for the first time (Krauss and Nyblade 2004). One continued to influence the other of course and when the popularity of one declined precipitously, so did the other. Nonetheless, for the first time in the postwar period, the LDP party leader was no longer perceived by the voters as only the creature of the party and its factional alignments—he had a distinct image that began to also influence the way people voted (Krauss and Nyblade 2004). And changes in LDP party rules in the 2001 election of the party leader to incorporate more grassroots party participation in the decision further reinforced the salience of party leader image.

The prime minister in whom these trends converged and culminated was Junichiro Koizumi (2001–2006). He came to power in 2001 as a result of the change in party rules. Not the leader of a faction (although a high-ranking member of the Mori faction), he used his iconoclastic personal image to build his popularity via television, becoming the highest rated prime minister in history with over 80 percent support for his Cabinet soon after taking office. Koizumi strengthened the connection between the party's fortunes and his personal image and program of "reform," and was the first prime minister to be able to use the policy councils created by administrative reform. Unlike the other predictions about the consequences of electoral reform, the enhanced potential for influence of the prime minister was barely commented on, but was to prove crucial to the transformations of Japanese democracy that were taking place.

Postreform: Organizational Continuity in the LDP

If the consequences of the new electoral system might have been predicted (and often were) by the nature of the system and its specific Japanese "zombie" variation, and trends like the greater influence of the prime minister were barely acknowledged, other predictions made in the first decade after electoral reform proved to be unfulfilled.

Some political scientists as well as some reformers expected that many organizational characteristics of LDP politics under the prior system would disappear because their existence was attributed solely to the nature of the SNTV electoral system. For example, *koenkai*, factions, and the specialization of Diet members in specific policy areas leading to the importance of *zoku* were all predicted to virtually disappear (citations found in Krauss and Pekkanen 2004).[4]

After a few years, and even a decade after the reform, it was clear that these predictions had not been fulfilled. The *koenkai* continued to exist and showed few signs of diminution. Indeed, during the two years between the passage of the electoral reform bill and the first election under the new system, several Diet members tried to "trade" *koenkai* members when the new boundaries placed their members in different districts. In Chapter 3 of this volume, Dyron Dabney also indicates that campaign styles reverted back after the first (1996) election.

Factions did appear to weaken. Indeed, Prime Minister Koizumi's reelection as LDP president in 2004 made it clear that factions no longer commanded the loyalty and discipline that they once had as some factions split on who they supported. Further, even Koizumi made a point of not appointing his Cabinet based on the factional balance or proportionality that had been the norm under the 1955 System. Diminished importance, loyalty, and discipline, however, did not mean that factions disappeared. Koizumi distributed sub-Cabinet posts (vice-ministers and secretaries) according to faction norms and factional representatives continued to control who was appointed to party and legislative posts.

Finally, *zoku giin* were still around and important even ten years after the reform. Indeed, many of Koizumi's major attempts at reform (such as the privatization of the highway system) were constantly resisted by *zoku* in these areas, which forced Koizumi to compromise his reform bills to get even a watered-down version through his own party before introducing them to the Diet.

As we have argued elsewhere, the reasons why the expected consequences of the new electoral system did not materialize are varied (Krauss and Pekkanen 2004). In the case of *koenkai*, for example, the maintenance of these organizations among LDP politicians seems to have been a question of "path dependence." The heavy prior investment and "sunk costs" of *koenkai* for LDP politicians under the prior system, and continuing or even "increasing returns" under the new system, meant that *koenkai* could continue to perform useful functions or be adapted to new ones given the fresh incentives of the newly introduced mixed-member system (Pierson 2004, 17–53).

In the new single-member district portion, for example, there was still a need to mobilize a personal vote with the continuation of highly restrictive campaign rules and as voters still voted for individuals in the single-member district portion. Further, with only one representative per district, a majority or at least wider plurality of votes was needed than under SNTV where the candidate could win by catering to a small segment of the district's voters. Consequently, it was usually necessary to gain the votes of even those who disliked the LDP. These voters might cast their ballot for other parties in the proportional representation portion but since most of the other parties except the DPJ had little chance of winning in most single-member district constituencies, they might still vote for the LDP candidate if they liked him, had a personal connection to him, or he could bring benefits to the district. Another indication of the continued importance of the personal vote is the continued success of hereditary candidates even after reform, as Naoko Taniguchi discusses in Chapter 4. Thus, although the number of *koenkai* and the financial resources available to them might have been weakened by reform (Carlson 2006), the *koenkai* remained a useful way to mobilize voters that the local party branch could not employ.

In the case of *zoku giin*, although the new electoral system put more of a premium on "generalist" single-member district representatives since they had to cater to the wider diversity of voters in the local district, the party continued to require specialists to produce policy after elections and the party's PARC divisions over time trained such specialists. As long as the party maintained a seniority system for attaining executive positions on these PARC divisions, and the party's rules required all legislation to be submitted to, discussed, and passed by them prior to going to the Cabinet and Diet, *zoku giin* could continue to have influence on legislation in their sector despite some reduced need for specialization with electoral reform.

Similarly, although factions by and large lost two of the primary functions for their members under SNTV—support for getting the party's district nomination and supplemental funding to maintain their *koenkai* and run their election campaigns—and thus were greatly weakened in their ability to retain loyalty and discipline among members, they continued to perform other important party functions for their members. Most significant was their lock-hold on the distribution of party posts below the Cabinet level. Such positions were allocated by bargaining among those who were essentially representing the party's different factions. If a Diet member wished to advance in his party and legislative career and attain important positions in terms of influence over policy and prestige, he or she had to belong to a faction. Those who did not were given the dregs of the party and legislative assignments after faction members were catered to.

Factions also retained their utility to the party as a means of organizing communication between party leaders and backbenchers and vice versa about policy and party strategy, and as a means to bargain over party leadership. In a governing party the size of the LDP with over 400 representatives, some means of vertical communication among smaller groups would have been necessary in any case. Although factions were not the only way that this might have been done, factions had always performed this function in the past.

In short, some of the forecasts about the consequences of electoral reform failed to allow for three important considerations. First, the particular form of Japan's new electoral system and the fact that it was being grafted onto organizations that had developed under the previous system would result in different consequences than if the single-member district and proportional representation systems had been de nouveau. Second, existing organizations such as *koenkai* could be and were adapted to reflect the new incentives that representatives confronted. Finally, as in Kaare Strøm's classic formulation of the goals of political parties, the parties were not just vote-seeking organizations, but also office- and policy-seeking organizations (Strøm 1990, 569–598; Müller and Strøm 1990). Thus, the PARC and policy specialists like *zoku giin* and factions might be weakened but nonetheless continue because of the non-vote mobilization goals of the LDP.

The 2005 Election

All of the trends above, the changes in party and electoral politics wrought by the 1994 electoral reform, the potential for the improved importance and influence of the prime minister, and the sometimes surprising persistence of 1955 System patterns of LDP organizational and behavioral continuity were all to converge in the September 11, 2005, general election. Indeed, their convergence and the exposure of contradictions is the story of this crucial election.

The origins of this election go back to Prime Minister Koizumi's desire to pass his most-preferred reform legislation: postal privatization. For over twenty years, Koizumi had been committed to the idea of reforming the vast postal services area. This involved much more than a desire to improve the delivery of mail and packages to residents. The postal system in Japan encompasses three parts: mail delivery, postal savings, and postal insurance. The latter two were massive and financially significant, with postal savings alone constituting the world's largest financial institution. For years the Ministry of Finance, which regulates banks, had seen postal savings as a favored institution that put private banks on an unequal competitive footing. Until Koizumi, few political leaders had ever tampered with this sacrosanct institution to back the ministry's and banks' desire to reform postal savings and postal insurance.

Perhaps one reason reform of the postal system never had much political support was because of the advantages that LDP politicians derived from it. Much of postal savings' deposits eventually went into the Fiscal Investment and Loan Program (FILP). This program was something of a "second budget" that allocated its funds to many infrastructural projects, including housing, transportation, and construction—in other words, sectors ripe for pork barrel manipulation by politicians.

Furthermore, within the LDP's PARC, there had grown up a powerful postal *zoku*. Many of these politicians used their influence to appoint part-time local postmasters in rural areas (of which there were thousands) and, in return, the latter would use their influence in the community to mobilize voters for the politician to whom they owed their loyalty and jobs (Maclachlan 2004, 303–313). To complicate matters even more, certain factions of the LDP were known to have more such postal *zoku* politicians than others. This was especially true of the former Tanaka faction that, for a long time, had been the largest in the LDP since the 1970s (Maclachlan, 296–299). Now called the Hashimoto faction,[5] it was the main rival to the Mori faction in which Koizumi had risen within the LDP. Another resister to postal reform was the Kamei faction, led by Shizuka Kamei. Policy and factional groups internal to the LDP that represented strong vested local interests were opposed to any change to the postal system's delivery or financial components.

Because of the politicized nature of the postal system, one reason for Koizumi's dedication to postal reform may not have been only to improve its economic efficiency, but also to bring about political reform. By breaking up and potentially privatizing the postal system, the aim of the bill Koizumi's government would introduce, Koizumi could simultaneously accomplish both economic and political reform. It would make the system operate more like a private corporation and save the government money. It also could additionally undermine pork barrel spending, and destroy one of the powerful *zoku* in the LDP—it was such *zoku* that previously had been forcing Koizumi to water down earlier reform proposals such as highway privatization. It could also undermine two factions, the Hashimoto and

Kamei factions, which were major rivals to the Mori faction from which Koizumi himself had sprung. Was Koizumi's pushing of postal privatization primarily to bring about economic reform? Political reform? Or, both? Only Koizumi knew for sure, but both types of his interests were aligned in this policy priority for him.

Sure enough, Koizumi's own party was split on the issue and, on July 5, 2005, the reform package barely passed the House of Representatives by only five votes (233 to 228). One reason that the vote was so close was that the opposition DPJ voted against the bill on its details rather than the concept itself, but they were joined by thirty-seven LDP Diet members (Izumi 2005, 42–46). Resistance in the LDP was led by the postal *zoku* as well as by some members of the anti-Koizumi factions. Interestingly, within these groups, there was a curvilinear relationship between becoming a *zōhan* (rebel) and seniority in the party. It appears that junior, electorally secure LDP representatives and more senior, anti-Koizumi LDP representatives were most likely to join in the rebellion, with those of in-between seniority least likely to join. It was exactly those in-between politicians, with careers much more dependent on their access to the key PARC and policy posts in the party, who apparently were reluctant to jeopardize those contacts and consequent advantages to their constituencies and own future by defying the party leadership (Nemoto, Krauss, and Pekkanen forthcoming).

Getting the reform package through the House of Councilors was to prove even more difficult. Koizumi and his ally, the LDP secretary-general Tsutomu Takebe, used both carrots and sticks (or, as the Japanese say, "whips and candy") to try to get it passed, staking the publicly popular Koizumi administration on its passage and stressing the importance of the reform. They also threatened to dissolve the Lower House (the House of Councilors cannot be dissolved by the prime minister as its members serve fixed six-year terms, like the US Senate) and call a general election if the bill did not pass, hoping that House of Representatives' members would put great pressure on their colleagues in the Upper House so as to avoid having to run for election prematurely. Whether they believed Koizumi's threat was a bluff or not, on August 8, 2005, twenty-two LDP members voted against the measure while another eight either abstained or did not show up for the vote and, when combined with other parties' negative votes, this was enough to cause the bill to fail by a surprisingly large margin of 125 to 108 (Foreign Press Center Japan 2005a, 2005b).

Koizumi now faced a difficult dilemma. He could stay in office, but his term as LDP president and thus prime minister would not end until a year later, in September 2006. His lower credibility after losing this vote and his failed promise to punish the "rebels" by dissolving the Lower House would immediately turn him into a very weak and humiliated lame-duck leader. Or, he could take a big gamble and call a general election and kick the rebels out of the party, with no certainty that the LDP and its remaining supporting candidates, along with its much smaller ally and coalition partner the New Komeito, would win enough seats to attain a majority again.

Koizumi gambled despite many in the party, including the former prime minister and Koizumi's mentor and faction leader, Yoshiro Mori, who urged him not to subject the divided party to a risky and potentially devastating election. The Koizumi government's coalition party, the New Komeito, also did not want the election because their normally well-honed electoral machine was not quite ready for a surprise election. Yet Koizumi called an immediate election, saying he would resign if the LDP and New Komeito failed to win a majority. He also lived up to his promise to punish the Lower House "rebels" who had voted against the postal reform bill, even though it passed in that House, and the party refused to nominate them to run as party candidates in the election, effectively kicking them out of the party. Five of the "rebels" decided not to run again, but thirty-two ran as independents, a few even with the support of their local LDP branches who also effectively went into rebellion against the central party. The LDP nominated candidates to run against them (Nemoto, Krauss, and Pekkanen forthcoming). Prior to this point, the decision as to which candidates to nominate in particular districts had been a rather decentralized affair involving factional representatives and local branch bargaining, but now Koizumi (along with his close political adviser, Isao Iijima) and Takebe took the unprecedented step of personally selecting the LDP's candidates in the election (confidential interview, 2005).

Especially among those chosen to run against the "rebels" in their districts, whom the media quickly labeled *shikaku* (assassins), were many accomplished women (whom the media dubbed "Madonnas!"). Some of these candidates already had high media profiles. Yuriko Koike was a popular former television and Arabic-speaking anchorwoman, and Horie Takafumi was a wealthy thirty-something media and Internet entrepreneur. In another surprising move, Koizumi listed a prominent international relations scholar and his ambassador to the disarmament talks in Geneva, but a political neophyte, Kuniko Inoguchi, to the only number one spot on the party proportional representation list in the Tokyo regional district.

The campaign was short, but intense. One dimension of the media coverage focused on each of the two main party leaders, Koizumi and the DPJ's young leader, Katsuya Okada. Okada and the DPJ were delighted with the turn of events. They had done very well in the 2004 House of Councilors election, winning a higher percentage of seats in the proportional representation section of that election than the LDP. Now, the LDP had split and the DPJ sensed the opportunity to finally take power away from the LDP, especially by ignoring postal reform and concentrating on issues like pension reform. Polls showed that the Japanese public, especially urban voters who were the core of the DPJ's support base, cared more about pension reform than postal privatization. So, Okada devoted many of his speeches to a wide range of issues including pension reform, the need for alternation in government, and criticism of Koizumi's record; postal reform remained secondary. Koizumi, however, hammered away at one theme: postal privatization. Newspaper content analyses of his speeches showed that Koizumi devoted over 80 percent of them to that one issue. This pattern repeated itself when all the party leaders met in sponsored debates.[6] Koizumi's focus on postal reform concentrated on three themes to the voters: explaining the need for it, designating the issue as the key to all future reform, and calling on voters to help him fulfill his previous promise to change the LDP (by supporting him and postal reform in this election).

The other dimension of media coverage was its extreme focus on the celebrity matchups of famous "assassins" against the key "rebels," while many other interesting races (particularly, of the DPJ versus LDP) were almost ignored. And finally, there was the paid sponsored advertising competition between the LDP and DPJ—only parties can buy media time, individual candidates cannot under election campaign law. The LDP's television ads were slick and skillfully constructed, portraying Koizumi, the party, and their individual local candidates as reformers. By comparison, the DPJ's ads seemed to lack a central theme and were listless.

As the September 11, 2005, vote neared and the short campaign drew to a close, polls began to show Koizumi's single-minded message of postal reform striking a surprising chord among the urban "floating voters" who normally preferred the DPJ. Polls showed the LDP doing surprisingly well among this strata ("Koizumi Gekijo" 2005, 3). Voter turnout was also up, indicating high interest in the election, especially in large cities ("Sosenkyo 2005" 2005, 2).

Indeed, as newspapers shouted the tabulated results in bold headlines on September 12, even the most optimistic LDP supporters had to have been shocked. The LDP won 296 seats with almost 48 percent of the popular vote, its greatest electoral victory in a quarter of a century and by far its best showing under the new electoral system. It had increased by eighty-four seats from before the election, after the party had been reduced by the loss of the "rebel" representatives, and had even increased by fifty seats since the last election when the "rebels" were part of the party. By contrast, the DPJ was devastated, winning only 113 seats with 36 percent of the popular vote, a fall of sixty-four seats. Sweetening Koizumi's victory was the fact that about half of the "rebels" lost and 80 percent of his "assassins" won election through either the single-member district or proportional representation portions ("Sosenkyo 2005" 2005, 1, 3). As can be seen in Figures 2.3a and 2.3b, the LDP overwhelmingly won single-member districts, but outdistanced the DPJ in proportional representation seats this time. Were it

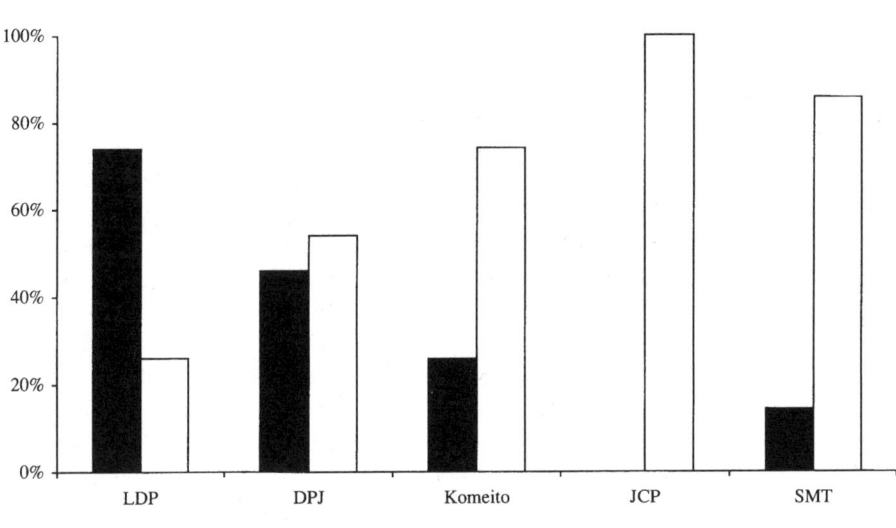

Figure 2.3a Percentage of Seats Gained by Party in the 2005 Election, Single-member District vs. Proportional Representation

■ single-member district　□ proportional representation

Source: Various newspaper reports after the election.

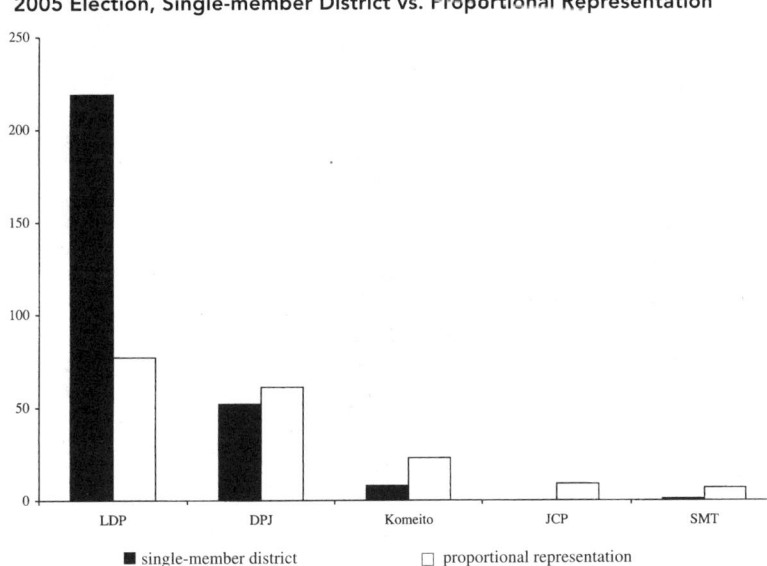

Figure 2.3b Number of Seats Gained by Party in the 2005 Election, Single-member District vs. Proportional Representation

■ single-member district　□ proportional representation

Source: Various newspaper reports after the election.

not for the "zombie" provision of the electoral system, the DPJ would have been even more devastated because many of its losing single-member district candidates remained representatives only by virtue of having been dual-listed in proportional representation districts.

Perhaps the most surprising aspect of the vote was the huge swing to the LDP among urban voters, traditionally their weakest constituency and the DPJ's strength. This is clearly seen in Figure 2.4, which shows the two parties' votes in Tokyo in this election and the two previous election periods. Indeed, one of the major reasons the LDP did so well in this election is that it held on fairly well to its perennial base in rural areas, winning seventy-two seats in the one-third most rural single-member districts, a drop of only five from the previous election (whereas the DPJ maintained only its miserable eleven seats in this group of districts), while greatly increasing its capture of seats in the one-third most urban and the one-third mixed single-member districts. The LDP increased from thirty-three to seventy-eight seats in the urban districts (the DPJ dropped from fifty-nine to eighteen), and from fifty-eight to seventy-five in the mixed districts (the DPJ dropped from thirty-six to twenty-three).[7]

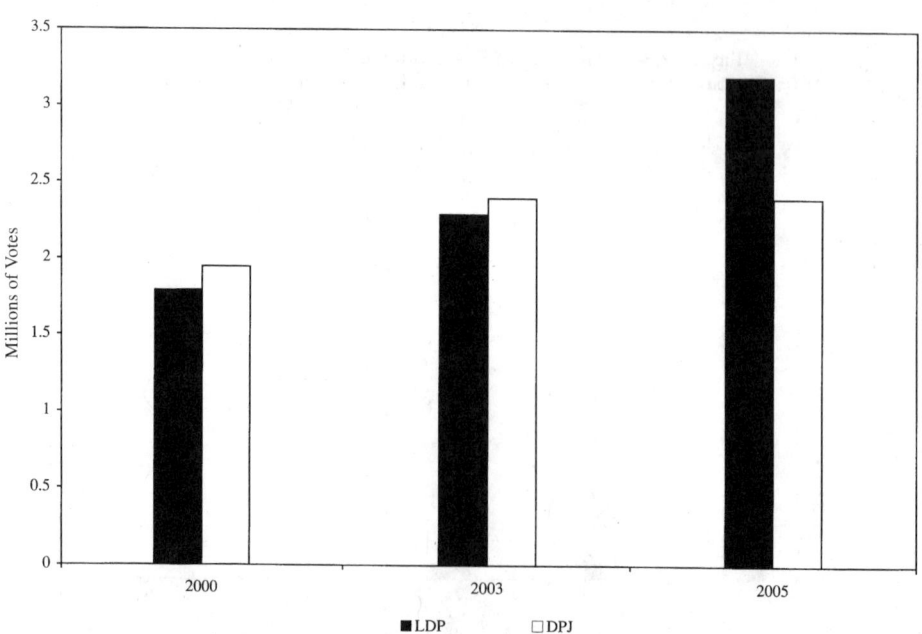

Figure 2.4 LDP vs. DPJ Votes Obtained in Tokyo Single-member Districts, Election Years 2000, 2003, and 2005

Source: Various newspaper reports after the election.

The LDP's overwhelming victory was, of course, partially due to the type of large swings an electoral system with a single-member district portion can bring. Recall that the LDP won this huge majority (61 percent of the seats) with less than a majority of the vote (48 percent). Indeed, it had picked up a "dividend" of 17 percent more single-member district seats than the last election with only a 3–4 percent increase in the vote, whereas the DPJ had lost about half of its single-member district strength, but had practically not lost any vote in those districts.

Whatever the reasons, Koizumi's gamble had paid off, and in a big way. With its coalition partner the New Komeito, which had lost three seats (to thirty-one) compared to its predissolution strength, the governing parties now controlled 327 seats out of the 480-seat Lower House, a little over a two-thirds majority. The latter is a key proportion because any constitutional amendment (e.g., Article 9, the famous "peace clause" in the Japanese Constitution) would require a two-thirds vote for passage before being sent to the people for a referendum. Soon after the election, Koizumi once again put his postal privatization bill to the Diet. Intimidated by the overwhelming victory—just as Koizumi had hoped—and by threats of party punishment if they did not change their vote and intimations of leniency if they did, many of the recalcitrant LDP members of the House of Councilors who had voted against the bill the first time, defeating it and bringing about the election, now switched their vote. Postal privatization passed the Upper House as well, making it law.

The key question, of course, was whether the changes that this election brought about and also represented—a newly powerful prime minister and party leaders who could initiate policy from above and bring their party along with them—could be institutionalized and survive Koizumi's retirement. Koizumi and Takebe wasted no time in beginning that process. In November 2005, less than two months after the election, they began to institute various changes in candidate selection, party unity, and policymaking. For example, there was a move to have the central LDP party take the lead in nominations of local party candidates, rather than the local branches, to try to establish a more coordinated policymaking structure between the PARC and the Cabinet, thus strengthening the government's role in policymaking within the party. Further, Koizumi began to urge newly elected representatives not to join factions (Yoshida 2005).

Japanese Democracy and the 2005 System

Assuming these trends continue, how can we say the new 2005 System differs from the 1955 System on our dimensions of democracy? First, representation has become a bit more equal. The electoral reform reduced malapportionment, but did not eliminate it. On the other hand, the LDP, especially with the 2005 election, has become more balanced and more of a true catchall party. LDP representatives are now equally divided among urban, rural, and mixed districts; previously 40 percent represented rural districts, and 30 percent each urban and mixed districts. There also are now more women represented in both the Diet and especially the Cabinet (Krauss, Nyblade, and Pekkanen 2007). In no case has inequality in representation been removed by any means, but there has been progress.

Second, accountability has become more complex. With the change to single-member districts and one Diet member per district, the representative has to respond to a broader diversity of constituents because he or she has to obtain a majority or large plurality of votes instead of the 15–20 percent to win election under the old system. This means more responsiveness to the "median voter" and less to one portion of the constituency or a narrow range of interest groups, and more to the broader "public interest" rather than narrow private interests. On the other hand, representation is also more distant than when a small part of the constituency held a representative so directly and personally responsive to their needs. Even now, there is personal representation—after all, the *koenkai* still exist—but the *koenkai* too represent a broader and more diverse stratum of voters in the district (Krauss and Pekkanen 2004).

Japan has become a little less pluralist if more competitive in its party system. Previously there was a broad spectrum of different ideological viewpoints represented in the party system. Now, the Communists and Socialists are marginalized, and the political spectrum is monopolized by three essentially centrist parties. Further, the LDP itself is on the way to becoming less decentralized and pluralist itself. The opposition has less "veto power" than it once did and, with the weakening of factions, more power is concentrated in the prime minister, party leaders, and the Cabinet.

On the other hand, we can say that the party system actually is more competitive in some ways. The very centrist nature of the opposition party means the ideological divide that separated the LDP and the major opposition party, the Socialists, under the 1955 System has virtually disappeared, and centrist and conservative voters can more easily cross over to the opposition party if they so choose. The "zombie" provision in the electoral system also means that even opposition party "losers" can still go to the Diet under the proportional representation system. The LDP single-member district representative has to be continually worried that the opposition candidate can come back next time and retake the single-member district—many opposition proportional representation representatives have become little more than single-member district candidates in waiting. Finally, despite the poor showing of the DPJ in the 2005 election, the election also demonstrated that small swings of votes can bring huge seat dividends in the single-member district portion creating artificial majorities, and this can give the opposition DPJ hope for the future (assuming it can overcome its weakness in rural areas). All of this makes the LDP, despite its apparent invincibility at the moment, potentially more vulnerable to opposition gains and thus makes the party system more competitive. The question is whether the DPJ can overcome the LDP's advantages in rural areas, and groom more "quality candidates" at the local level who would make better Diet candidates (Scheiner 2006).

Koizumi stepped down in September 2006 and the LDP selected Shinzo Abe as his successor. Abe is a grandson of a prime minister and son of a foreign minister. Being a hawk on security policy, and especially toward North Korea, gave him an appeal to conservatives. It is likely that no prime minister in the future will be successful without having the ability to project a popular image and to manage the television media, and Abe has proven this. After an auspicious beginning with 60 percent popularity ratings, his ratings fell to the 30–40 percent range after a series of personnel scandals, government errors, and a seeming inability to capture the popular imagination with visions of further reform. Although he clung on in the wake of electoral defeat, he then resigned, to be replaced by Yasuo Fukuda. Candidates unable to project a popular media image might come to power, and it is unlikely any leader will be able to reverse the changes that have occurred even if they want to, but those without such qualities are unlikely to be as successful in the job as those who have them. It remains to be seen whether a future leader will be able to push both reforms and the centralization of the LDP even further than Koizumi did.

Abe took power at a crucial juncture in the postwar history of the LDP and of Japanese democracy. Future prime ministers will have to do more than just possess the popularity to assume power, keep the LDP in power, and govern. They will have to consolidate and institutionalize the changes that Koizumi wrought with the new capabilities of the system if the LDP is to permanently change toward a more unified, less decentralized and fragmented, and policy-effective party and stay in power over the long term. In short, the LDP will have to permanently become a more "normal" party in the parliamentary democratic world. If the LDP can do this, the question might then be raised: Although this may be good for the LDP, will it be as good for the future of Japanese democracy? Or, alternatively, will the DPJ assuming power and alternation in government be more functional for Japanese democracy?

Because of the majoritarian nature of the single-member district portion of the electoral system, as we have indicated, the DPJ could come back strongly with only a return of the urban "floating vote" that it lost in 2005. Having said this, though, the DPJ's victory in the 2007 Upper House election was partly due to winning rural votes. The DPJ now needs to solidify this support and develop a stronger organizational base in rural areas in order to overcome the LDP's great stronghold in the rural areas and become a truly "national" party. The DPJ could do so through a personal and perhaps pork barrel–based appeal to the rural areas, which might then endanger its image as a "reform party" and lose its more natural support base in the urban areas. That, in turn, might mean less support for fixing the still-reprehensible malapportionment in the electoral system. We can ask another similar question: Doing what the DPJ needs to do to assume power will be good for the DPJ, but will it be good for Japanese democracy?

The answers to the above questions, of course, depend on which dimension of democracy is valued more: party competitiveness or equality in representation. As we mentioned at the beginning of this chapter, there is no ideal democracy, but only trade-offs along different dimensions of democracy. The interesting thing is that, after fifty years of LDP rule, Japanese democracy is truly experiencing choices among these trade-offs, perhaps for the first time.

Notes

We thank Jessica Louise Leithem for her research assistance. We also thank Ethan Scheiner for sharing data with us. This research was assisted by a grant to Robert Pekkanen from the Abe Fellowship Program administered by the Social Science Research Council and the American Council of Learned Society in cooperation with and with funds provided by the Japan Foundation Center for Global Partnership. Our Japanese Legislative Organization Database (J-LOD)—upon which Robert Pekkanen, Benjamin Nyblade, and Ellis S. Krauss 2006; Kuniaki Nemoto, Ellis S. Krauss, and Robert Pekkanen forthcoming; and Robert Pekkanen, Benjamin Nyblade, and Ellis S. Krauss 2007 are based—was expanded thanks to support from a University of California Pacific Rim Research grant awarded to Ellis S. Krauss.

1. J. Mark Ramseyer and Frances McCall Rosenbluth 1993, especially pp. 31–34, originally argue that the policy specialization route to deliver pork barrel benefits to the district was most prevalent. Masahiko Tatebayashi and Margaret McKean's (2002) and Masahiko Tatebayashi's (2004) analyses confirm that the PARC did serve a vote division function, but challenge this notion of "pork specialization." They did find some specialization for representatives, but found it geographically. Those with *jiban* (concentrated geographical bases) delivered pork to their districts, but did not specialize while those who specialized in policy did not necessarily do so with pork.

2. See also Yutaka Tsujinaka (2003) and Robert Pekkanen (2006) for analyses of pluralism that focus on associations and the representation of organized interests. See also Yuko Kawato and Robert Pekkanen's discussion of the changes wrought in civil society by the 1998 Nonprofit Organization Law in Chapter 10 of this volume.

3. For ideological purposes, the JCP tends to run a candidate in all districts even if he or she has no chance of winning.

4. See Ray Christensen (1996) for more realistic scholarly predictions.

5. Led by Ryutaro Hashimoto, prime minister in the mid-1990s who failed in challenging Koizumi in the LDP's party presidential race in 2001.

6. For example, on the final afternoon before the election, September 10, 2005, Koizumi devoted 92 percent of his speeches to postal reform and only 8 percent to

other themes, whereas Okada, the leader of the DPJ, devoted only 1 percent to postal reform, 35 percent to pension reform, 33 percent to tax and fiscal issues, and 31 percent to other themes (*Mainichi Shimbun*, September 11, 2005, p. 1).

7. Data from Ethan Scheiner is gratefully acknowledged.

CHAPTER 3

Campaign Behavior: The Limits to Change

Dyron Dabney

MORE THAN THREE DECADES HAVE PASSED SINCE THE PRINTing of Gerald L. Curtis's comprehensive study on Japanese election campaign behavior, *Election Campaigning, Japanese Style* (1971). Curtis's study of one candidate's campaign behavior for the 1967 Lower House election remains one of the few contributions to election studies entirely dedicated to election campaign strategy. It also was one of the first commentaries on democracy through the electoral process. Only within the past ten years have new studies on election campaign behavior (Otake 1998; Park 1998a; Curtis 1999; Christensen 1998; McKean and Scheiner 2000; Reed and Thies 2001, to name a few) emerged as contemporary updates of Curtis's 1971 study.

Inspired by the passage of the 1994 election reform (particularly, the electoral uncertainty it introduced to a once-routine, predictable campaign process), these studies, as well as the research presented here, represent a revival of attention to and appreciation for electioneering in Japan. Moreover, these studies fundamentally explore the impact of the new mixed-member system—a hybrid of proportional representation and single-member district systems adopted as part of the reform package (see Ellis S. Krauss and Robert Pekkanen in Chapter 2 of this volume)—on election campaign behavior, and its meaning for Japan's democratic future.

One of the underlying considerations of this study is the impact of the single-member district and proportional representation electoral system on the political culture and ethics of Japanese election campaigns, especially the new electoral system's ability to produce "good election campaigning," defined by electoral reform architects as a party-centered, issue-oriented campaign strategy. Good election campaigning, by extension, fosters improved responsiveness during the course of the resultant administration because it has committed itself to the issue positions and promises stated during the campaign period. Such campaign strategy purportedly utilizes a medium for voter mobilization that does not induce undue reliance on old-fashioned, patron-client politics condoned under the multimember district electoral system. Recall from Gill Steel and Sherry L. Martin in Chapter 1 of this volume that the impetus for the change to the electoral system was decades of problematic representative governance attributed to questionable political and electoral practices fostered by the former multimember district electoral system. The multimember district electoral system encouraged electoral competition among candidates—frequently from the same party (i.e., the Liberal Democratic Party [LDP]). At the same time, it stifled competition over policy issues and political party platforms. Victories were scored, often through ethically questionable campaign practices, by mobilizing just enough votes to guarantee a seat. Both of these features of the multimember district electoral system motivated candidates to pursue illicit or ethically questionable campaign practices to score election victories. Since candidates from the same party (predominately LDP candidates) no longer would compete against each other in the same district under the reformed electoral system, political candidates' electoral fates were expected to be decided on policy issues and party identification instead of over constituency favors and services that invite money politics. Thus, the new electoral system—particularly the single-member district component of the system—was expected to advance good governance by making candidates and parties more directly accountable to a broader base of electoral support. A two-party system would replace Japan's multiparty system, and the two parties would compete for votes fought over well-articulated policy manifestos or issue platforms (Seligmann 1997; Christensen 1998). Competitive single-member district races between two major parties on issue platforms would obligate candidates to broaden their public outreach in order to win a plurality of votes, thereby meeting the accountability test described by Ellis S. Krauss and Robert Pekkanen in Chapter 2 and Robin M. LeBlanc in Chapter 9.

An important claim posited in this chapter is that electoral reform itself could change campaign behavior only so much. In addition to the sociopolitical, cultural, structural, and institutional incentives or disincentives at play to weaken the desired effect of electoral reform, a candidate's political and electoral maturation (hereafter referred to as "political life cycle") equally complicated any full realization of desired campaign behavior.

The political life cycle represents the accumulation of a candidate's campaign experiences and political experiences (tenure of public, elected office) over time that is employed in an election campaign strategy. Krauss and Pekkanen's use of the accountability and competitive dimensions to evaluate democracy in Japan are particularly relevant to the political life cycle argument (Chapter 2). Fundamentally, candidates running for office seek to win. The political life cycle (depending on a candidate's stage along the life cycle) may discourage, or encourage, a strategy known to exact accountability (i.e., greater public exposure, scrutiny, or direct interaction with voters) or competitiveness (i.e., opportunities for opponents to gain public favor) in order to ensure election victory. Because a goal of election reform is the production of accountability and competitiveness (as well as representation and pluralism), a candidate's political life cycle potentially stands in the way.

Since the adoption of the system in 1994, four Lower House elections—1996, 2000, 2003 and 2005—have taken place under the current single-member district–proportional representation electoral system. Politicians, however, have been slow to respond to (if they have not resisted) the so-called dictates under the mixed-member district system. The findings presented in this chapter suggest that the reform-induced change in election campaign behavior predicted by political observers and pundits was not completely off base. Indeed, campaign behavior for the 1996 general election was altered by the new electoral system—after all, the unfamiliarity of the mixed-district system instinctively provoked candidates to alter their campaign behavior. Yet these alterations were not durable or lasting. Instead, campaign behavior observed in the 2000 general election reflected a political life cycle effect that was stronger than the forces of institutional change. In other words, the candidates were not motivated by the incentives of the new electoral system—at least not after the initial general election in 1996. Instead, their election campaign behaviors were prompted by political and electoral maturation between each election. Among all of the forces at play on strategy choice from one election to the next—new political parties, geographic location, demographic composition, the degree of challenge mounted by the opponent, election rules, and the new electoral system—rarely has the political life cycle been evaluated.

The conclusion spelled out in this chapter on the limited impact of institutional change on behavior is particularly relevant to the inquiry into the quality of democracy in Japan. The electoral system reform in and of itself and candidates' initial strategic and tactical deference to the new electoral system are important, progressive testimonials about representative democracy; they represent concrete attempts to improve constituent-politician representation, political competition, and political accountability in Japan. However, has this institutional change strengthened democracy in Japan? And does the campaign behavior witnessed under the new electoral system elevate democracy in Japan? The findings, at least based on data generated from the case studies, do not offer clear answers to these questions.

The case studies presented in this chapter are a distillation of election campaign behavior observed across three general elections: one before the election reform (in 1993) and two following election reform (in 1996 and 2000) among three candidates. The three candidates competed in three different classes of districts: urban, suburban, and rural. The urban candidate is Noboru Usami. Usami competed in the Tokyo Second, Third, and Fourth Districts in the 1993, 1996, and 2000 Lower House elections, respectively. The suburban candidate is Shigefumi Matsuzawa. Matsuzawa competed in the Kanagawa Second District in 1993 and the Kanagawa Ninth District in 1996 and 2000, respectively. Finally, the rural candidate is Koichiro Genba. Genba competed in the Fukushima Second District in 1993 and the Fukushima Third District in 1996 and 2000. All three politicians selected for this study possess similar biographic profiles—a methodological strength of a study beset with variability. They are all young, ideologically progressive-conservative (opposition party–supported) graduates of elite Japanese universities and the prestigious Matsushita Institute of Government and Management. Moreover, each possesses prior political preparation for a career in politics. Usami was a Diet secretary while Matsuzawa and Genba were prefectural politicians before running for national office. Additional biographic details about these candidates, including political experience and the districts in which they competed, are presented later in the chapter. The multiwave, longitudinal nature of the study is designed to bring to light valuable facts about the immediate, short-term effects and long-run effects of election reform on candidates' campaign behavior. Additionally, the inclusion of candidates across three different sociodemographic district types aids the delineation of campaign behavior motivated by the district's demographic makeup vis-à-vis the election reform and the political life cycle.

Intensive interviews, print and electronic media analyses, and participant observations of candidates and voters are employed to explore campaign behavior attributed to election reform and new party formations (period effects), political maturation and election campaign experience (political life cycle effect), and district type (demographic effect). The framework used to measure the candidates' responses to the election reform has two elements: the direct mobilization strategy (DMS) and the indirect mobilization strategy (IMS).[1] By examining the extent of the DMS and IMS employed by the candidates, we can understand whether candidates focus on issue-, candidate-, or party-centered election campaigns.

Candidates who employ the DMS directly seek voter support through the use of various forms of the mass media, including broadcast, print, and telecommunication services (e.g., telephone, facsimiles, and the Internet). Informal and formal public greeting speeches; rallies (*gaito enzetsu, enzetsukai*, and *shukai*); sound truck canvassing (*gaisensha no yusei*); door-to-door canvassing; and mail and telephone solicitation are additional ways that candidates try to directly appeal to voters. Whereas the DMS centers on tactics that allow the candidate to appeal directly to voters, the IMS centers on intermediaries between the candidate and voters. A broad web of electoral support is essential to execute an IMS-rich election campaign. Candidates who make use of the IMS rely on an influential local authority or institution as the vehicle for voter support. Such local notables commonly broker votes for candidates from within organizations, such as enterprise-based labor unions, professional organizations, neighborhood associations, interest groups, as well as the *koenkai* (a mass-based, candidate support organization).[2] Collectively, these intermediaries represent the candidates's election campaign *keiretsu* (a body of individuals who amass a gathered vote on behalf of the candidate). Examining the extent of the DMS and IMS in election campaigns wherein issue, candidate, and party orientations are expressed offers insight into the scope of electoral and political engagement candidates and voters seek from each other. That is, strategy choice sheds light on how candidates seek to engage voters and how voters seek to be engaged by candidates.

Political candidates typically do not limit themselves to either the DMS or the IMS. In fact, it was the desire of the candidates observed for this study to do both that complicates the assessment of the observed candidates' campaign behavior. Nonetheless, the conventional strategy prescription among inexperienced challengers is the DMS, while the strategy prescription for experienced incumbents or experienced challengers is the IMS. The DMS is the strategic language most political challengers speak, but it is not a language foreign to political incumbents: incumbents, unlike challengers, are strategically bilingual. Moreover, the candidates' choice between the IMS and DMS is guided by geographic and demographic characteristics of the district. Each case study presented in this chapter offers important insights on how campaign strategy was negotiated under prereform and postreform conditions in light of the established wisdom for the rural, suburban, and urban district-based campaigning.

According to conventional wisdom, the election campaign in a rural district is defined by candidate image (personality and reputation) and organized political machines (networks of local politicians, organizations, and associations). In an urban election district, on the other hand, the election campaign is defined by party ID (party labels) and issues. In other words, candidates located in rural settings adopt a campaign strategy that places personality and networks at the center, while candidates in urban settings adopt a campaign strategy that places issues and the party at the center. Candidates behave in these ways in response to the political culture of the city and countryside.[3] In terms of reaching and mobilizing voters, candidates invariably consider the practicality and suitability of the strategy in the light of the physical size of the district, the distribution of residents in the district, the scale of gathering points or hubs of activity (e.g., shopping plazas, parks, and train stations) in the district, and the sociopolitical norms and efficacy of the district. Among the case studies presented, the rural district candidate, for example, concluded that there simply was not a market for the retail politics style of the DMS in his district. That is, the DMS was inefficient at and insufficient for getting out the vote. Accordingly, candidates observed running in a rural district tend to rely on the IMS, while candidates running in an urban district tend to rely on the DMS. First-time challengers competing in rural districts, however, are often more conflicted about campaign strategy than their urban counterparts.[4] Challengers (first-time, or experienced) usually are more resource (monetarily, credentially, etc.) poor than are incumbents. Consequently, the scope of their outreach to and mobilization of voters is limited to the DMS. Conversely, experienced incumbents typically are more resource rich relative to challengers. The scope of their outreach and access to voters as well as their mobilization of voters is extensive. Thus, logically the gravitational pull of the DMS is stronger for an inexperienced challenger than the experienced incumbent because the production cost is less. A challenger can conveniently and efficiently mobilize voters via the DMS at a fraction of the resources needed by an incumbent to mobilize voters via the IMS. The case studies below underscore the common sense of these strategy prescriptions according to district type and experience, and the conflict the new electoral system posed to candidates' former strategy decisions.

Three Case Studies of Campaign Behavior

Japan's 1993 Lower House election was the first national-level election campaign for Usami, Matsuzawa, and Genba. All three were victorious in 1993. Competing in a five-member election district, Usami finished fifth in a field of ten candidates in the Tokyo Second District, Matsuzawa finished fourth among nine candidates in the Kanagawa Second District, and Genba finished third among ten candidates in the Fukushima Second District in the 1993 Lower House election. All three politicians claimed Lower House seats in 1993 with nearly the same percentage of votes—Usami garnered 12.8 percent of the vote; Matsuzawa, 13.1 percent; and Genba, 12.7 percent. Their electoral fortunes for the next two general elections, however, were quite different: Usami lost the single-member district and proportional representation races in the 1996 general election, and again in 2000; Matsuzawa won the single-member district seat in 1996 and 2000 with increasingly larger vote margins; and Genba lost the single-member district contest in 1996 (he picked up the proportional representation seat in 1996), but reclaimed it in the 2000 general election. All three politicians eventually were endorsed by the litany of new, progressive-conservative opposition parties—New Party Sakigake, the Shinsei Party, the New Frontier Party, and the Democratic Party of Japan (DPJ)—between 1993 and 2000.[5] Moreover, all three were among the youngest politicians elected to the Lower House in their respective districts in 1993 and in Japanese election history.

Noboru Usami (Urban District)

Usami entered the 1993 Lower House campaign without the sufficient electoral capital to get elected. He possessed limited *kaban* (campaign funding), *kanban* (name recognition), and *jiban* (a support base). Usami's election victory upset the conventions for electoral success, and reignited the debate about democracy in Japan through the lens of election campaign strategy as the gateway to political office. The Tokyo Second District was home to familiar political figures like LDP incumbents, Ishihara Shintaro and Shokei Arai, who repeatedly were returned to office, thereby limiting the seats contestable for any general election to three seats in the five-member election district. The district also consisted of voters who entrusted the established political parties to govern so, as a first-time challenger, Usami was not favored to win a multimember district seat. All the same, he won a Lower House seat in the five-member Tokyo Second District in 1993. Handicapped by a resource poor campaign, Usami's 1993 Lower House election victory resulted from an intelligent, efficient vote-targeting campaign driven by the DMS that was augmented by a new party endorsement and a sellable policy platform.

Usami had to shape his campaign strategies to suit a densely populated, socioeconomically diverse, and young constituency in the Tokyo Second, Third, and Fourth Districts in which he ran in the 1993, 1996, and 2000 general elections. The nonpartisanship and declining turnout among voters in the district prompted Usami to adopt the campaign strategy that would maximize his reach with voters in the district, particularly younger voters who were immune to partisan mobilization and nonvoters. The IMS proved ineffective with these members of the electorate. In fact, these voters—typically young voters—often were outside the reach of the IMS-defined conventional tactic of organizational mobilization. Consequently, Usami appealed to voters through an issue-oriented, yet candidate-centered (i.e., image) campaign managed via the DMS, and based on a new party (New Party Sakigake) platform, a vibrant personality, and a policy message of responsible governance and political transparency.

The most interesting tactics corresponding to the DMS that Usami used in each election campaign was Momotaro-style canvassing. This tactic targeted uncommitted, nonpartisan, and nonvoting members of the electorate through direct, vibrant personal appeals. The Momotaro was big on candidate image, though attention to issues was integral to the execution of the tactic. The tactic gets it name from the popular Japanese fable about Momotaro (Peach Boy). Akin to the fable, the goal of the tactic is to attract electoral support from voters to gain access to the Lower House, much like Momotaro drew on supporters to overtake the evil demon threatening his village. Usami and a small staff of young volunteers canvassed the district on foot for some 30 to 50 kilometers each day during the official campaign period, meeting and greeting passersby and distributing political pamphlets. Most of these passersby could not be converted into a hard vote as a result of an encounter with Usami. Rather, they represented a soft vote, potentially convertible through his image and direct appeal for election support. Momotaro was most effective as an image-building tactic. In the few minutes or less that Usami spent with passersby, he tried to leave a lasting positive image that impressed upon voters that he was a young, physically and intellectually vibrant, candidate. Because of Usami's sudden candidacy, and lack of campaign preparation in 1993, Momotaro was the wild card among campaign tactics.

In 1996 and 2000, Usami still continued to target nonvoters and floating voters under the Sakigake and DPJ party labels, respectively, and via the Momotaro tactic. However, the energy and priority put on Momotaro for the 1996 and 2000 election campaigns were principally limited to the official election campaign period. Because the single-member district contest in the Tokyo Third and Fourth Districts in 1996 and 2000 was highly competitive, Usami realized the imperative of mobilizing support beyond the DMS. Usami continued to rely on the DMS, particularly outdoor speeches at train stations to reach voters, but the noticeable addition to the DMS were reasonably developed *koenkai,* and organized support allied with the DPJ—tactics central to the IMS.

One source of support not fully realized until the 2000 Lower House election was the mobilization know-how of a network of local politicians, or election *keiretsu* as mentioned above. Usami did not organize a machine of local political operatives to gather votes on his behalf for the 1993 general election. By the time he fully appreciated the value of an electoral *keiretsu* for the 1996 general election, it was too late. The single-member district of the mixed-district system adopted for the 1996 general election had raised the cost of doing business with local politicians. Usami's candidacy vis-à-vis other candidates was too politically costly for most local politicians to support. Although Usami managed to enlist some local politicians for the 1996 general election, most local politicians who sought a reliable, direct pipeline to national-level politicians did not want to invest in, or absorb the cost of, supporting a less competitive candidate. Usami was certainly a quality candidate, but he lacked the competitive edge and political viability vis-à-vis other candidates competing for the single-member district seat.

While local politicians did not extend support to Usami for the 1993 and 1996 Lower House elections, Usami also claimed that he did not especially desire, or solicit the support of local politicians to organize votes. According to Usami, the unusual absence of the electoral *keiretsu* and strong political networks in his election campaign was tied to his deeply democratic view about constituency representation and the effect that the electoral *keiretsu* has on equitable constituency representation. For most candidates, an electoral *keiretsu* rarely comes without a cost, namely, political favors in exchange for election support. The *keiretsu* system conflicted with Usami's belief about political accountability. He reasoned that he could overcome the need for the electoral *keiretsu* and political networks in 1996 by appealing to voters with a "not-in-the-pocket politician" campaign platform. Voters who frowned on the traditional methods for getting elected, he believed, would find his candidacy attractive. Thus, an element of political machine backlash was included in Usami's election calculation. The best strategy for capturing these voters was to remain as disconnected as possible from local and regional political machines and the political and business elite greasing the machines. Resisting these electoral arrangements, however, eventually proved equally costly for Usami. In fact, it sealed his political fate in the 1996 Lower House election. Usami underestimated the importance of networks and overestimated the behavior of floating voters and nonvoters in 1996. He also misjudged the public's attitude about so-called in-the-pocket politicians. It seems that voters were far more pragmatic about the relationships among politicians and political support organizations. Usami's poor performance in the 1996 Lower House race reflected, among other things, these miscalculations.

The freshness and viability of the New Party Sakigake had faded by the 1996 election. Sakigake lost some of its fresh appeal and influence with voters (and, thus, Usami lost some of his voter support) when it settled for a tripartite alliance with the Liberal Democratic Party and the Social Democratic Party of Japan (SDPJ) to govern Japan. Usami, however, still projected a strong, fresh public image that was bolstered by the DPJ recommendation (the DPJ did not run a candidate in the Tokyo Third District in 1996), the last new party to emerge in 1996 to challenge the LDP. Yet neither his fresh image nor the fresh image of the DPJ was enough to overcome the challenge of the single-seat constituency fight against the LDP and New Frontier Party (NFP) contenders. The single seat went to the LDP, and the second- and third-place finishers were the NFP and Japan Communist Party (JCP), respectively.

By all accounts, the 2000 Lower House election was Usami's best election campaign showing. He was endorsed by a viable, competitive political party, the DPJ, and his campaign behavior reflected political maturity from the perspective of a calculated combination of the DMS and IMS. While he failed yet again to get elected, his campaign behavior perhaps is less responsible for his failure. Usami was simply "outcampaigned" by his opponents in the 2000 general election.

Shigefumi Matsuzawa (Suburban District)
Matsuzawa entered the 1993 Lower House election with a modicum of political and campaign experience. He had served two terms in the Kanagawa Prefectural Assembly before the 1993 election (a noteworthy departure from Usami's political experience), which translated into a limited, but transferable voter and local politician support base, and the campaign "insurances" (campaign funding and name recognition) deemed necessary for his Lower House candidacy. Still, akin to Usami's campaign strategy in 1993, Matsuzawa relied on the DMS in 1993. Moreover, he also competed for the Lower House in 1993 on an issue- and party-centered campaign platform, drawing on the new party fervor and political reform rhetoric of the time. Matsuzawa's party centeredness for the 1993 general election was afforded by the party endorsement he received from the Shinsei Party. In fact, backing from the Shinsei Party, like the backing Usami received from the New Party Sakigake, was an important contribution to the formulation of Matsuzawa's strategy. Placing the party at center of his campaign gained him the attention of voters who were charmed by the new political parties and the policy objectives professed by new political parties. The same new-party rationale applied for Matsuzawa's continued party-centered campaign appeals during the 1996 and 2000 Lower House elections via endorsements by the NFP and the DPJ, respectively. In the 1996 Lower House election, Matsuzawa's decision to compete in only the single-member district was a turning point in his campaign behavior. Although it was a decision equally made by his fellow NFP members (NFP members opposed the dual single-member district and proportional representation listing permitted under the new electoral system), it was a personal statement about his ability to win the single-member district seat on the strength of the votes he could claim. The single-listing was one of many significant campaign decisions Matsuzawa would make for the 1996 general election. The decision to limit his candidacy to the single-member district seat forced voters to vote decisively. Significantly, voters perhaps undecided about the dual-listed candidates or the political parties that endorsed them could not split their vote by casting the proportional representation vote for one party and the single-member district vote for a candidate representing a different party (see Krauss and Pekkanen in Chapter 2 of this volume for a review of the dual-listing arrangement of the single-member district and proportional representation electoral system).

Matsuzawa's tactical and strategy priorities shifted between the 1993 and 1996 Lower House elections. The presumed cause of change in his campaign behavior was the new election reform, which was overwhelmingly defined by geographically smaller single-member and proportional representation seats. Matsuzawa now had to capture a larger percentage of a smaller electorate. Cherry-picking likely supporters in the district (a viable option exercised under the multimember district electoral system) offered little guarantee of election victory. The new Kanagawa Ninth District in which he competed consisted of simply three wards (down from the seven wards and four cities of the previous Kanagawa Second District under the multimember electoral system). Yet the demographic and geographic diversity of this suburban district (e.g., small, independent business owners; big industry employees; small farmers; young, single, and nonpartisan men and women; long-term residents; and transient, less sociopolitically integrated communities) meant adopting a complex campaign strategy conventionally prescribed for urban or rural election districts.

Matsuzawa made a number of electoral system–driven adjustments to his campaign behavior that were intimately tied to his 1996 election victory. Among the most important of these electoral system–driven adjustments defining Matsuzawa's 1996 campaign strategy was aggressive organization and social network expansion. Expediting the attainment of the organizational support he desired were the de facto inheritance and cooperative exchanges of support from NFP incumbents no longer possessing any electoral stake in the new Kanagawa Ninth District. For example, since Yuuichi Ichikawa, a former Komeito rival in the 1993 Lower House election, became an ally in the 1996 election (Komeito was subsumed under the NFP label in 1996), and limited his candidacy to a proportional representation seat, Matsuzawa inherited a generous portion of Komeito-Ichikawa voter support. Ichikawa, due to his alliance with the NFP, and other incumbents, due to district reassignments (seventeen single-member districts were carved from the original five multimember districts), created a vacuum of competition for Matsuzawa for the 1996 election. They represented electoral conditions (the consolidation of opposition parties under the NFP and the assignment of incumbents to other districts) that created an environment for Matsuzawa to begin a shift toward the IMS. An imperative of this shift to the IMS was organization and association expansion.

Yet the single, dominant, and dependable organized support Matsuzawa secured for the 1996 election was former Komeito support (technically absorbed by the NFP), the political arm of the religious organization, Soka Gakkai. Kawasaki City (the Kanagawa Ninth District consisted of three wards of Kawasaki City) had one of the largest Soka Gakkai memberships in Japan, and consequently active representation in local politics. Soka Gakkai members' and the Komeito's tacit commitment to NFP candidates offered Matsuzawa a well-organized, disciplined election support base. Both Komeito supporters and Komeito-backed local politicians were reliably mobilized on Matsuzawa's behalf in 1996. His political and party relationship with Soka Gakkai and Komeito did not sit well with some supporters, but Matsuzawa was able to overcome this problem by appealing to some voters on personal ties and a candidate-centered platform. This was evident in his presentations to, and interaction with, different audiences. In either case, his personal image and vitality were strong crossover points. Similar to the 1996 election, Matsuzawa's organizational network solution for the 2000 election rested in part with the endorsement he received from the DPJ. Membership with the DPJ (the NFP was defunct by 1997) guaranteed him enterprise–labor union endorsement. At the same time it undercut his support from Komeito members (Komeito had reconstituted for the 2000 general election).[6]

Soka Gakkai support was impressive, but it was not sufficient to get Matsuzawa elected for the 1996 general elections. Given the emphasis on social network and organization expansion for the 1996 general election, Matsuzawa invested the political capital earned as an incumbent to solidify support from many small- and medium-sized businesses, associations, and clubs in the district. Facilitating these gains was a team of three district staff members, one for each ward in the district, who canvassed the district daily to maintain relationships with existing supporters and gather new commitments from local merchants and business and community leaders.

The biggest vote payoff for Matsuzawa's expansionary effort for the 1996 Lower House election occurred in one of the three wards, Takatsu Ward, of the Kanagawa Ninth District. Prior to the 1996 election, Takatsu Ward voters had consistently given their support to LDP candidates, in large part because of ties to agriculture in the ward and the historical political relationship between farmers and the LDP. It was here that Matsuzawa directed his campaign efforts in order to win the single-member seat. Matsuzawa faired well in Takatsu Ward for the 1993 general election (the percentage of votes he received in 1993 actually exceeded that received by the LDP candidate), but a repeat of 1993 was not guaranteed for at least two reasons. First, the political landscape in 1996 was very different from that of 1993. Second, there was uncertainty over whether conservative-minded voters who supported his Shinsei Party–endorsed candidacy in 1993 would do so again in 1996 under the NFP label. The LDP candidate, Eiichi Ogawa, was a clear threat to Matsuzawa in 1996 in the new Kanagawa Ninth District and, in particular, Takatsu Ward, the weakest of the three wards making up the district. All the same, Matsuzawa more than doubled his votes in Takatsu Ward as well as claimed the most votes in all three wards. What proved to be an important asset for his campaign was incumbency (Matsuzawa was the only incumbent running in the Kanagawa

Ninth District in the 1996 general election). When placed in the context of the aforementioned discussion on organizational support coordination, political and electoral experiences were extremely valuable to his election victory in 1996. Moreover, the organizational support Matsuzawa ascertained between 1993 and 1996 positioned him to negotiate a coordinated exchange of constituency support with former political rivals. Made possible by a shared membership in the NFP and the redistribution of incumbents into different election districts, two of Matsuzawa's biggest political rivals, Eiji Nagai and Yuuichi Ichikawa, became important allies. Nagai competed in the Kanagawa Tenth District, and Ichikawa contested only one of the proportional representation seats. What's more, as the only incumbent in the race for the single-member district seat and a competent, well-liked politician, Matsuzawa was viewed by many voters as the most appropriate political choice. The unexpected support of one of the LDP's own prefectural assembly (Takatsu Ward) members, Yuuki Saito, solidified Matsuzawa's strength in the district. Saito became a vital and well-enlisted member of Matsuzawa's political *keiretsu*, and the support he gained in a once-well-guarded territory was a tribute to Matsuzawa's efforts to expand his web of ties in the district.

Matsuzawa's adoption of the IMS in 1996 and 2000 to strengthen his political foothold with organizations was not at the expense of the DMS. He still maintained his commitments to the DMS for the 1996 and 2000 Lower House elections. Unquestionably, the most important tactic Matsuzawa made full use of for both the 1996 and 2000 general elections was outdoor public speeches. Preemptive, regular outdoor canvassing set Matsuzawa apart from his opponents who admitted that their electoral defeat was aided by a less than aggressive pursuit of votes to establish connections with voters. Matsuzawa admitted that he did not particularly delight in the hustle associated with this tactic to gain voters' attention and support, but he was skillful at it—much more so than any of his opponents. LDP challenger Eichi Ozawa acknowledged in a post-2000 election interview that he underestimated the electoral value of the DMS tactics like outdoor presentations during his 1996 and 2000 election campaigns to safeguard and gain voter support. What's more, Ozawa acknowledged that he miscalculated the effectiveness of the DMS in the Ninth District to amass voter support in 1996 and 2000. Matsuzawa purportedly conducted 2,000 public speeches in front of train stations, supermarkets, and shopping centers by the 1996 general elections. Weekdays and weekends, early mornings and afternoons were devoted to greeting constituents during their commutes and daily activities. The tactic served to increase Matsuzawa's name recognition in the district and express to voters his political commitment and diligence to his job and constituents. He even exploited this commitment by formally including his speechmaking achievements in his election campaign literature. By the 2000 general election, the number of Matsuzawa's public speeches had reached 2,500.

Koichiro Genba (Rural District)

In 1993, Genba ran for one of the five Lower House seats up for grabs in the Fukushima Second District. The Fukushima Second District conforms to the classic example of a rural election district in Japan. Communities were socially cohesive and hierarchical. Voters possessed an ideologically pragmatic, yet conservative bias. They went to the polls regularly (until the 1993 Lower House election, the turnout in the Fukushima Second District remained solidly above 80 percent), and voted for candidates frequently on the recommendation of a local notable or organization. The conservative bias of the Fukushima Second District is a manifestation of domestic geopolitics—the LDP has consistently championed the concerns of the farming communities who heavily populate the district in exchange for votes on election day. Most Fukushima Second District residents had ties to farming or construction. The conservative bias of the district is a manifestation of the conservative attitudes of the dominant age groups—middle-aged baby boomers and mature voters—who inhabit the district and regularly participate in politics. Genba's campaign behavior and support targets for the 1993, 1996, and 2000 general elections were especially attentive to these factors. His candidacy for the Lower House was preceded by one term in the Fukushima Prefectural Assembly. He was a conservative, independent local politician and remained an independent challenger when he ran for the Lower House in 1993. Political independence ensured his adoption of a solidly candidate-centered campaign posture. Unlike Matsuzawa and Usami who jump-started their careers in the Lower House via membership with new political parties, Genba began his career in the Lower House as an independent politician, albeit a conservative independent.[7] His victory in the 1993 Lower House election was only the second time since 1955 that a candidate won a seat without official political party endorsement.[8] Genba's 1993 victory defied the conventional wisdom in the rural Fukushima Second District by showing that success was possible as a political independent. Paradoxically, the penalty for political independence in the rural district was sufficiently difficult to determine because most party-endorsed candidates secured a sufficient number of votes through personal and gathered votes. Genba relied on his personal image, *koenkai*, and backing from local organizations and associations as well as his legislative experience at the prefectural level to secure a seat in the Lower House in 1993. Following his 1993 Lower House victory, Genba accepted membership with the New Party Sakigake for three main reasons: (1) campaign funding, (2) popular image of the party, and (3) committee appointments enhanced by party attachment. His tenure with Sakigake was short lived, however, much like the political appeal of the party. He left Sakigake in September 1996, then joined the DPJ, hoping that the party's popularity and charismatic leadership would draw greater attention and credibility to his 1996 election campaign.

Genba's shift between political parties (like the party shifts that occurred with Usami and Matsuzawa) did not particularly damage his support base in the district. Why? First, a number of members of the DPJ were previously Sakigake members. Second, Genba's strongest support base was not party centered, but instead candidate centered. Theoretically, membership in either the New Party Sakigake or the DPJ did not matter with voters in the Fukushima Third District since the political interests of these two progressive-conservative parties were considered similar. What matters with voters was the ability of a party to advance politics and policy favorable to their interests. Voters' uncertainty about the DPJ—according to Genba, the DPJ fervor in 1996 failed to reach the Fukushima Third District—legitimized Genba's anxiety about winning the single-member district seat for the 1996 general election. Historically, the LDP had dominated politics in the rural Fukushima Second District under the multimember district electoral system, and it was expected to do so under the single-member district and proportional representation system in the Fukushima Third District in which Genba competed. As champions of interests and issues relevant to many members of the electorate, the LDP candidates had a competitive edge with voters over an unproven party like the DPJ. Genba's best strategy for securing conservative votes was to expand his *koenkai* base, electoral *keiretsu* base, and organization-association base. He succeeded in all three without much personal effort.

In accordance to the election reform, the Fukushima Second District was parceled into three new districts—Fukushima Second, Third, and Fourth Districts—for the 1996 Lower House election. Genba was reassigned to the Fukushima Third District. By far the best expression of Genba's support base expansion effort in this new election district was represented by the formation of additional *koenkai* chapters and an acquisition of additional organizational endorsements. An appreciable portion of the support Genba secured, however, was inherited from "friendly" rivals with whom he brokered deals for voter support forfeited following reassignment to different election districts. One such friendly rival was the career politician Kozo Watanabe, who secured the most votes in the Fukushima Second District in 1993. Genba received the support base Watanabe left behind when he was assigned to the Fukushima Fourth District. The support harnessed from Watanabe's political favor, as well as the onset of fewer political rivals competing for the single seat in the Fukushima Third District, positioned Genba to build a winning support base for the 1996 Lower House election.

Genba's 1996 election campaign was well organized and well orchestrated with respect to his application of the IMS, but it was not enough to win the single-member district seat. The reform-induced reductions to competition left one rival, LDP incumbent Hiroyuki Arai, in the Fukushima Third District. In the 1996 Lower House election Arai claimed the single-member district seat. Genba, however, picked up one of the Tohoku bloc proportional representation seats. He was not defeated on the basis of his choice of strategy. Rather, he lost the single-member district seat because of deficient campaign coordination and communication among his network of supporters and overconfidence in his certain victory. Arguably, supporters who were convinced that Genba would win the single-member district seat were demobilized and did not turn out on election day. Another explanation for Genba's failure to take the single-member district seat was that he did not reach out to voters assumed to be too difficult to mobilize or considered to be the hard votes of his political opponents.

The lesson learned from the election loss in 1996 was not lost on Genba, evidenced by the single-member district seat he reclaimed in the 2000 general election. He won by building on the campaign strategy put into practice for the 1996 election.[9] He defined his 2000 election campaign as a *koenkai*-centered campaign. Rather, the *koenkai* was at the head of the IMS strategy. By Genba's estimate, his *koenkai* roster included some 70,000 names, each of whom he credited as a reliable supporter. The opportunity to advance his support base through the partisan support waned in 2000. Having only limited faith in the allure of the DPJ in 2000, Genba retreated from the partisan-based voter mobilization effort he began in 1996 in favor of the reliability of rural campaign traditions. Although the DPJ endorsement offered his campaign additional political continuity and the organizational alliance with labor unions, his organizational support-building effort was largely defined by *koenkai*. Still, some important fine-tuning of his campaign applied to the DMS. Taking a page from his urban and suburban contemporaries—Usami and Matsuzawa, respectively—he engaged in more *kojin enzetsukai* (personal public addresses), more household visits, and more pamphlet distribution. This part of his campaign behavior was applauded by supporters because it celebrated the place of open, public political engagement (as opposed to closed, political arrangements) in the electoral process in the rural Fukushima Third District. Genba also focused his reelection efforts on penetrating weak areas of support. Unlike 1996, he was much more aggressive about approaching organizations and communities that were considered the hard vote of his opponents. He had a stronger, more organized team of local politicians and organization leaders supporting his election campaign in 2000 to challenge the political hold that the LDP had in certain parts of the district.

Analysis of Campaign Behavior

Election reform critics' suspicions about the single-member district and proportional representation electoral system were confirmed following the 1996 Lower House election when the candidates' campaign behavior did not fully comply with reform architects' vision for campaign behavior. The ubiquity of support organizations, especially candidates' *koenkai* in urban and rural election districts, remained unchanged because of their demonstrated record for winning elections. Increases in *koenkai* membership and consolidation of *koenkai* initiated for the 1996 general election are strong evidence that candidates were not willing (or able) to give up this candidate-centered tactic. The *koenkai* is unlikely to wane as long as local party branches—the only challenge to the *koenkai*—remain weakly supported and organized.[10] In all three case studies, dependence on *koenkai* and other nonpolitical organizations increased for the 1996 election. Moreover, the candidate-centered, personality-driven campaign behavior remained intact in no small part due to the limited policy-issue differentiation among candidates or political parties (see Otake 1998; Christensen 1998, Seligmann 1997; Park 1998a). The beginnings of a discernible pattern shared by all three candidates that supports the life cycle explanation for campaign behavior occurred by the close of the 2000 general election.[11] A graphic illustration of Usami's, Matsuzawa's, and Genba's campaign behaviors (as described above) is presented in Figure 3.1. The figure is a composite of the candidates' behavior along a DMS-IMS continuum for each general election. An aggregation of each candidate's behavior is included for each election year to show the collective shift between the DMS and IMS. Conclusions about the location of each candidate along the continuum were determined by quantifying candidates' self-reports on past and present campaign strategy during repeat interviews and their day-to-day campaign tactics witnessed as a participant observer (see Figure 3.2 in the chapter appendix for a complete description of coding system). Campaign behavior is defined according to a 7-point scale where 1 is a completely direct mobilization strategy and 7 is a completely indirect mobilization strategy.[12] The graph shows how candidates shifted along the DMS-IMS continuum for each election. The behavioral shifts between the 1993 and 1996 Lower House elections were motivated by the tug of the new electoral system. A countervailing undercurrent present in each election, however, was the reflexive correction exacted by the political life cycle effect on the candidates.

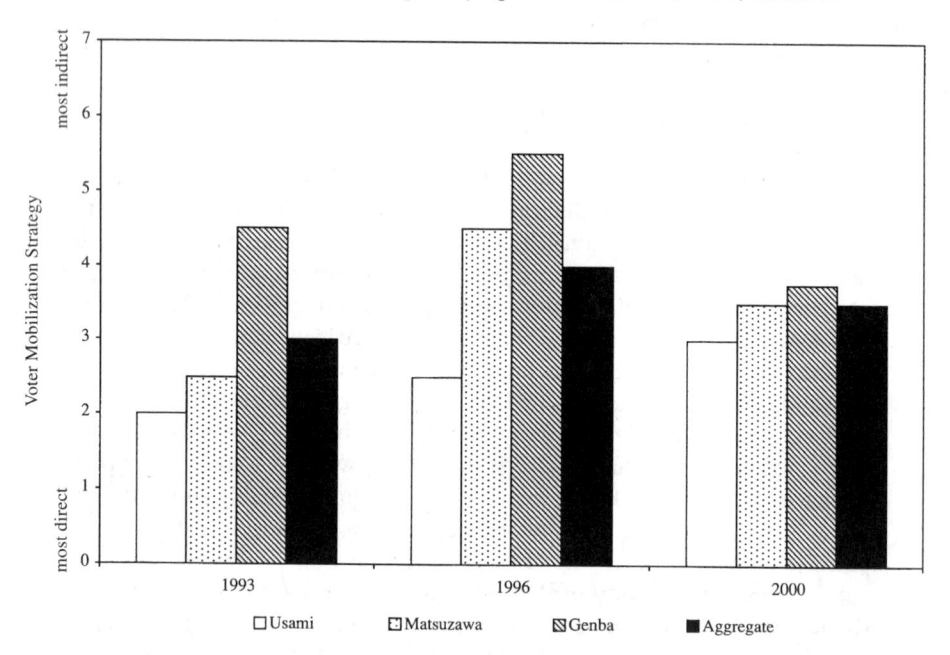

Figure 3.1 Politicians' Evolving Campaign Behavior, 1993, 1996, and 2000

□ Usami   ▨ Matsuzawa   ▨ Genba   ■ Aggregate

Political Life Cycle Change and Behavioral Convergence

Usami, Matsuzawa, and Genba continued to experience urban, suburban, and rural district-specific challenges each election. District type is one explanation for the candidates' different campaign strategies observed in 1993, but their campaign behaviors seem less constrained by the district type in the 2000 general election. Three factors figure prominently in the candidates' campaign behaviors across the three elections: (1) political challenger and newcomer versus incumbency; (2) the electoral system; and (3) political maturity, or political life cycle. In 1993, the most expedient explanation for the campaign behavior for Usami, Matsuzawa, and Genba was the challenger status.[13] When these politicians first campaigned for Lower House seats in 1993, the cornerstone of their campaigns was the DMS. As political challengers, Usami, Matsuzawa, and Genba took to tactics within the DMS simply because they were in short supply of the provisions for the IMS. In 1996, the most expedient explanation for campaign behavior was the new electoral system, particularly as it related to candidates' speculations about how to get elected under a new electoral system. Unlike Matsuzawa and Genba, Usami's campaign behavior in 1996 (still largely DMS) reflected his unyielding reformist idealism about election campaigning, but equally his limited accessibility to resources to consider the IMS. Matsuzawa and Genba, on the other hand, were more reactive to the new electoral system than Usami. Their 1996 election campaign behaviors reflected a one-time, exogenous response to the new electoral system that exaggerated their behavior. The new electoral system prompted a premature campaign behavior for the 1996 general election, which called into question the candidates' behavioral authenticity for the 1996 Lower House election. Indeed, the immediate anxiety associated with competing under the new electoral system caused many candidates to step outside their strategy comfort zones. The assumption was that the only way to win in 1996 was the IMS—paradoxically a behavior inconsistent with the intended goals of election reform. Matsuzawa and Genba succeeded in exploiting the IMS for the 1996 election, but it was unsustainable. The modulation of their campaign behavior for the 2000 general election suggests as much. The modest retreat from the IMS to the DMS by Matsuzawa and Genba, and the unidirectional shift of Usami from DMS to IMS following the 1996 general election reflect the final expedient explanation for campaign behavior in the 2000 general election: a life cycle effect. Paralleling the more forced, unauthentic pursuit of resources (i.e., organizational endorsements, local politician backing, and *koenkai*-building) incited by the new electoral system was the more unforced accumulation of resources incited by incumbency. Perhaps the most telltale indication of a life cycle effect is how the candidates' initially divergent campaign behaviors converge by the 2000 general election contest. Even the district type, a plausible explanation for these candidates' campaign behaviors in the 1993 Lower House election, has less explanatory power by the 2000 general election. The greater similarity observed among the candidates' campaign behaviors by the 2000 general election suggests parsimony between the DMS and the IMS induced by each candidate's political life cycle. Interestingly, even these self-described "new style" political reformists, fond of the DMS, realized the attraction of the IMS. Though the IMS conflicted with their ideals about campaigning for votes, the IMS was consistent with their political and electoral maturation.[14]

Conclusion

The electoral maturity that occurred with each candidate between the 1993, 1996, and 2000 general elections permitted a more flexible choice between the DMS or IMS. Use of the IMS was inevitable as the candidates expanded their social network sphere by penetrating previously inaccessible sources of organizational support that enhanced the overall quality of their candidacy with voters (see Scheiner 2006). Finally, the modest, but positive financial balance sheet established after the 1993 general election permitted the candidates to finance certain tactics tied to the IMS. Electoral and political maturation addressed many of these earlier deficiencies. From the standpoint of the political life cycle, a litmus test of authenticity lies with the direction taken by the candidates along the DMS-IMS continuum. Matsuzawa's and Genba's campaign behaviors shifted from the IMS to the DMS between 1996 and 2000. Logically speaking, a candidate who is able to confidently conduct the IMS should be less inclined to pursue the DMS. Matsuzawa's and Genba's 1996 campaign behaviors can only be viewed as premature and therefore unsustainable from the standpoint of political life cycle considering the modest return to the DMS in 2000. The timidity and tentativeness of Matsuzawa's and Genba's choice between the DMS and IMS in the 1996 general election reflected the fact they were no longer novice politicians, but they were not yet seasoned veterans with respect to the traditional political life cycle of a career politician. What's more, the emphasis on the IMS in the 1996 election was an overestimation of the appropriate campaign behavior to get elected. The correction occurred with the 2000 general election. Matsuzawa's and Genba's modest shifts from the IMS to the DMS between the 1996 and 2000 general elections illustrate this correction. In fact, all three candidates' locations along the DMS-IMS continuum in 2000 reflect the equilibrium points for rural, suburban, and urban candidates running their third consecutive election campaigns.[15] That is, their use of the DMS was tempered by an increasing ability to employ the IMS.

With respect to a critique of the effects of electoral reform, two of the three observed candidates (Matsuzawa and Genba) responded to the election reform, so election reform did induce a behavioral modification as some pundits had predicted. However, this behavioral modification was a short-lived period effect of the "newness" of the new electoral system in 1996. Matsuzawa and Genba even acknowledged that the hype surrounding reform and the expectations to modify their behavior for the 1996 Lower House election was a distraction. The perceived necessity for politicians to change strategies exceeded the real necessity for candidates to change strategies for the 1996 Lower House election. Although a degree of behavioral change was required, the candidates quite possibly overestimated how much they needed to shift to the IMS. The 2000 election campaign behavior was a corrective step back toward the "natural" order of things for politicians like Matsuzawa and Genba with some political and electoral resources at their disposal.

The underlying assumption of the life cycle effect is that all candidates eventually gravitate to the IMS as they amass experience and build a reliable coalition of supporters beyond a fixed time like that observed in the 1996 election. Usami's three election campaigns offer evidence that candidates—even urban candidates, or electorally progressive candidates purportedly predisposed to the DMS—eventually gravitate to the IMS. Given that Usami's, Matsuzawa's, and Genba's candidacies were initially built on progressive electioneering, consideration should be given to the possibility that personal limits existed (based purely on the principle of electoral responsiveness to voters) for these candidates where use of the IMS is concerned. By the same token, because veteran politicians tend to make less use of the DMS over time (a consequence of accumulated electoral capital), consideration should be given to their decreasing desire to conduct the DMS to mobilize voters.

While the single-member district and proportional representation election failed to exact an immediate transformation in Lower House candidates' campaign behaviors, it succeeded at exacting a change in the relationship between Lower House candidates and local politicians. Prior to election reform, local politicians frequently benefited from the multimember district system by negotiating with Lower House candidates (typically LDP candidates) from the same party for campaign support and political favors. The single-member district component of the electoral system appears to constrain local politicians' ability to self-servingly shift their loyalty between Lower House candidates (thereby ratcheting up potential for corruption) because political party endorsements are limited to one candidate per district (Park 1998a). The single-member district system closed the door to these kinds of opportunistic exchanges between local and national politicians. Albeit a peripheral goal of reform, the modest change in the nature of the support *keiretsu* of local politicians is a valuable contribution of the new electoral system to political accountability and responsible government.

Election campaign strategy fundamentally speaks of who gets into office (based on the strategy adopted) and the policies pursued by election victors once in office. Political life cycle, however, speaks of how candidates engage or alienate voters by way of their strategy choices. Whether or not Lower House members are elected under the multimember district system, or the single-member district and proportional representation system, the political life cycle appears to impact strategy decisionmaking. For candidates like Usami, Genba, and Matsuzawa who attained broader access to the IMS with time, the study raises an important question about the consequences of political maturation on the advancement of democracy in Japan in terms of turnout and public interest in politics. Candidates frequently turn inward as they mature and gain comfortable, reliable margins of electoral support and accumulate political resources advanced through incumbency. Consequently, voter mobilization through the more dynamic DMS (dynamic in terms of public outreach) diminishes with political maturity—a matter overlooked by election reform.

Appendix

Figure 3.2 Scale for Direct Mobilization Strategy and Indirect Mobilization Strategy

This scale takes into consideration the type (experimental, new, or traditional) and volume of tactics conducted under the direct mobilization strategy (DMS) and the indirect mobilization strategy (IMS). Additionally, stylistic differences in the execution of the tactics were examined. Some of these tactics were limited to the official campaign period due to regulatory reasons, but many were conducted between elections. Arguably, any action on the part of a candidate can have electoral implications. The list provided here is limited to the more familiar tactics within the election campaign repertoire.

Observed tactics (subsumed under the DMS) conducted between 1993 and 2000 include outdoor and indoor political speeches and rallies (*gaito enzetsu kai*); indoor large and small speeches and rallies; sound truck canvassing (*gaisensya yuzei*); election district "blitzing" (*rolla sakusen*); phone bank calls (*denwa sakusen*); policy study meetings (*benkyo kai*); and outdoor district canvassing.

1   0–10
2   11–20
3   21–30
4   31–40
5   41–50
6   51–60
7   61+

Indirect Mobilization Strategy: *Koenkai*

Number of *koenkai*:

1   0–2
2   3–4
3   5–6
4   7–8
5   9–10
6   11–12
7   13+

Koenkai membership:

1   0–500 members
2   501–1,000
3   1,001–3,000
4   3,001–5,000
5   5,001–10,000
6   10,001–20,000
7   20,001+

continues

Koenkai member solidarity and expansion activities/events:

1 0–2
2 3–4
3 5–6
4 7–8
5 9–10
6 11–12
7 13+

Party membership and party machine: 0 = no party membership/independence; 7 = party membership/endorsement.

Organizational endorsement (Religious organizations, such as Soka Gakkai, labor unions, farmers' and construction associations, neighborhood associations and merchant associations, and local and national clubs)

1 0–5
2 6–10
3 11–15
4 16–20
5 21–25
6 26–30
7 30+

Local politician support/endorsement (*electoral keiretsu*) (Local politicians, such as town and city council and prefectural assembly members, mayors, and governors)

1 0–1
2 2–3
3 4–6
4 7–9
5 10–12
6 13–14
7 15+

A score of 1 represents a purely DMS. The candidate only makes use of tactics defined within the DMS. Tactics that are logistically easy to execute figured prominently in the election campaign.

A score of 2 indicates that the DMS dominates the election campaign, but some tactics within the IMS have been adopted.

A score of 3 reflects a near equal application of the DMS and the IMS. The candidate relies on both strategies to mobilize voters, but still has great appreciation for the DMS because it has been mastered by the candidate during repeated campaigns for office.

A score of 4 indicates stronger reliance on the IMS. The IMS is increasingly more pronounced because it has become easy to effectively and efficiently execute.

continues

A score of 5 indicates that the IMS dominates the election campaigns. Only the most well-recognized/popular tactics within the DMS are employed in the election campaign.

A score of 6 indicates limited use of even the most popular tactics within the DMS. A strong admiration for the DMS developed from earlier elections decreases.

A score of 7 represents a purely IMS. No candidate, however, conducts a purely IMS.

The number assigned to each candidate each election year represents one participant observer's subjective evaluation of campaign behavior for each election. However, due diligence has been given to fairly and appropriately evaluate each candidate's record of tactics. The self-reports/self-evaluations provided by the candidates about their campaign behavior during interviews and via surveys substantiate the assignment of the candidates on the scale.

Notes

1. The candidates' overall application of the DMS and the IMS in both quantity and intensity serves as the "measure" of the strength of political life across the observed elections (see Figure 3.2 in the chapter appendix for a complete description of the framework of the DMS and the IMS).

2. The *koenkai* is the US equivalent of the "citizens for candidate X" organization, except the *koenkai* is comprised of voters who are organized and maintained by the candidate. Debates exist over whether or not the *koenkai* actually is a tactic within the IMS since the candidate directly presides over it. Although established by the candidate, the *koenkai* functions as any other voter mobilization organization.

3. A candidate's personal preference for a party-, personality-, network-, or issue-driven campaign is unlikely to override the political culture of the district. Most preferences manifest themselves in the absolute volume or intensity of a campaign tactic that corresponds to a party-, personality-, network-, or issue-driven campaign.

4. Exceptions to the rule exist, however. Some incumbents, regardless of geographic location, simply prefer the DMS to the IMS. Likewise, some first-time challengers are poised to make use of the IMS. Subsumed within both of these strategy choices are the resources required to execute each of them.

5. Genba secured a seat in the Lower House in 1993 as an independent candidate. However, he received an official party recommendation by the New Party Sakigake. His official membership with the New Party Sakigake came shortly after his 1993 Lower House election victory.

6. Recall that labor union support in the district was not available (at least not in any reliable, cohesive manner) to Matsuzawa because of the SDPJ's and DPJ's franchise in the election districts in 1993 and 1996. Matsuzawa, however, was able to collect former Democratic Socialist Party (DSP) support (an NFP acquisition) in 1996.

7. In truth, Genba was a political moderate. That is, his policy position was near the center of the conservative-liberal continuum. The culture of conservatism in the Fukushima Second District, however, encouraged Genba to present himself more conservatively to the electorate.

8. Initially, Genba was a member of the LDP. His membership in the LDP followed his election to the Prefectural Assembly. When Genba decided to run as an independent in the 1993 Lower House election, he managed to hold on to some of his LDP support base.

9. Genba's 2000 election victory perhaps was facilitated by the "Costa Rica system" adopted by the LDP. The Costa Rica system is a proportional representation and single-member district rotation system used by the LDP to satisfy the problem associated with the surplus of LDP incumbents following the shift from the multimember district to single-member district system. Under the Costa Rica system, single-member district and proportional representation legislators alternate candidacy with each Lower House election. Consequently, Genba avoided a repeat contest against Hiroyuki Arai in 2000.

10. Generational replacement of candidates in effect may help Japan realize the goals of election reform as incumbents used to the old ways of doing things are replaced with new politicians who know of no other campaign behavior (i.e., way to campaign for office).

11. Preliminary findings for the 2003 Lower House election campaign behavior for Genba and Usami (not included here) point to the candidates' slow, but steady advance toward the IMS. (Matsuzawa did not seek reelection in 2003; he contested and won the gubernatorial race for the Kanagawa Prefecture in 2002.)

12. The number assigned to each candidate in each election year represents one participant observer's subjective evaluation of campaign behavior for each election. However, self-reports/self-evaluations, which allowed the candidates to voice opinions about their campaign behavior during repeated interviews and surveys, substantiate the assignment of the candidates on the scale.

13. The most expedient explanations for Usami's, Matsuzawa's, and Genba's electoral victories in 1993 rest with their endorsement by new political parties, the multimember district system that made it easier to win a seat with fewer votes, and political freshness from the standpoint of an absence of any ties to corrupt politics.

14. The 2003 Lower House election further confirmed the similar trajectory of Usami's and Genba's election campaign behaviors. Matsuzawa's campaign behavior is unavailable because he did not seek a third term of office as Kanagawa Ninth District representative in order to run in Kanagawa Prefecture's gubernatorial election.

15. A question remains over whether or not Usami's, Matsuzawa's, and Genba's 1996 election campaign efforts actually advanced their location along the continuum in 2000 at a much faster pace than that expected for junior politicians.

CHAPTER 4

Diet Members and Seat Inheritance: Keeping It in the Family

Naoko Taniguchi

THE AIM OF THIS CHAPTER IS TO EXAMINE THE RELATIONSHIP between hereditary politics and democracy in Japan. The prevalence of Nisei (second-generation politicians),[1] typically consisting of a child or grandchild of a former politician, is a common characteristic of contemporary Japanese politics. Around 30 percent of the members of the House of Representatives, and as high as 40 percent of the Liberal Democratic Party (LDP) Diet members, are currently second-generation politicians.[2] In the 2000 general election, 12 percent of all candidates and one-third of the LDP candidates had a father, father-in-law, or grandfather who served as a Diet member. Moreover, second-generation politicians are also disproportionately common among Cabinet members and key posts of the LDP, including the prime minister.

One explanation for this proliferation of second-generation legislators is that they are able to inherit from their political family or relatives various political resources, including the "3-bans": *jiban* (support base), *kanban* (name recognition), and *kaban* (financial support) (Tanaka 2001, 11–12), which may also include personal connections with political, administrative, and business leaders. Such resources can increase the possibility of winning or keeping a seat, or generally succeeding as a politician even without directly inheriting a seat.

Although Japan has a stable democracy, its democratic system consists of a large proportion of second- and third-generation politicians. This phenomenon, unheard of in any other developed nation, is in need of further investigation when we think of the "quality" of democracy in Japan. Tomoaki Iwai (2003) perceives both negative and positive consequences of such second-generation Diet legislators. On the negative side, they are regarded as obstacles for newcomers to win seats, resulting in inertia in Japanese democracy. Yet Diet members who inherit seats are considered a more sophisticated generation of the political elite, possessing great political resources.

Second-generation politicians are actually quite popular among the public. This is indeed ironic given that the prime ministers who have led a number of drastic reforms in the political, economic, and social realms during the "lost decade" of the 1990s (i.e., Morihiro Hosokawa and Junichiro Koizumi), are themselves second- and third-generation politicians, the sons and grandsons of politicians who established such schemes. And the public seems to welcome such reforms. In other words, there is apparently an "odd" sort of democracy in Japan, where the public expects political reforms to be undertaken by hereditary politicians, who have certainly benefited from the old political scheme.

Based on such premises, this chapter will discuss the following topics: Why does the Japanese political system have so many hereditary legislators? How much advantage do hereditary politicians have in winning elections or gaining governmental spending? Have such advantages changed in any way after the various political reforms? Finally, has Japanese hereditary politics affected the quality of Japanese democracy?

Proliferation of Second-generation Legislators

Trends over Time

To begin, this chapter presents an overview of the increasing trend in the number of second-generation Diet members. Figure 4.1 shows the change over time of the percentage of such members in the narrow sense of the term.[3] Figure 4.1 refers to members of the House of Representatives with the proportion of second-generation legislators represented by the bold line. The figure shows that the ratio of second-generation Diet members increased from 1958 to 1980. This linear increase can be explained by the gradual retirement of legislators elected in the early postwar period who gave their seats to successors. Since 1980, the ratio of second-generation Diet members has maintained a stable level at around 20–25 percent. However, it must be noted that, because the ratio includes only second-generation Diet members in the narrow sense, it will increase even more if those in the broad sense are incorporated.

Figure 4.1 also shows that second-generation legislators are a predominant element in the LDP, accounting for 40 percent of all LDP Diet members in 1993. The downturn after 1993 might be attributed to the secession from the LDP during the political realignment in the same year. The overall

DIET MEMBERS AND SEAT INHERITANCE 67

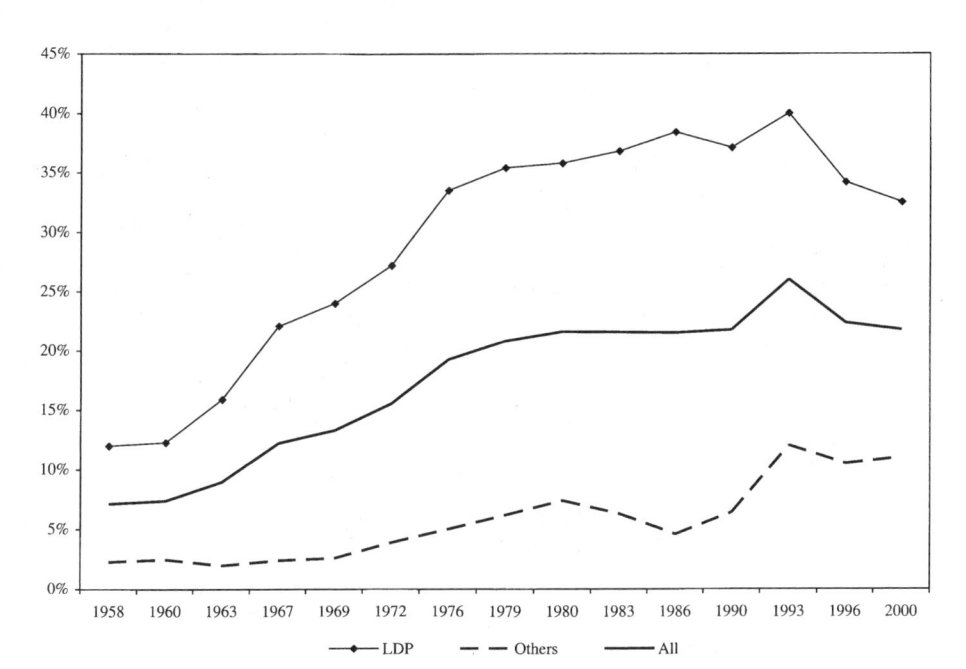

Figure 4.1 Proportional Changes of Second-generation Members of the House of Representatives Among Parties, 1958–2000

Source: Based on Matsuzaki (1991); Asahi Shimbun Senkyo Honbu (1980–1997); Kensei Shiryo Hensan Kai (1978); Shugiin and Sangiin (1960–1963); Shugiin and Sangiin (1990); Nichigai Associates (1999); and local newspapers.

percentage of second-generation Diet members in the LDP has decreased, but has increased in other parties.

Coincidentally, Ireland is another country known to have a large number of second-generation politicians in its legislature. Twenty-five percent of all politicians in Ireland have relatives in politics. This fact has been attributed to the similarity of its electoral system to that of Japan, specifically the single nontransferable vote (SNTV) system and candidate-centered campaigns (Ishibashi and Reed 1992, 366–379).

Additionally, the United States, with an electoral system much different from that of Japan, has several well-known "political families" such as the Bush family. In the 1960s, 54.1 percent of members of the US Congress had relatives in politics, although only 5.9 percent had relatives who had served in Congress. In the early days of Congress, the latter percentage was around 20 percent, which means that the percentage of second-generation politicians has actually decreased in the Congress (Ishibashi and Reed 1992, 367). Reasons for this decrease in Congress have included the following:

(1) serving in Congress has come to be regarded as a job that does not pay well compared to the enormous cost of running for election (Suzuki 1989, 108); (2) there have been frequent changes in the electoral system (such as changes in reapportionment); (3) there has been public criticism against hereditary seats; and (4) there is a decentralized relationship between the federal and state government. On the other hand, in local politics, there have been cases in state legislatures where second- and third-generation politicians have occupied the majority of seats (Ishibashi and Reed 1992, 367). Moreover, many of the recent US presidential candidates have been close relatives of prominent politicians, for example, former vice president Al Gore, Senator Hillary Clinton (D–NY), and former governor Mitt Romney (R–MA). It may be possible to deduce from these facts that, in candidate-centered elections, hereditary politicians are more likely to win seats regardless of differences in the party system or political culture.

Why Has the Number of Hereditary Politicians Increased in Japan?

Let us turn our attention back to Japan for an overview of the factors related to the proliferation of second-generation Diet legislators. According to Taiichi Ichikawa, the rise in the number of second-generation politicians, particularly second-generation Diet members belonging to the LDP, has resulted from the following factors: (1) the stable politics (less competition) due to LDP's long reign, (2) the SNTV system and the presence of *koenkai* (support organizations), (3) the financial dependence of the local government on the national government, (4) the indifference of the electorate toward politics, and (5) the difficulty in recruiting new legislators (1990, 289–293).

Among these, the SNTV system and the presence of *koenkai* has been pointed out by many as a major factor behind the proliferation of second-generation legislators. That is, the LDP's weak organizational structure at the lower end of its hierarchy as compared to other parties has forced candidates to form support organizations by themselves, binding supporters together in order to successfully compete in electoral campaigns. This method is particularly effective (and is, in fact, the only option) under the SNTV system in which intraparty competition is unavoidable. Conversely, in some cases, support organizations seek out hereditary candidates who will benefit their interests. At this point in time, Diet seats, in which a huge amount of money has been invested, have become a valuable resource not only for the politician and his family, but also for the support organization itself.

Another important factor contributing to the proliferation of second-generation legislators may be the hierarchical organization of the LDP's internal structure. In the past, when a politician was forced to retire at short notice, his spouse or secretary typically ran as a successor. Gradually, however, it more often has become the case that a child or grandchild has taken over as successor. This has been based on the LDP's internal organization, in which a Diet member climbs the ladder based on how many times he or she has been elected. The seniority system encourages successors to enter politics at a young age and continuously return to the Diet as many times as possible so as to rise to a high intraparty position (Tanaka 1989, 81). Other researchers have pointed out that the rise in the ratio of second-generation candidates has occurred in connection with the LDP presidential elections. When leaders of intraparty *habatsu* (factions) sought to strengthen their support base, they apparently turned to the recruitment of new second-generation candidates (Ichikawa 1990, 247). Another driving factor may be the problem of political funds. When a politician is left with a large debt, he or she may retire and allow a successor to take over so as to convince the creditors that the debt will be repaid on an *arutoki barai* no *saisoku nashi* basis, that is, the funds will be repaid when they are available so that the creditors will not put pressure on the debtor (Iwai 1990, 140–141).

In the meantime, the voters' indifference toward politics and the difficulty in recruiting new legislators, as mentioned above, suggest that electorates also play a role in the proliferation of second-generation legislators. Japanese voters hold a negative view of politicians in general, and indifference toward politics is the norm. A consequence is that few young people wish to enter the political world. But at the same time, voters are eager to support second-generation legislators. This is based on economic rationality (so as to make use of the politician as a channel for attracting interest and subsidies from the central government), political passivity (typically seen in people's tendencies toward unchanging support), and a weakness for members of the political elite who have clean, sophisticated images (Taniguchi [Onizuka] 2003). Therefore, it may reasonably follow that not only the circumstances faced by the political elites, but also the preferences on the part of the electorate have contributed to the rise in the number of second-generation legislators.

Performance of Hereditary Politicians in Elections

The increasing number of hereditary politicians is in itself evidence of the fact that they have a good chance of winning elections. Michihiro Ishibashi and Steven R. Reed (1992) focus on "when" and "how" a support organization is passed on to a successor, and point out that a successor is more likely to win an election if he or she inherits a support organization from a "winning" incumbent. Yoshiaki Kobayashi shows that the relationship between candidates' electoral campaign pledges and their subsequent vote shares is affected by whether or not the candidate is the hereditary successor of a politician (1997, 46–68). Also, analysis of second-generation politicians conducted by the Kabashima Ikuo Seminar (2000a, 2000b) focuses on vote share, political funds, and the possibility of withdrawing from the party, and demonstrates candidates' election strategies and advantages that accrue to them in winning elections.

How much of an advantage do second-generation candidates actually have in elections? The results of recent Lower House elections are shown in Table 4.1.[4] In the 1990 and 1993 elections, which were executed under the SNTV system, there was a total of around 950 candidates, which means that roughly half of all candidates won a seat. Then, in the 1996 general election, when the mixed-member district system with single- member districts and proportional representation was newly adopted, an upsurge in the number of total candidates was seen.[5] This boom subsided as candidates who had little or no chance of winning refrained from running. It should be noted, however, that the overall victory rate of 20–30 percent under this system is much lower than under the SNTV system (53 percent). This is mainly due to the fact that the percentage includes a considerable number of candidates who do not seek to win under the single-member district system (e.g., candidates of the Communist Party and dual-listed candidates).

In contrast with the low victory rate for all candidates, the victory rate for second-generation candidates has remained as high as 80 percent, both before and after the implementation of the SNTV system. Moreover, it should be noted that, although the number of second-generation candidates has remained stable, the ratio of second-generation candidates against the total number of candidates has risen steadily. This may be explained as follows. Under the SNTV system, an LDP incumbent was no less likely to lose in the next election because he or she had to fight for the same piece of pie, or conservative votes, against other LDP candidates and independent con-

Table 4.1 Victory Rates for Hereditary vs. Nonhereditary Politicians, 1990–2003

	1990	1993	1996[a]	2000[a]	2003[a]
Total number of candidates	953	955	1,261	1,199	1,026
Total victory rate (%)	53.7	53.5	23.8	25.0	29.2
Number of hereditary candidates	169	158	162	152	150
Ratio of hereditary candidates (%)	17.7	16.5	12.8	12.7	14.6
Victory rate of all hereditary candidates (%)	74.0	83.5	75.3	72.4	81.3
Victory rate of hereditary newcomers (%)	—	64.7	36.8	50.0	45.6

Source: Asahi Senkyo Taikan Books and the CD-ROMs of the 2000 and 2003 general election data, edited by *Asahi Shimbun.*

Note: a. Results for the single-member district system only.

servative candidates. However, under the single-member district system only one candidate may be awarded the party nomination, and the single-member district system discourages independent conservative candidates from standing for election. Therefore, it follows that incumbent candidates have a high chance of winning.

In turn, this may result in an increase in the victory rate for LDP incumbent candidates because the LDP consists of a large number of incumbent second-generation politicians. On the other hand, the single-member district system has led to a decrease in the victory rate for new candidates, including second-generation newcomers; their victory rate has dropped from 65 percent (before implementation of the single-member district system) to 45 percent (after implementation). Of course, this percentage is much higher than that of non-second-generation newcomer candidates. Therefore, it may be safe to say that second-generation candidates thus far have been in an advantageous position both before and after the adoption of the single-member district system.

Next, let us turn to the types of newcomer hereditary winners. Figure 4.2 shows the victory rates for second-generation challengers classified by

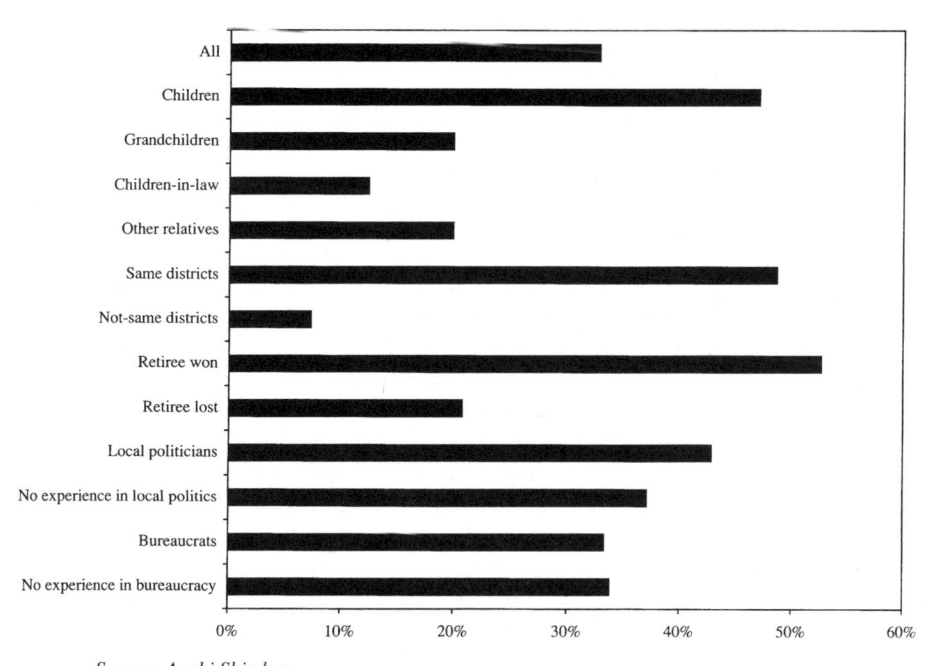

Figure 4.2 Victory Rates for Second-generation Candidates Running for the First Time (percentage)

Source: Asahi Shimbun.

their attributes. According to the figure, children of predecessors clearly have by far the highest victory rate, followed by grandchildren and other relatives (i.e., spouses and brothers or sisters of predecessors). Compared to these two types of winners, children-in-law have a much lower victory rate. Another line of reasoning, as Ishibashi and Reed (1992) point out, is that chances of success are much higher when the newcomer inherits the predecessor's *jiban* (i.e., runs from the same district as the predecessor) and when the newcomer runs while the predecessor is still in his or her term. Previous work experience of the newcomer, such as having been a bureaucrat or a local politician, has little, if any, effect on the victory rate.

Figure 4.2 shows victory rates for second-generation candidates in the narrow sense who are running for an election for the first time, whereas Table 4.1 shows the percentages of second-generation candidates in the broad sense who had not yet won a seat (survey conducted by the *Asahi Shimbun*). By including candidates who have run a number of times, the percentages in Table 4.1 result in a higher victory rate for newcomer second-generation candidates. Figure 4.2 highlights second-generation candidates who are running for the first time based on the idea that the most effective way to compare and analyze (between various types of second-generation politicians) the advantages of being a second-generation politician should be to focus on the first election in which they ran.

To sum up, the most important factor for a newcomer hereditary candidate to win an election is the blood relationship between the candidate and the predecessor. It is also important that a newcomer inherits the predecessor's support base and the *koenkai* while the predecessor still has a strong political influence. In short, what matters most is the second-generation candidate's relationship with the predecessor, rather than the candidate's capability.

Success in the Political World

Apparently, second-generation politicians inherit and maintain the predecessor's robust support base as they win consecutive elections, thereby climbing the ladder to political success. In this section, we will take a look at how second-generation politicians gain success.

Table 4.2 shows the results of a logistic regression analysis of LDP candidates in the 1996 general election. In the LDP, it is said that whether a person can rise to a Cabinet minister position depends on how many times he or she has won elections. Most of the LDP Diet members can enter the Cabinet for the first time following their fourth or fifth electoral victory; however, whether this politician can continue as a Cabinet member depends on his or her competitiveness. Table 4.2 supports this claim, showing that the number of victories affects the progression toward becoming a Cabinet member. A more interesting fact is that, even after controlling for the num-

Table 4.2 Ministerial Experience and LDP Candidates' Performance in the 1996 Lower House Election

	Dependent Variables					
	Ministerial Experience		The Highest Vote Share		Winner	
	B	sig.	B	sig.	B	sig.
Independent Variables						
Number of victories	0.943	0.000	0.095	0.000	−0.001	0.968
Hereditary candidate factor	0.646	0.000	1.255	0.000	1.271	0.000
Ministerial experience			0.209	0.149	1.460	0.000
Highest vote share					2.630	0.000
Constant	−5.217	0.000	0.175	0.002	−1.299	0.000
Cox & Snell R square	0.521		0.092		0.333	
N	3,228		3,227		3,227	

Source: Data from the Asahi Senkyo Taikan Books and the CD-ROMs of the 1996 general election data, edited by the *Asahi Shimbun*.

Note: See Table 4.5 in the chapter appendix for details of the variables.

ber of electoral victories, the hereditary candidate factor has a significant effect. In other words, if two politicians win elections the same number of times, the second-generation politician will have a higher chance of winning a Cabinet seat than the non-second-generation politician.

Effects of the hereditary candidate factor are overwhelming when it comes to forming a support base (i.e., winning the largest vote share in an area). In the 1996 House of Representatives election, when either a second-generation LDP or New Frontier Party candidate competed in a given district, the other party ran a newcomer with little political experience so as to avoid an "unwinnable war." This seems to have led to many major second-generation candidates winning "a perfect victory" (i.e., winning the largest number of votes in every municipality in the district). This may be good evidence of the robustness of a second-generation politician's support base. Moreover, in terms of an LDP candidate winning or losing an election, the hereditary factor has a positive effect in raising the chance of winning, along with winning the highest vote share in a municipality and Cabinet experience. This means that if two politicians have a support base of a similar robustness, and if the two have the same number of positions as a Cabinet member, then a second-generation candidate can contribute more to the LDP winning than a non-second-generation candidate.

Slicing the Central Government Spending Pie

As mentioned earlier, second-generation politicians gain support from their loyal constituencies so that they can win consecutive elections, and then experience a Cabinet position in the early stages of their political career, thereby steadily working their way up the political ladder. However, the bulk of the support base probably would stop supporting the respective political family if their locality did not receive a substantial profit allocation. Let us consider next the success of second-generation politicians in terms of profit allocation.

As Ichikawa (1990) points out, there is a theory that the local government's financial dependence on the national government has accelerated hereditary succession within the LDP. It is well known that the long-ruling LDP in Japanese politics finds its strongest support in nonurban areas with a weak economic base. Numerous studies have been conducted to identify the LDP's political impact on the distribution of subsidies (e.g., Kobayashi 1985, 1990, 1997; Cho 1993; Taniguchi [Onizuka] 1997; Natori 2002; Horiuchi and Saito 2003a, 2003b). Second-generation politicians in the LDP serve as conduits, established by their predecessors, to channel funds from the central government to their constituencies.

Table 4.3 reports only the significant findings of a multiple regression analysis of the difference that electing an LDP or second-generation politician has on the financial transfer (local allocation tax, special local grants, and national treasury subsidies) from the central government to each local government in 1997. The first line of the table indicates the effects on revenue increase where LDP candidates gained the highest vote share, while the second line exhibits the same effects where LDP second-generation candidates gained the highest vote share. Each result is controlled by elements illustrated in the census of 1995 (i.e., the population growth rate, the popu-

Table 4.3   The Effect of First- and Second-generation Politicians on the Revenue of Local Governments

	Local Allocation Tax		Special Local Grants		National Treasury Subsidies	
	B	t	B	t	B	t
LDP candidate	**0.030**	2.306	**0.046**	2.070	**−0.128**	−5.638
Nisei candidate	**0.029**	2.060	**0.059**	2.470	−0.040	−1.631

Notes: N = 3,227.

The models included social and financial condition control variables. See Table 4.5 in the chapter appendix for details of the variables. The parameters (B) in **bold** indicate that the effects are significant.

lation density, the primary industries rate, the financial index) as well as a dummy variable for a government ordinance-designated city (ODC) and a dummy variable indicating areas damaged by the Great Hanshin Earthquake in 1995.

Table 4.3 also shows that, when we compare (1) LDP politicians who have garnered the highest vote share and (2) LDP second-generation politicians with the highest vote share, there is almost no difference between the two in the increase in the shares of local allocation of tax revenue that they were able to deliver to their districts. If we look at special local grants revenues, however, LDP second-generation politicians scored higher.

It is commonly thought that the allocation of special local grants is more susceptible to political influence than the local allocation of tax. The results shown in Table 4.3 confirm this view by implying that second-generation legislators could exercise a greater influence in the allocation of special local grants.

Table 4.4 shows the effects of hereditary succession on the financial conditions of local governments, namely, how much each local government's financial condition improved from 1997 to 1998. Two cases in the 1996 general election are considered here: (1) instances in which an LDP Diet member scored the highest vote share, and (2) those when an LDP second-generation Diet member gained the highest vote share.

Table 4.4 shows that the scale of local finance (the fiscal strength index [FSI]) tends to increase more in the latter cases (i.e., when an LDP second-generation Diet member gained the highest vote share). However, as to the improvement of the ratio of recurring profit (RRP), which indicates financial rigidity, there is almost no difference between these two types of politicians. In short, second-generation Diet members play an important part in expanding the scale of local public finance, but not in putting local public finance on a healthy footing.

Table 4.4 The Effect of Second-generation Politicians on the Growth Rate of Local Finances, 1997–1998

	Growth Rate of the FSI		Growth Rate of the RRP	
	B	t	B	t
LDP candidate	**0.060**	**2.678**	−0.003	1.114
Nisei candidate	**0.068**	**2.880**	−0.002	0.657

Notes: N = 3,227.
The results models included social and financial condition control variables. See Table 4.5 in the chapter appendix for details of the variables. The parameters (B) and (t) in **bold** indicate that the effects are significant.

The results reported in Table 4.4 imply that LDP or second-generation legislators contribute to aggravating the already increasing local public finance deficits. And for local residents, supporting second-generation Diet members suggests that obtaining immediate budgets is more important than establishing sound finances. Therefore, it may follow that Japanese electorates do not expect second-generation politicians to execute a reform in the true sense of the term. Rather, what they expect of second-generation politicians is to leverage their advantages as such and secure profits for their district amid the severe economic and social conditions.

Conclusion

Being a second-generation politician does not only mean a high probability of winning elections. It also means that a politician is already equipped with the many advantages required to get along in the political sphere. Second-generation LDP Diet members, compared to non-second-generation LDP Diet members, are more capable of forming a support base; they also have a higher probability of serving in a Cabinet position. This implies that second-generation LDP Diet members benefit from the hereditary factor in their efforts to become influential Diet members. In this sense, considering the fact that the two prime ministers after Koizumi (Shinzo Abe and Yasuo Fukuda) had a Diet member as father or grandfather, it may be likely that Japan will continue to have hereditary politicians in its top leadership positions in the upcoming years.

As for their relationship to political reforms, second-generation candidates have, at least for the time being, an advantage in winning elections. As discussed in this chapter, their victory rate is as high as 80 percent, even after the implementation of the new electoral system. To be more precise, the ratio of second-generation candidates among all candidates dropped after the implementation of the new system, but has gradually recovered in recent elections. This may be due to the fact that the single-member district system works in favor of incumbents; therefore, it may be more likely for second-generation incumbent candidates to win seats.

This fact should have important implications in considering the effects of the new single-member district–oriented system on the competitiveness of Japanese democracy. The single-member district system is considered in general to lead to a two-party system, which in turn increases the possibility of administration change (Duverger 1954). This is actually the ongoing case in Japan, where a two-party system is gradually emerging. Some have pointed out that such a situation in which two major parties are seeking to hold office has promoted competitiveness, at least at the party system level (McKean and Scheiner 2000). However, it should be noted that the possibility of an administrative change actually taking place will remain low unless the two major parties (the LDP and the Democratic Party of Japan [DPJ]) have equal power. As Ellis S. Krauss and Robert Pekkanen suggest in Chapter 2, under the single-member district system, a narrow defeat in the district level may lead to a landslide defeat in the overall result, which is why the DPJ has failed to hold office in spite of its increase in the vote ratio. On the other side of the same coin, in the 2005 Upper House election, the LDP won narrow victories in many of the districts, thereby leading to a massive overall victory. And such possibilities also hold true in the case of incumbent and newcomer candidates under the single-member district system: it is difficult for a newcomer to win a seat over an incumbent. Therefore, it may be said that competitiveness has not been promoted at the district level.

If elections become more competitive in the future, then the resources needed to successfully compete in such elections will naturally increase. Some support second-generation legislators on the basis that they are capable of reducing the election costs and maintenance costs of their support bases, and consequently are able to allot more time and funds to high-politics matters. In this respect, it may follow that the progress of democracy in Japan will lead to the flourishing of second-generation legislators.

However, this is not to say that second-generation politicians have no need to care about maintaining their support bases. Rather, if their support base is located in an area with poor financial conditions, they are faced with a greater requirement to gain more financial transfers from the government—which is what the support base expects them to do. In areas where second-generation LDP candidates won with the highest vote share, they play an important part in increasing local public finances, but not in putting local public finance on a healthy footing as shown in Table 4.4.

It is true that the ability to bring about great improvements in local public finances is one measure of a competent politician. However, it is also true that politicians who seek to improve local public finances by governmental transfers, as well as electorates who favor such circumstances, lead to a "tragedy of the commons" in national finance. Moreover, the current critical state of governmental finance is producing "smaller pieces of pie" and seems to be accelerating politicians' moves to secure ever-smaller pieces. This may be a good reason for supporting second-generation legislators who, even in this age of calls for reform, are representative of "stability" and "lack of change."

Finally, I must comment on the relationship between Japanese hereditary politics and the quality of democracy. The current high victory rate of hereditary candidates along with the high proportion of hereditary politicians in the Cabinet is by no means desirable in terms of the ideals of democracy (i.e., it should be refined through constant competition and innovation). It is often the case, however, that in low-income areas second-generation politicians are expected more than anything else to win financial transfers from the government, and that in urban areas second-generation politicians gain their electoral support due to a sophisticated and clean image. As long as the public views second-generation politicians in this manner, it is highly likely that they will disregard hereditary politicians' potential to degrade democracy. Such consequences are already apparent in the public's indifference toward hereditary politicians, despite the fact that it is increasingly becoming a major phenomenon in the political sphere.

In order to decide whether hereditary politics is in fact degrading democracy, further examination will be required to determine what kind of negative effect it actually has. For example, it is not only hereditary politicians who execute pork barrel projects or practice corruption. The influential former prime minister Kakuei Tanaka, who is most strongly associated with such elements, was not a hereditary politician. On the contrary, hereditary politicians seem to succeed in driving reform with their clean and sophisticated public image—as was demonstrated in the recent reforms led by former prime minister Koizumi, a third-generation politician.

Also requiring further consideration is the psychology behind public support for hereditary politicians. If a hereditary politician should succeed in carrying out reforms that meet public expectations, then such performance may have to be understood as one characteristic of Japanese democracy.

* * *

Appendix

Table 4.5 Measuring the Impact of Hereditary Seats

Variable	Source
Social and financial variables	
Population (log)	*Jumin Kihon Daicho Jinko Yoran* (Kokudo Chiri Kyokai)
Population growth rate (log)	*Kokusei Chosa* (Somusho Tokeikyoku)
Population density (log)	*Kokusei Chosa, Zenkoku Todofuken Shikuchoson Menseki Shirabe* (Kokudo Chiri In)
Primary industries workers ratio	*Kokusei Chosa*
Taxable income per capita (log)	*Kojin Shotoku Shihyo* (Nihon Marketing Center)
Local revenue per capita (log)	*Shichoson-betsu Kessan Jyokyo Shirabe* (Chiho Zaimu Kyokai)
Local allocation tax per capita (log)	*Shichoson-betsu Kessan Jyokyo Shirabe* (Chiho Zaimu Kyokai)
Special local grants per capita (log)	*Shichoson-betsu Kessan Jyokyo Shirabe* (Chiho Zaimu Kyokai)
National treasury subsidies per capita (log)	*Shichoson-betsu Kessan Jyokyo Shirabe* (Chiho Zaimu Kyokai)
Fiscal strength index (FSI)	*Shichoson-betsu Kessan Jyokyo Shirabe* (Chiho Zaimu Kyokai)
Ratio of recurring profit (RRP)	*Shichoson-betsu Kessan Jyokyo Shirabe* (Chiho Zaimu Kyokai)
Cities designated by ordinance=1, others=0	*Kokusei Chosa* (Somusho Tokeikyoku)
Cities damaged by the 1996 earthquake=1, others=0	*Kokusei Chosa* (Somusho Tokeikyoku)
LDP candidate dummy variables	
Hereditary candidates=1, others=0	Data collected by Asahi Shinbunsha
Winners=1, others=0	*Asahi Senkyo Taikan* (Asahi Shinbunsha)
Getting the highest vote share=1, others=0	JED-M Data: The General Elections Database (L.D.B)
Winning with the highest vote share=1, others=0	JED-M Data: The General Elections Database (L.D.B)
Hereditary candidates winning with the highest vote share=1, others=0	
Candidates with minister experience=1, others=0	*Asahi Senkyo Taikan, Nippon no Naikaku* (Kokusei Mondai Chosakai)
Number getting elected	*Asahi Senkyo Taikan*

Sources: Horiuchi and Saito (2003a); data obtained from the Nikkei NEEDS database from www.nikkeieu.com/needs/data/d corporate.html.
Note: Districts and areas where there was no LDP candidate running are not included in the analyses.

Notes

I thank Ellis S. Krauss, Moriwaki Toshimasa, Steven R. Reed, Taniguchi Masaki, and anonymous reviewers for their helpful comments. I am also grateful to Habara Kiyomasa and the Asahi Shimbun Company for their support in collecting the data on Japanese candidates. I acknowledge the support from Ross D. Schaap and Narita Ayumi, and the grant from the Abe Fellowship.

1. In this chapter, "second-generation politician" in its narrow sense refers to politicians who have inherited an electoral base from a politician relative, whereas in its broad sense it refers to politicians who simply have a politician as a relative. Various researchers have defined the term differently. Some define "second-generation politicians" as politicians (1) who have inherited the retiree's electoral base (i.e., those who run in the same electoral district as the retiree, or those who run in the same area at a different election level than his or her predecessor); (2) who are running immediately after the predecessor's retirement (or, the inheritor is running early enough for the *koenkai* to be maintained); and (3) who are an offspring of a lineal family of the predecessor (this applies to cases where a lineal family is regarded as being more important than a collateral family, such as an adopted child, daughter's husband, wife, and other relatives). Others define "second-generation politician" as any Diet member and candidate whose relative is a politician (some critics use this definition for "hereditary politicians"). For example, Taiichi Ichikawa applies the concept of the political family, a term coined by W. L. Guttsman, meaning an English family whose members have consecutively served as members of the Lower House, Cabinet member, or ambassadors for three generations, and defines a "hereditary Diet member" as "a Diet member who has had relatives as national level politicians for two preceding generations" (Ichikawa 1990, 2–5). However, Tetsuhisa Matsuzaki (1991) defines the "second-generation Diet member" as "professional politicians who have inherited, from a relative, an electoral base to run for the House of Representatives, and have won," and uses the term "quasi–second generation Diet member" for those who have not inherited the electoral base (1991, 34–37). This may be enough to show that the definition of the term "second-generation" and the scope of analysis depend largely on the aim of study.

2. Tomoaki Iwai (2003, 97) seems to be using the broad sense of the term.

3. Christopher T. North (2005) views the LDP's seniority system as the most important factor that has increased second-generation Diet members in that party.

4. In the 1996 House of Representatives election, the LDP won 239 seats, recovering its strength as the ruling party. Although the Social Democratic Party of Japan and the New Party Sakigake then enjoyed a position of non-Cabinet participation, this election led to the loss of half of their seats—to only seventeen seats. Therefore, analysis shall be based on the fact that distribution of subsidies was chiefly done by the LDP. Additionally, in this chapter, subsidies include local allocation taxes as subsidies. Although there is disagreement regarding this point, they have been included on the basis that the calculation methods of local allocation taxes are subject to discretion, they supplement national treasury disbursements, and they are related to changes in local loans. Local loans are also included in subsidies with a focus on their subsidy-like nature.

5. Needless to say, further discussions on this matter require a more detailed analysis of the effects of the election outcomes under the proportional representation system, as well as the effects of "zombie" winners (Pekkanen, Nyblade, and Krauss 2006) benefiting from the dual candidacy system.

CHAPTER 5

Policy Preferences and Party Platforms: What Voters Want vs. What Voters Get

Gill Steel

OBSERVERS HAVE BEEN QUICK TO DISMISS JAPANESE DEMOCracy as a "spectator democracy" in which citizens are characterized as uninvolved in and apathetic toward politics. Commentators argue that parties do not discuss policies and citizens do not use their own policy preferences to guide their vote choice.[1] Voters simply "deliver" their vote when requested to do so by local notables, and bureaucrats and the Liberal Democratic Party (LDP), in cahoots with business, make policy in what they profess to be the national interest (see Hrebenar 2000; Kohei, Miyake, and Watanuki 1991; Richardson 1991).

The old electoral system had been blamed for many of the ills in Japanese politics, particularly the money-based nature of politics and the lack of focus on policy issues (see Otake 1998). Politicians, perhaps fearing for their own livelihoods, enacted a series of reforms that were supposed to end corrupt politics, and produce a freer and fairer system. A part of this reform package, as Ellis S. Krauss and Robert Pekkanen discuss in Chapter 2 of this volume, involved amending the Public Office Election Law to create a new electoral system that has been described in detail elsewhere (see, e.g., Christensen 1998; McKean and Scheiner 2000). The new "side-by-side" or mixed-member system combines 300 first-past-the-post single-member districts with 200 (later reduced to 180) proportional representation seats from eleven regional blocks. The system also provides unsuccessful candidates with a much-criticized "second chance": candidates who fail to be elected in their single-member district race can be transferred to their party's proportional representation listing (the so-called zombie or resurrected winners).

The system was intended to provide incentives for voters and parties to focus more on parties and their platforms, and less on individual candidates. Part of the rationale behind introducing the single-member district portion of the system was that candidates would run for election in larger constituencies—no longer running against members of their own party—so they neither would need, nor be able to rely on, only a personal vote. In the proportional representation portion, the constituencies are even larger than are the districts in the single-member district portion, which also necessitates an electoral base beyond the *koenkai* (candidates' personal support networks), since voters can vote for a party. As voters become used to the system, they will decreasingly focus on individual politicians, and instead focus more on parties.[2] But the dual system and the "zombie" provision cloud the issue. As Krauss and Pekkanen point out in Chapter 2, most candidates are dual-listed candidates and two-fifths of all proportional representation representatives are "zombie" winners. This large number of legislators need to focus on their constituencies, rather than on platforms or their parties.

To what extent have the reforms actually made any difference to the business of politics? Some analysts are optimistic. Brian Woodall (1999), for example, suggests that, as voters, parties, and candidates become used to the system, distinct party platforms may develop. Krauss and Pekkanen (2004) comment that the reforms have forced LDP representatives to think more about the median voter, but that the system continues to provide incentives for a personal vote strategy. However, Margaret A. McKean and Ethan Scheiner (2000) argue that the technicalities of the system will transform the proportion representation representatives into locally based politicians who will rely on the personal vote, rather than on party- or policy-based politics. Three case studies of 1996 election campaigns suggest McKean and Scheiner may be right. Hideo Otake (1998), Masahiro Yamada (1998), and Cheol Hee Park (1998a) all found that networks continued to be as important as ever in vote mobilization, candidates actually spent more money during their campaigns than they had previously spent (although these authors expect this to decline in the future), and that party platforms had little impact on the election.

In contrast, authors of other case studies (e.g., Dyron Dabney in Chapter 3 of this volume) and some politicians are convinced that the new electoral system has fundamentally changed the way that politicians campaign (politicians discussed this in personal interviews I conducted in 2004 and 2005). Their views accord with the received wisdom on the incentives that proportional representation and single-member districts produce. Larger single-member districts, and even larger proportional representation blocs, provide incentives for candidates to cast their net beyond a personal vote. As candidates try to attract more voters, they should be more responsive to voters' policy and ideological preferences.

While it is true that responsiveness requires linkages to ensure that governments respect the preferences of the governed, one step in this process is to narrow the gap between the policy preferences of citizens and those of politicians. In this chapter, I examine the correspondence between citizens' ideologies and policy preferences and those of politicians. I look first at long-term trends and show that, over time, parties have become more responsive to voters. I then examine short-term trends to ascertain whether electoral reform has heightened this process. I demonstrate that, overall, parties behave according to Downsian logic, that is, parties move their ideological positions and policy platforms toward the preferences of the median voter as a vote-maximizing strategy (Downs 1957). And one effect of the pursuit of votes is an increase in the responsiveness of parties to citizens' preferences, that is, an improvement in democratic responsiveness. However, politicians have not completely given up the pursuit of the personal vote in favor of the kind of politics in which parties make clear policy or ideological commitments, and we should not expect them to do so. Nonetheless, the dual-listing provision does complicate matters: rather than choosing either to pursue a personal vote or to cast their nets widely, the incentives in the current system mean that a rational candidate or party should simultaneously engage in both of these strategies. It also is unrealistic to expect dramatic, immediate change given that parties and voters are used to the standard operating procedures developed under the old system and the incentives in the current system do not encourage politicians to cast off these procedures, but rather to develop complementary strategies.

In this study, I used large-scale public opinion surveys and ideological surveys of politicians to examine citizens' ideological beliefs and citizens' perceptions of parties' ideological positions. I then examined the correspondence between citizens' and politicians' policy preferences. Finally, I analyzed the role of policy preferences in the 1986, 1996, and 2003 Lower House elections to see whether citizens' policy preferences played a greater role in their vote choice after electoral reform had been enacted. I chose the 1986 election as a baseline because no policy issue dominated this election: choosing, for example, a scandal-dominated election or an issue-dominated election would have provided too unusual a baseline for comparison.

Data Used in This Study

My main source of data was the Akarui Senkyo Suishin Kyokai ([ASSK] Society for the Promotion of Clean Elections) House of Representatives election surveys from 1972 to the present. The ASSK is a cross-sectional survey that is conducted after each election. The respondents are drawn from a stratified nationally representative sample, and the interviews are conducted face-to-face. In the postreform period, I examined politicians' ideological self-placements and policy preferences, using data from ideological surveys of politicians conducted in 1998, 2003, and after the 2005 election. The 1998 ideological survey of legislators was jointly conducted in November and December 1998 by the Political News Department of the daily newspaper, the *Yomiuri Shimbun*, and the Kabashima Research Group at the University of Tokyo's Faculty of Law. The response rate was 59 percent (297 members of the House of Representatives and 150 members of the House of Councilors). The Kabashima Research Group jointly conducted the 2003 and 2005 ideological surveys with the Political News Department of the *Asahi Shimbun*.

Politicians' and Citizens' Ideological Self-placement

Parties began changing ideologically long before electoral reform occurred, partly in response to the changing post–Cold War international environment and partly in pursuit of support from the median voter. Under the 1955 System, with the marginalization of the left and the dominance of the LDP at the national polls, the political map was straightforward for decades. Despite its lack of success in general elections, the Japan Socialist Party (JSP) functioned successfully as a "party of pressure," occasionally setting the agenda for national discussion and legislation. Yet the system was not static: although marked by some degree of policy consensus and conservative dominance in national elections, all parties underwent fundamental shifts in ideology and policy platforms.

When asked to locate the parties on a 10-point (or 5-point) left-right or progressive-conservative scale, ranging from 1 (*most progressive*) to 5 (*most conservative*), citizens placed the parties far apart in the 1960s. But when surveys asked voters the same question in the 1980s and in the 1990s, citizens thought that the parties were becoming ideologically closer (see Figure 5.1). See also Ikuo Kabashima and Yoshihiko Takenaka (1996).

This shift in the parties' ideological positions makes sense electorally because the median citizen thinks of himself or herself as neither conservative nor reformist, but as neutral (see Figure 5.1). The ASSK surveys ask citizens, "When you think about national politics, do you consider yourself conservative, progressive, or neutral?" I recoded the responses from 1990 and 1993 to conform to this pattern (see Figure 5.6 in the chapter appendix). Since the early 1970s, around 40 percent of citizens describe themselves as conservative, whereas less than 20 percent describe themselves as reformist. The parties' shift can be described in classical Downsian terms, that is, converging toward the position of the median voter, but fear of losing extremist voters prevents parties from becoming identical (Downs 1957, 140).

The electoral system was adopted with the expectation that it would provide incentives for the development of a two-party system, where parties

Figure 5.1 Voters' Perceptions of Parties' Ideologies vs. Position of Median Voter, 1967, 1983, and 1996

1967	JCP	JSP	ý Komeito		LDP
1983		JCP	JSP	ý Komeito	LDP
1996			JCP	JSP ý	LDP
	1	2	3	4	5
	most progressive		neutral		most conservative

Sources: Japanese Election Study, Robert Ward and Akira Kubota, principal investigators, Interuniversity Consortium for Political and Social Research, no. 7294, available from http://www.icpsr.umich.edu/; Japanese Election Survey (JES I, 1983), Joji Watanuki, Ichiro Miyake, Takashi Inoguchi, Yoshiaki Kobayashi, and Ken'ichi Ikeda, principal investigators, available from http://www.bokutakusha.com/ldb/ldb databank.html; Japanese Election and Democracy Study (JEDS 1996), Aiji Tanaka, Ken'ichi Ikeda, and Yoshitaka Nishizawa, principal investigators, available from http://ssjda.iss.u-tokyo.ac.jp/en/.

Notes: ý = median ideological self-placement.
Question wording and orginal codes are not identitcal; see Table 5.1 in the chapter appendix.

offer voters alternative platforms from which to choose. Yet the contemporary party system does not fit well this idealized model. On average, the ideologies of the major parties are moving toward the center, but much intraparty ideological variation exists. The Democratic Party of Japan (DPJ), formed in 1996, and reconstituted in 1998, emerged as the major opposition party, having absorbed some of the Socialists, some smaller parties, and some conservative politicians. This union of politicians from across the ideological spectrum inevitably lacks a coherent ideology. The LDP, too, has classically been a "catchall" party that includes politicians with a broad range of ideologies.

In addition, with the broader international "postideology" environment coupled with fundamental changes in the Japanese party system during the 1990s, we could expect voters to be confused by parties' ideology and to be less inclined to think in ideological terms. During the 1990s, seemingly unconnected to ideology, a dizzying array of parties formed, dissolved, and reformed. Coalition governments comprised of ideologically strange bedfellows, ranging from a few parties to almost all parties from across the ideological map, governed Japan. Such cooperation made it harder to distinguish between the parties. Yet despite this and the parties' lack of emphasis on ideology, citizens do actually think in ideological terms, and a majority of voters can identify the parties' changing ideologies.

Turning from citizens' perceptions of parties to the actual self-placement of Diet members on a progressive-conservative scale shows that DPJ Diet members have taken a rational course of action and increasingly located themselves closer to the LDP. This makes sense because it is close to the position of the median voter. The *Yomiuri Shimbun*–Kabashima Research Group survey asks Diet members their opinions on a number of policy issues and to place themselves ideologically on a scale that ranges from 1 (*kakushin*) (*most progressive*) to 10 (*hoshu*) (*most conservative*).[3]

Figure 5.2 presents the average Diet members' ideological self-placements for each of the major parties in 1998, 2003, and following the 2005 election. Since 1998 the LDP legislators have moved in a more progressive direction (although they are weighted toward the conservative side). Komeito politicians have positioned themselves more centrally, but have been moving in a slightly less progressive direction (toward the LDP).[4] The DPJ legislators also have moved in a more conservative direction, closer to the LDP.

The average placements of the legislators fail to show the diversity within the parties, thus Figure 5.3 presents the legislators' ideological placement in the form of distribution curves. In 2005, the ideological self-placements of the LDP Diet members show the divisions within the party: the more numerous old guard peaking at around 7 in Figure 5.3, while the "reformers" are visible as a slight rise around the number 3. The DPJ,

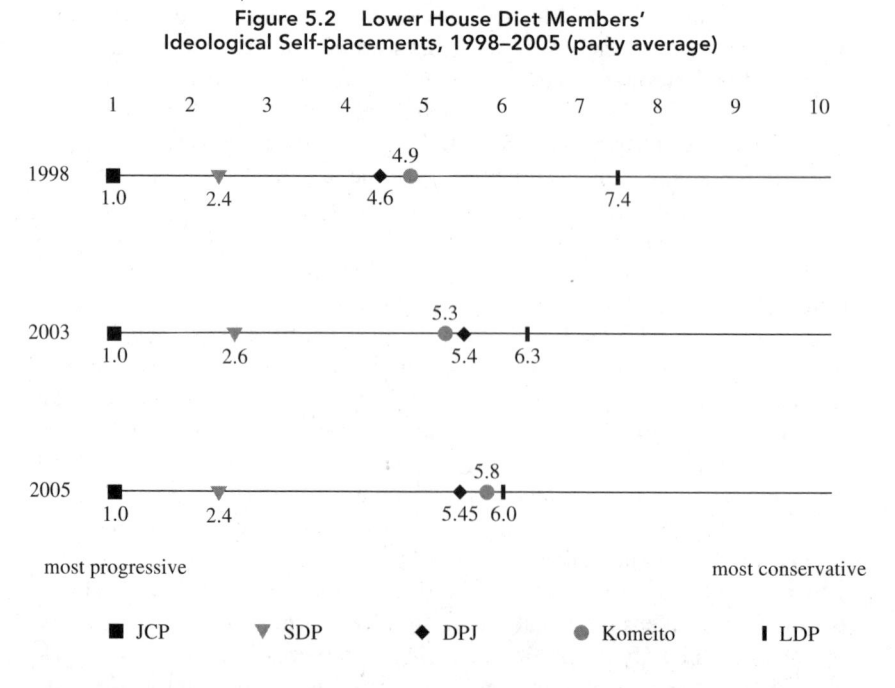

Figure 5.2 Lower House Diet Members' Ideological Self-placements, 1998–2005 (party average)

Year	JCP	SDP	DPJ	Komeito	LDP
1998	1.0	2.4	4.6	4.9	7.4
2003	1.0	2.6	5.4	5.3	6.3
2005	1.0	2.4	5.45	5.8	6.0

most progressive ← → most conservative

■ JCP   ▼ SDP   ◆ DPJ   ● Komeito | LDP

Sources: Survey conducted in 1998 by *Yomiuri Shimbun* Political News Department and the Kabashima Research Group at the University of Tokyo, Faculty of Law; 2003 and 2005 surveys conducted by *Asahi Shimbun* Political News Department and the Kabashima Research Group.

POLICY PREFERENCES AND PARTY PLATFORMS 87

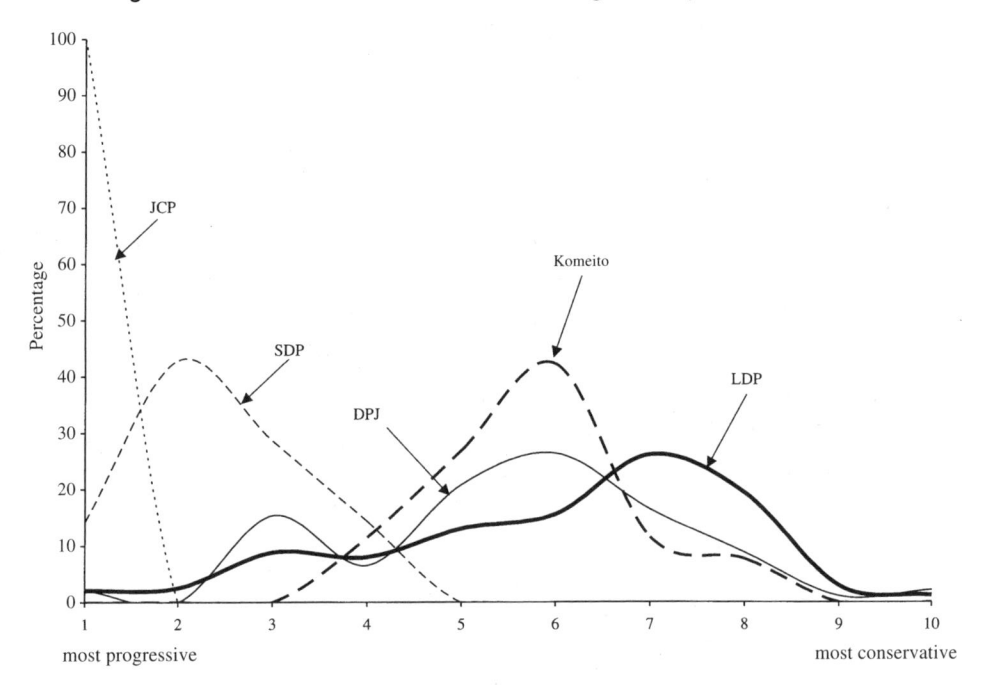

Figure 5.3 Lower House Diet Members' Ideological Self-placements, 2005

Sources: Survey conducted in 1998 by *Yomiuri Shimbun* Political News Department and the Kabashima Research Group at the University of Tokyo, Faculty of Law; 2003 and 2005 surveys conducted by *Asahi Shimbun* Political News Department and the Kabashima Research Group.

unsurprisingly, lacks cohesiveness because of the diverse origins of its legislators, but what is absolutely obvious from the figure is the considerable overlap between the ideology of the LDP and that of the DPJ.

These ideological placements seem to accurately reflect policy preferences, with the old guard of the LDP supporting policies that are designed to protect uncompetitive sectors of the economy, maintain spending on public works, and postpone or abandon privatization plans. The reformers, on the other hand, favor "structural reform," by which they mean deregulation, disposal of bad loans, and privatizing public corporations.

Party Platforms and Citizens' Policy Preferences

This shift toward the median voter is also somewhat visible in the shifts of party platforms. Over the long term, the LDP has famously followed a pragmatic approach to its policy platform, and this pragmatism is increasingly evident. The LDP emphasized social issues in the mid-1950s, then moved to lifestyle issues before returning to social issues in the 1970s, and subsequently shifted to foreign affairs in the 1980s. But the electorate may not particularly associate the LDP with these policies because the correlation between the emphases in its platform and government expenditures has been weak (Kobayashi 1997).

The advent of the manifesto in Japanese politics, again exactly in line with Anthony Downs's theories, meant that the LDP and the DPJ did not produce two distinct platforms. The policy platforms located the parties in the area of overlapping policies, near the middle of the scale, so that the parties resemble each other and the manifestos lack overall clarity. Downs explains this ambiguity as follows: "This tendency towards similarity is reinforced by deliberate equivocation about each particular issue" (1957, 141). Fostering ambiguity is a rational vote-maximizing strategy.

The Social Democratic Party of Japan (SDPJ), formerly the JSP, is now committed to social democracy, rather than to socialism, having dropped some of its more radical policy positions. According to Yoshiaki Kobayashi's (1997) content analysis of party documents, the JSP focused on lifestyle issues until the mid-1960s and then focused more on social issues in the 1970s. In the 1990s, the SDPJ finally dropped its long-standing opposition to the Japan-US Security Treaty and the Japan Self-Defense Forces. This makes sense electorally, as we have seen that these issues interest only a small minority of the population. The ideological survey of politicians shows that even between 1998 and 2005, the SDPJ politicians had modified several of their positions. In 1998, the SDPJ strongly opposed strengthening defense capabilities, strengthening the Japan-US security arrangements, possessing nuclear weapons, and small government. But in the space of five years, the party's positions had become more moderate on all issues except for nuclear weapons (*Asahi Shimbun* and Kabashima Research Group Ideological Survey of Diet Members 2003), thus moving toward the mainstream and away from the more radical policies that are popular only with activists.

The Japan Communist Party (JCP), once intent on creating a communist Japan has also changed its rhetoric over time. Rather than working toward a socialist revolution, the JCP now proposes a "democratic revolution," stressing freedom and democracy. But JCP Diet members are still ideologically cohesive and have barely shifted their policy preferences. In 2005, JCP politicians maintained their progressive ideology and policy positions. To some extent, the JCP has gone down the path of many other Communist Parties and reformed its basic ideological stance to improve its electoral fortunes. The questions on the survey, however, reflect the continued commitment of the JCP Diet members to highly progressive policies.

Komeito has followed an ad hoc approach to its policy platform that seems to be aimed toward gaining support. Originally committed to a radical policy platform, the Komeito has jettisoned much of its former radicalism. During the 1960s, the Komeito emphasized lifestyle and foreign affairs, locating itself fairly close to the JCP in these respects (Kobayashi 1997, 38). Even between 1998 and 2005, Komeito lawmakers' positions on foreign policy became more neutral. Once a steadfast supporter of the Constitution, by 1998, lawmakers were neutral on the question of revision (Kabashima 1999), even though Komeito's official policy is opposition to constitutional revision.[5] By the 1990s, Komeito had been part of various coalition governments, and had achieved some significant policy successes in the area of welfare.

Surveys of Diet members show the ideological shifts and changes in policy preferences. The Ideological Survey of Diet Members conducted by the *Asahi Shimbun* and the Kabashima Research Group after the 2005 election shows that in the 2005 Lower House, compared with its predecessor, a number of the new Diet members favored reform but, at the same time, were more conservative on a number of policy preferences, with slightly more Diet members who favored strengthening Japan's defense capabilities and revising the "peace clause" of the Constitution.

Legislators rated their own positions on fourteen basic policy issues using a 5-point scale that ranges from 1 (*agree*) to 5 (*disagree*). Broad agreement among the legislators regardless of party existed on the issues of providing a stronger say for the emperor in government affairs and possessing nuclear weapons; virtually all of the legislators opposed both. A broad consensus existed on the issues of improving social welfare and implementing reforms to elevate the status of women. All the parties leaned toward support for improving social welfare, reforming systems to elevate the position of women, and carrying out administrative reform.

More variation in opinion existed on the neoliberal agenda of achieving small government, promoting self-reliance, and raising the share of indirect taxes. The Liberal Party was the most strongly in favor, followed by the LDP, while the DPJ, Komeito, SDPJ, and JCP were more negative. Wide variation is evident among the parties on the strengthening of Japan's defense capabilities and of its security arrangements with the United States, a permanent seat for Japan on the UN Security Council, and revision of the Constitution. The Liberals were the most heavily in favor of strengthening Japan's defense capabilities, followed by the Liberal Democrats. Unsurprisingly, both the SDPJ and the JCP were definitively opposed, and the DPJ and Komeito legislators had intermediate views that leaned toward opposition.

To what extent do the parties' platforms correspond with voters' policy preferences? Although data do not exist to allow a direct test, qualitatively comparing citizens' and Diet members' preferences adds to our overall understanding of this issue. The ASSK surveys ask the respondents what issues they had in mind when they made their vote choice (they are given a "show card"). Unfortunately, the questions do not ask for direction of preference, nor are the closed-set responses identical to the questions on the survey of Diet members, so direct tests are difficult. Nonetheless, a more qualitative comparison of citizens' policy concerns with those of Diet members is still illuminative. The issues that are directly connected to voters' own livelihoods unsurprisingly concern them most. Since 1972, between 20 percent and 55 percent of voters have considered welfare, prices, and taxation when making the vote choice (ethics periodically concerns voters during scandals).[6] I present the percentages of citizens who considered the various policy issues that I include in the regression analysis in Figure 5.4. Issues that fairly consistently concerned only a minority of citizens are the environment, the Constitution, and commerce. Issues that were included only on the 2003 survey and on which politicians focus (e.g., fiscal reform, structural reform, and political reform) concerned between 6 percent and 20 percent of voters.

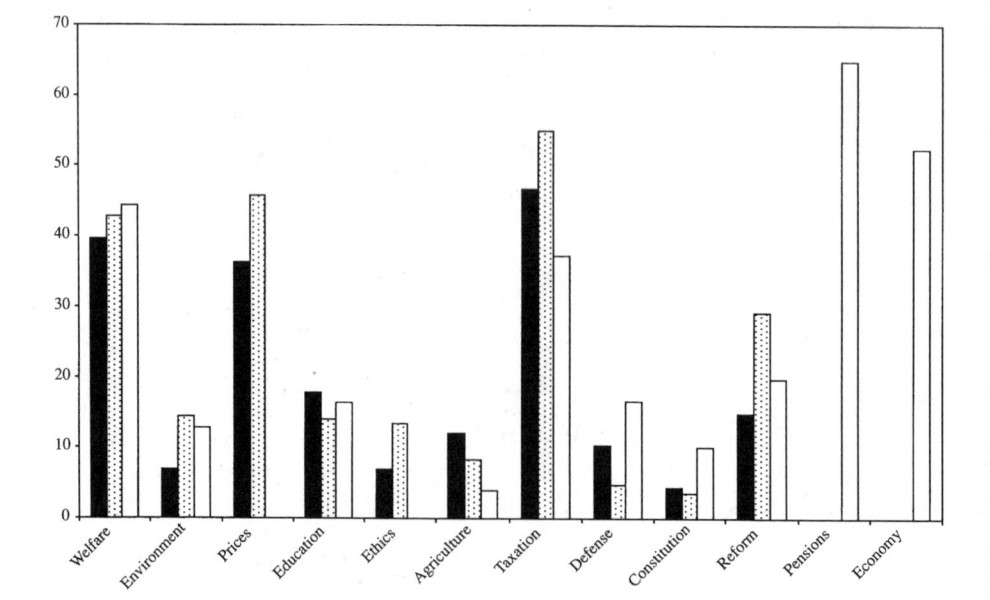

Figure 5.4 Percentage of Citizens Who Consider Policy Issues in Their Vote Choice

Source: Akarui Senkyo Suishin Kyokai Shugiin Giin Sosenkyo (Society for the Promotion of Clean Elections House of Representatives election) studies from the years 1986, 1996, and 2003, made available through the Leviathan Data Bank, Tokyo.

What do voters get? Politicians from the two major parties—the LDP and the DPJ—have remarkably similar policy preferences. The LDP reformers, in common with the DPJ, broadly favored economic reform—deregulation, fiscal restraint, and the privatization of public corporations—issues that concerned few citizens. The LDP and DPJ Diet members' levels of support for various policy issues reported in Figure 5.5 emphasizes the remarkable closeness of the two parties on other policy issues, making it even more difficult for citizens to distinguish between the two.

In sum, although most parties do not usually emphasize policy platforms or ideology at election times—even the more recent "manifesto elections" were not particularly clarifying—the parties have all shifted ideologically and voters are aware of the ideological shifts. Furthermore, over the long term the parties' policy platforms have shifted considerably.

Since citizens do care about policy issues, why do parties seem to place so little emphasis on platforms? To examine whether citizens' policy preferences have become more influential in the vote choice in the postreform

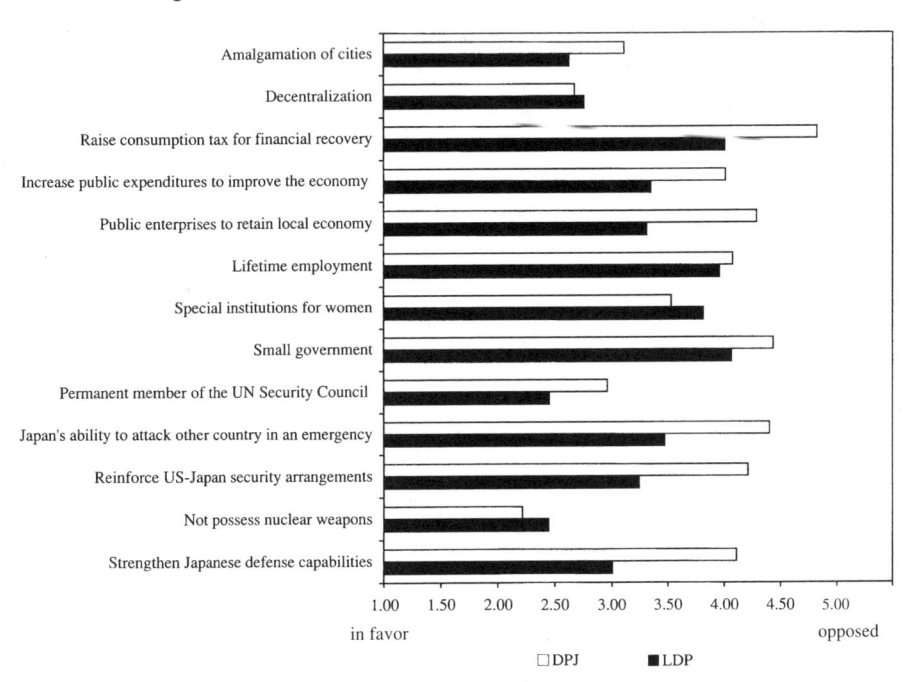

Figure 5.5 LDP and DPJ Politicians' Policy Preferences, 2003

Source: Survey conducted in 2003 by *Asahi Shimbun* Political News Department and the Kabashima Research Group.

period, I analyzed the influence of issue preferences on the vote choice in Lower House elections in 1986, 1996, and 2003.

If it were the case that electoral reform has changed the way citizens decide how to vote, we would expect that, before reform, citizens' policy preferences would not influence their vote choice but, after reform, policy preferences would weigh more heavily. I chose these three elections because they were not dominated by any single issue that would unusually influence voting preferences. For each election, I estimated a multinomial logistic regression model, with the *respondent's reported vote* as the dependent variable. This is a three-category variable: the LDP, leftist parties (the JSP and the JCP), and other parties. I included the following variables in the analysis to gauge their influence on the vote decision:

Policy issues. Whether the respondent considered agriculture, prices (1986 and 1996), pensions (2003), welfare, taxation, education, defense, the environment, the Constitution, reform (fiscal reform 2003), ethics, and economics (2003) in the vote choice (1 if considered, 0 otherwise).

Measures of network integration. As "control" variables, I included membership in a community network, professional association, trade union, *koenkai* or a religious alignment (1 if member, 0 otherwise), social integration: length of residence (four-category variable) and community size (five-category variable).

Sociodemographic variables. Age (six-category variable in 1986 and 1993; eight-category variable in 2003); education (1988 elementary, middle, upper; 1996 four-category variable; 2003 five-category variable); gender (1 if female, 0 otherwise); and white-collar status (1 if white-collar, 0 otherwise). (See Figure 5.6 in the chapter appendix for the exact question wording.)

I present the results of the multivariate analysis of voter choice in Table 5.1 in the chapter appendix. The results demonstrate that policy preferences only occasionally influenced the vote choice, after taking into account other causes of the vote. Overall, comparing the prereform 1986 election with the postreform 1996 and 2003 elections demonstrates that policy preferences did not become more influential in voting preferences as a result of the reforms. Despite the incentives in the electoral system that had the potential to encourage politicians to focus on policies, and the introduction of manifestos into election campaigns, only a few policy preferences had a modest, and occasionally substantial, impact on the vote choice, and most issue preferences did not play a role.

I do not convert these coefficients to probabilities because it is sufficient to note that there is no large and substantial change in the influence of policy preferences in the elections after reform. Concern over welfare stands out; prior to 2003, citizens who were concerned about welfare were less likely than were others to vote for the LDP. But by 2003, they were more likely to vote for the LDP than for other parties. The DPJ has failed to associate itself with welfare policy in ways that the old leftist parties did. Since the LDP is in coalition with Komeito, and Komeito has been able to push through a number of pro-welfare reforms, Komeito's pro-welfare image may have "rubbed off" on the LDP.

Defense was prominent in the anti-LDP vote in 1986 and 1996, and decreased the LDP vote by around 1 percent. Yet by 2003, the DPJ was unable to capitalize on this issue in the way that the traditional leftist opposition did. Surprisingly, for a party that has been linked with agricultural interests and support for farmers, concern over agriculture only benefited the LPD in 1986, when the average citizen who was concerned was 0.92 percent more likely to vote LDP than was his or her nonconcerned counterpart.

Most issues do not influence the vote, but citizens do claim to be interested in policy issues. If parties were to offer strong policy platforms, they may be able to garner votes. But this is a difficult strategy. Japan, in common with a number of Western societies, has no socioeconomic or cultural cleavage more important and stable than others that politicians could draw on to garner votes. The electorate is capable of a number of splits along policy lines, so politicians have to decide which of the potential splits will be more effective and advantageous to them as vote-garnering strategies. As Bernard Manin (1997) points out, the convergence between candidates proposing a line of division and the audience (i.e., electorate) responding is a constant process that involves trial and error.

Discussion

Depictions of Japanese voters as unconcerned by either ideology or policy issues are not wholly accurate. Many voters do think ideologically and have specific policy preferences, and some of these preferences have a marginal effect on their vote choice. The majority of policy issues, however, do not influence vote choice, and electoral reform has made little difference in this respect. Several commonly cited factors such as the "catchall" nature of the LDP, the former electoral system, and the waning of the sharply bifurcated political division of the 1960s may have impeded the development of issue-based politics. But these factors have not prevented voters from distinguishing between the parties on the basis of their policy platforms or ideologies. In addition, the divergent incentives of the current electoral system discussed earlier mean that politicians should be responsive to the median voter but, at the same time, should cultivate a personal vote that relies more on the distribution of benefits than it does on firm policy commitments.

Despite pressure from inside the LDP for internal reform, the old guard opposes change. Perhaps with good reason. R. Michael Alvarez and Jonathan Nagler (1995), using the 1992 US presidential election as an example, demonstrate that the movement of candidates' ideologies is not always a sound electoral strategy. If a party moves ideologically toward one group of potential supporters, it risks alienating those who supported the previous platform or ideology. As the LDP moves away from the "politics of redistribution," it risks undermining the party's support base (much of the structural reform program cuts into the LDP's traditional base), and further reform—in either direction—could be a risky strategy.

The findings I present in this chapter highlight questions that are at the heart of democratic politics, namely, the extent to which citizens are able to control their political representatives and the factors that influence the extent of politicians' accountability to citizens. To put it more concretely, in a situation in which citizens care about policies but don't vote on policy issues, how do they get politicians to adopt the policies they support, that is, how do they ensure responsiveness?

Some theorists argue that institutional constraints are necessary to ensure responsiveness. In Japan, proponents of electoral reform thought that a different electoral system would alter the practice of politics in Japan, but electoral reform has not caused a sharp break with past practice. However, over the long term, politicians have gradually moved toward the central ground that is occupied by voters. Two remarkably similar catchall parties—the LDP and the DPJ—have emerged that have in common similar ideologies and policies. As Gerald L. Curtis points out, "Japanese politicians seeking the support of as many voters as possible end up sounding very much like each other" (1999, 164). Overall, the parties are moving toward the rational outcome that Downs (1957) hypothesizes for a two-party system. For Downs, parties move toward the center of the issue space to maximize their vote share, in effect becoming more responsive to the median voter. Ironically, however, the parties' increasing responsiveness leads to a lack of choice for voters: as the two largest parties move to the center, voters are offered less, rather than more, choice. Even the alternatives that the SDPJ and JCP offer are not attractive choices for the strategic voter, given the marginalized status of these two parties. In the single-member districts, the LDP and DPJ have squeezed out smaller parties, but the proportional representation portion of the system ensures that the smaller parties have not been completely eliminated, allowing voters some choice.

Although it is true that the LDP is a catchall party, and its closeness to the DPJ adds confusion, this has not resulted in a blanket absence of interest in policies among the electorate. But when it comes to the vote choice, many other factors are influential. Furthermore, as much previous research demonstrates, the link between platforms and policymaking is weak, so it makes sense for voters to not rely on what largely have become unfulfilled promises to guide their vote choice.

Appendix

Figure 5.6 Coding and Sources of Variables

Question and response category wording are exact across years, unless otherwise noted.

Vote
Question: 1990–1993: "In the House of Representatives Election, could you please tell me which party the person you voted for belongs to?" 1996: "In the election in your electoral district, could you please tell me which party the person you voted for belongs to?" Coding: 1 if LDP; 0 if otherwise.

Gender
Coded by interviewer. Coding: 1 if female; 0 if male.

Occupation
Question: "What is your occupation? (Even if you're what we call housewife, and you help in the family business at home, enter family business.)" This variable was recoded into binary (dummy) variables.

Education
Question: "Until when did you go to school? (Leaving a particular school before having graduated is counted as graduating.)" 1986: (1) Elementary; current system middle school graduate; (2) Previous system middle school; current system high school; (3) Previous system high school, junior college, university; new system university graduate. 1996: In order to preserve basic comparability, the 4-item responses were recoded into the same 3-item categories. Unclear responses and don't know: system missing.

Age
Question: "What is your age in full?" 1986 and 1996: 6-category variable. 2003: 8-category variable. 20–24 = 1; 25–29 = 2; 30–39 = 3; 40–49 = 4; 50–59 = 5; 60–100 = 6.

Community Size
From sample information: 1986: (1) Tokyo; (2) The other nine large cities; (3) Towns with a population greater than 100,000; (4) Towns with a population less than or equal to 100,000; (5) Villages. 1986: (1) Tokyo; (2) The other ten large cities; (3) Towns with a population greater than 100,000; (4) Towns with a population less than or equal to 100,000; (5) Villages. 1983: (2) The other ten large cities; otherwise as 1972–1976. [1990]: (2) The other eleven large cities; otherwise as 1972–1976. 1993–1996: (2) The other twelve large cities; otherwise as 1972–1976.

continues

Length of Residence
Question: "About how many years have you lived in this City (Prefecture, Town, Village)?" 1986–1996: (1) Three years or less; (2) More than three years; (3) More than ten years; (4) More than twenty years (ever since birth). Unclear and don't know responses: system missing.

Issues
Changes to question: 1990–1993: "In the last election, what kinds of issues did you think about when choosing how to vote? If they appear on this list, please say." 1996: "In the last election, what kind of issues did you consider? If they are on this list, please say." Changes in response categories: 1986: Environmental pollution. 1990–1996: Environmental pollution; environmental problems. 1972–1990: Prices. 1993–1996: Prices; business. 1990–1996: The education issue. 1983-1996: Taxation (*zeikin mondai*). 1983–1990: Political ethics (*seiji rinri*). Coding: 1 if yes; 0 if otherwise.

Trade Union Membership
Question: "Are you a member of a trade union?" Coding: 1 if yes; 0 if otherwise.

Group Membership
Question: "Are you a member of any of these kinds of groups?" List includes: neighborhood groups (*Chonaikai, Burakukai, Jijikai*); 1972–1990: Women's association and young people's association; 1993–1996: Women's association, *koenkai*, PTA, religious groups, farmers' unions, trade and commerce associations.

Community Network
Variable coding: 1 if member in one or more of the following community-based networks: neighborhood associations, PTA, women's associations, *koenkai*, or leisure groups; 0 if otherwise. Trade union: 1 if member of a trade union; 0 if otherwise. Professional union: 1 if member of one of more business, commerce, farming or fishing association; 0 if otherwise.

Questions from JES I, JES II, and JEDS[a]
Q21 [Ideology]: We frequently use the words "Conservative" or "Progressive." Which of the following categories best describes you? (1) Conservative; (2) Somewhat conservative; (3) Moderate; (4) Somewhat progressive; (5) Progressive.

This question is only used in 1990 and 1993, and is recoded so that the choices are comparable across years. The question for the other years is shown below.

Q21SUP [Ideology]: When you think about national politics, do you consider yourself conservative, progressive, or neutral? (1) Conservative; (2) Progressive; (3) Neutral; (4) Other/DK.

JES (1967)[a]
VAR 0090 Q.28(C): [If yes to Q.28(A)] Where would you say the Liberal Democratic Party is? (1) Right; (2) Moderate right; (3) Center; (4) Moderate left; (5) Left; Other, D.K., N.A., INAP; system missing.

VAR 0091 Q.28(D): [If yes to Q.28(A)] Where would you say the Socialist Party is? (1) Right; (2) Moderate right; (3) Center; (4) Moderate left; (5) Left; Other, D.K., N.A., INAP; system missing.

continues

VAR 0093 Q.28(F): [If yes to Q.28(A)] Where would you say the Komeito party is? (1) Right; (2) Moderate right; (3) Center; (4) Moderate left; (5) Left; Other, D.K., N.A., INAP; system missing.

VAR 0094 Q.28(G): [If yes to Q.28(A)] Finally, where would you say the Communist Party is? (1) Right; (2) Moderate right; (3) Center; (4) Moderate left; (5) Left; Other, D.K., N.A., INAP; system missing.

JES I[a]

Q50: Then what about the following political parties? Where would you place the political position of each political party?

Q50-1 [LDPIDE]: (a) Liberal Democratic Party: (1) Progressive; (2) Somewhat progressive; (3) Neutral; (4) Somewhat conservative; (5) Conservative; DK, NA; system missing.

Q50-2 [DSPIDE]: (b) Democratic Socialists: (1) Progressive; (2) Somewhat progressive; (3) Neutral; (4) Somewhat conservative; (5) Conservative; DK, NA; system missing.

Q50-3 [CGPIDE]: (c) Clean Government Party: (1) Progressive; (2) Somewhat progressive; (3) Neutral; (4) Somewhat conservative; (5) Conservative; DK, NA; system missing.

Q50-4 [JSPIDE]: (d) Japan Socialist Party: (1) Progressive; (2) Somewhat progressive; (3) Neutral; (4) Somewhat conservative; (5) Conservative; DK, NA; system missing.

Q50-5 [JCPIDE]: (e) Japan Communist Party: (1) Progressive; (2) Somewhat progressive; (3) Neutral; (4) Somewhat conservative; (5) Conservative; DK, NA; system missing.

Sources: Data from the Akarui Senkyo Suishin Kyokai Shugiin Giin Sosenkyo (Society for the Promotion of Clean Elections House of Representatives election) studies from the years 1972, 1976, 1979, 1983, 1990, 1993, and 1996, made available through the Leviathan Data Bank, Tokyo (my translation).

Notes: a. Japanese Election Survey (JES I), Joji Watanuki, Ichiro Miyake, Takashi Inoguchi, Yoshiaki Kobayashi, and Ken'ichi Ikeda, principal investigators, available from http://www.bokutakusha.com/ldb/ldb databank.html; Japanese Election Survey (JES II), Ikuo Kabashima, Joji Watanuki, Ichiro Miyake, Yoshiaki Kobayashi, and Ken'ichi Ikeda, principal investigators, available from http://www.kh-web.org/research/archive/jes2; Japanese Election and Democracy Study (JEDS), Aiji Tanaka, Ken'ichi Ikeda, and Yoshitaka Nishizawa, principal investigators, available from http://ssjda.iss.u-tokyo.ac.jp/en/; Japanese Election Study (JES 1967), Robert Ward and Akira Kubota, principal investigators, available from http://www.icpsr.umich.edu/.

Table 5.1 Influences on Voting, 1986, 1996, and 2003

	1986 LDP	1986 Other	1996 LDP	1996 Other	2003 LDP	2003 Other
Issues						
Welfare	−0.602*	−0.322	−0.570*	−0.725*	0.281**	0.282**
	[0.148]	[0.192]	[0.209]	[0.197]	[0.127]	[0.138]
Environment	0.163	0.022	−0.026	−0.056	−0.079	−0.171
	[0.269]	[0.330]	[0.278]	[0.261]	[0.185]	[0.203]
Prices	0.085	0.332	0.406**	0.09	−0.05	−0.406*
	[0.153]	[0.198]	[0.204]	[0.191]	[0.125]	[0.136]
Education	0.359	0.275	0.553	0.438	0.185	0.297
	[0.193]	[0.238]	[0.306]	[0.290]	[0.180]	[0.187]
Ethics	−0.5	−0.097	−0.869*	−0.355	—	—
	[0.280]	[0.333]	[0.275]	[0.245]		
Agriculture	0.918*	0.365	0.5	−0.289	0.219	0.049
	[0.262]	[0.375]	[0.375]	[0.372]	[0.313]	[0.359]
Taxation	−0.263	−0.124	−0.27	−0.1	0.062	0.133
	[0.152]	[0.198]	[0.205]	[0.193]	[0.133]	[0.144]
Defense	−1.242*	−0.778*	−1.113*	−0.53	−0.197	−0.147
	[0.229]	[0.288]	[0.428]	[0.369]	[0.169]	[0.182]
Constitution	0.151	−0.225	−0.415	−0.516	−0.301	0.206
	[0.344]	[0.423]	[0.476]	[0.428]	[0.217]	[0.218]
Reform	0.051	−0.027	0.114	0.056	−0.12	−0.122
(Fiscal reform 03)	[0.201]	[0.255]	[0.228]	[0.214]	[0.153]	[0.166]
Pension	—	—	—	—	−0.23	−0.243
					[0.138]	[0.149]
Socioeconomic variables						
Cohort	0.154**	−0.082	0.255*	−0.1	0.164*	0.029
	[0.064]	[0.081]	[0.083]	[0.076]	[0.048]	[0.051]
Education	0.038	−0.273	−0.054	−0.14	−0.106	−0.128
	[0.124]	[0.160]	[0.113]	[0.106]	[0.067]	[0.074]
Gender	−0.181	−0.492**	0.302	0.451**	0.135	0.218
	[0.158]	[0.204]	[0.209]	[0.197]	[0.127]	[0.139]
White-collar	0.287	0.102	0.276	−0.166	0.02	−0.02
	[0.152]	[0.195]	[0.217]	[0.205]	[0.131]	[0.141]
Integration						
City size	0.101	−0.304*	0.291*	0.017	−0.120**	−0.089
	[0.065]	[0.084]	[0.085]	[0.079]	[0.051]	[0.055]
Duration	0.123	−0.231**	0.270**	0.075	0.128	−0.146
	[0.084]	[0.100]	[0.116]	[0.102]	[0.079]	[0.077]
Network membership						
Trade union	−1.609*	−0.767*	−0.441	−0.076	−0.454	−0.468
	[0.216]	[0.258]	[0.318]	[0.282]	[0.309]	[0.332]
Religious	−0.448	1.971*	0.231	0.172	—	—
	[0.398]	[0.368]	[0.567]	[0.541]		
Community	−0.184	−0.346	−0.101	0.055	0.056	−0.119
	[0.178]	[0.223]	[0.228]	[0.213]	[0.122]	[0.133]
Koenkai	1.052*	0.716*	1.046*	0.762**	0.740*	0.397
	[0.207]	[0.256]	[0.328]	[0.321]	[0.198]	[0.228]
Professional	0.077	−0.547	0.107	−0.214	0.739*	−0.145
	[0.241]	[0.373]	[0.356]	[0.354]	[0.248]	[0.324]
Constant	0.162	2.790*	−1.544**	2.797*	−0.557	0.929**
	[0.584]	[0.716]	[0.707]	[0.632]	[0.445]	[0.457]
Observations	1,567		2,063		1,736	

Source: Akarui Senkyo Suishin Kyokai Shugiin Giin Sosenkyo (Society for the Promotion of Clean Elections House of Representatives election) studies from the years 1986, 1996, and 2003, made available through the Leviathan Data Bank, Tokyo.

Notes: Cells are multinomial logit coefficients with standard errors in brackets.
Leftist parties (1986, 1993) and DPJ (2003) are the comparison groups.
1996 and 2003 single-member district vote; 1986 is a vote for the LDP or the NLC; 2003 is a vote for the LDP or the CP.
** significant at .05; * significant at .01

Notes

I would like to thank Professor Ikuo Kabashima for incredibly helpful comments and access to survey findings. I also appreciate the assistance of Koji Yamamoto and comments from Sean Richey.

1. Research conducted in the 1960s found that the correlation between issues and the vote was lowest in elections at the House of Representatives level (Miyake, Kinoshita, and Aiba 1967). Yoshiaki Kobayashi argues that the possible exception to this is the consumption tax (1997, 197–198). The consumption tax issue was of dramatic but transient significance, as described by Edward G. Carmines and James A. Stimson with their impulse-decay model (1989). The ASSK datasets do not ask a consumption tax–related question. Other notable exceptions include the LDP's antipollution measures and expansion of social welfare policies during the early 1970s.

2. In contrast, Margaret A. McKean and Ethan Scheiner (2000) argue that the technicalities of the system will transform the proportional representation representatives into locally based politicians who will rely on the personal vote, rather than on party- or policy-based politics.

3. In Japan, the term "progressive" is generally taken as being the opposite of conservative and referring to the forces, thinking, and policies of left-wingers, socialists, and those of a similar bent. One problem with the term is that it means favoring reform of the status quo, but it does not in itself indicate the direction of the desired change. Therefore, it is possible for a conservative to be progressive as well. And in fact, some of the legislators we surveyed labeled themselves "highly progressive" even as they declared their support for the strengthening of Japan's defense capabilities and revision of its pacifist Constitution, two major planks of rightist thinking. But the vast majority of our respondents followed the traditional definition of progressive versus conservative

4. Officially this is the New Komeito, having reconstituted itself in 1998, four years after formally merging into the now-defunct New Frontier Party (NFP). Komeito was the political arm of the Soka Gakkai (the lay organization of the Nichiren Shoshu Buddhist Sect), one of the new religions in Japan. The two have been formally separate since 1970, but still maintain close ties. Analysts estimate that around half of the Komeito votes come from affiliates of the Soka Gakkai. See Joji Watanuki (1991).

5. Komeito seems to be divided on this: in June 2005, a Komeito politician whom I interviewed was convinced that lawmakers would move to support constitutional revision.

6. Although I do not report the findings here, it is interesting to note that leftist voters were more likely than LDP voters to consider issues such as the Constitution, the regime, defense, and the Japan-US Security Treaty. These issues also concern the right, but the effects of some of these issues were not "canceled out" by rightist voters considering these issues and voting for the LDP. On the whole, LDP voters did not prioritize issues in the vote decision as much as supporters of other parties.

CHAPTER 6
Reforming the Bureaucracy
Eiji Kawabata

SINCE THE EARLY 1980S, THE JAPANESE GOVERNMENT HAS instituted major reforms, each of which, led by the prime minister, brought about major changes to government policymaking. Prime Minister Yasuhiro Nakasone (1982–1987) privatized major government corporations, such as Nippon Telegraph and Telephone (NTT), and deregulated the telecommunications market. Prime Minister Ryutaro Hashimoto (1996–1998) drastically reorganized the bureaucracy. Prime Minister Junichiro Koizumi (2001–2006) succeeded in privatizing the postal business and national highway construction. Because each reform reflected dissatisfaction with politics prevalent among citizens at that time, it attracted a great deal of public attention as well as public support. However, each reform also faced intensive resistance from the Liberal Democratic Party (LDP) and government ministries, and reformers had to engage in extensive negotiations. All of these reforms involved political showdowns, and were major political events in Japan.

The bureaucracy was at the center of each reform because reformers regarded the bureaucracy as their central target and sought to fundamentally change its role in policymaking for mainly the following three reasons. First, reformist politicians alleged that the bureaucracy's strong control over economic activities damaged the economy. In the conventional view of the Japanese bureaucracy, (career) bureaucrats in the national government act as a dominant elite in policymaking. When Japan was recovering from the destruction caused by World War II and the economy was developing rapidly, bureaucratic control was not questioned and some scholars attributed Japan's economic success to the economic bureaucracy's effective guidance (Johnson 1989a). However, as the Japanese economy matured, bureaucratic control came to be viewed as an obstacle that prevented economic actors from freely engaging in activity that would contribute to development. Reformist politicians sought to lessen bureaucratic control.

Second, reformist politicians criticized the bureaucracy in conjunction with the "subgovernment" system that channels government funds to pork barrel projects. Each subgovernment exists in a specific policy area (such as agriculture, road construction, and medicine), and consists of *zoku* (policy tribe) politicians, the bureaucrats of the ministry in charge of the policy area, and interest groups (companies and semigovernment organizations that operate in the policy area). *Zoku* politicians are a group of LDP Diet members who work to allocate government funds to their policy area and to protect any vested interests held by their subgovernment. Whereas *zoku* politicians are important in determining fundamental aspects, the bureaucrats are instrumental for smooth micromanagement, which includes day-to-day operation of subgovernmental activities, the formulation of budget plans, and writing legislative bills. In return for *zoku* politicians' activities, the interest groups provide them with monetary contributions and campaign support during elections. For the bureaucrats, member companies and organizations of the interest groups offer lucrative postretirement jobs. This subgovernment system promotes increases in government spending while making it difficult for government leaders to cut spending, causing budget deficits and inefficient resource allocation. As a part of their attempt to resolve budget deficits, reformers sought to dismantle vested interests in subgovernments and fought against bureaucrats who resisted changes along with *zoku* politicians.

Third and finally, reformers called for the reform of the bureaucracy to improve government operations. Since the bureaucracy, unlike private sector companies, usually does not face market competition, it lacks incentives to cut costs, provide better customer service, and pursue managerial and other innovations; the bureaucracy is likely to be wasteful, stagnant, and unpopular among the public. To solve this problem, reformers sought to infuse the bureaucracy with cost-consciousness and entrepreneurship. Also, as mentioned above, bureaucrats maintain stable relationships with companies and government organizations, and often the relationships become so collusive that interest group members bribe or lavishly wine and dine bureaucrats. In fact, a series of corruption scandals occurred that involved bureaucrats as well as politicians. The public was not only frustrated at the bureaucracy's aloofness, but also outraged about corruption, prompting reformist politicians to engage in the rectification of the bureaucracy as an essential part of reform.

In the early 1980s, the reform of the bureaucracy came to the fore of political discussion. Although some prime ministers made more efforts than others, most took up reform as their core political agenda and the prime minister's contribution to reforms has became an important indicator of his performance in policymaking. Reformers have formulated and implemented a number of bureaucracy reform measures and significantly changed government regulation and operation. But has the bureaucracy improved in a broader and fundamental sense? More specifically, have reforms improved the democratic quality of the Japanese bureaucracy? This chapter provides an answer to this question by examining the impact of the reforms on the Japanese bureaucracy's role in policymaking.

John Campbell provides an insightful analysis of the relationship between the Japanese bureaucracy and democracy, a topic closely related to the central question of this chapter, covering various aspects of the post–World War II Japanese bureaucracy up to the 1980s. He points out some undemocratic characteristics of the Japanese bureaucracy: the legacy of the bureaucracy's undemocratic past is rather intact, bureaucrats' attitudes emphasize their importance in policymaking pertinent to the national interest, and the bureaucracy's organizational cohesiveness minimizes the impact of outside forces (Campbell 1989, 114–122). Nonetheless, Campbell questions the conventional view that emphasizes bureaucratic dominance and therefore regards the Japanese bureaucracy as an antidemocratic institution beyond the control of the public. Examining the bureaucracy's control over its environment, he shows that the conventional view does not accurately portray the reality of the Japanese bureaucracy. Contrary to the conventional view, more and more societal interests influence policymaking and LDP politicians, particularly *zoku* politicians, and intervene in the bureaucracy's activities (Campbell 1989, 122–134). To this extent, he demonstrates that the Japanese bureaucracy is more consistent with democracy than in the conventional view.

In this chapter, I extend Campbell's analysis in two ways. Conceptually, I evaluate the relationship between the bureaucracy and its environment, using three criteria for the measurement of the quality of democracy, namely, responsiveness, accountability, and capability. Empirically, I provide a longitudinal analysis of the impact of government reform on the democratic quality of the Japanese bureaucracy. I show that the reform of the bureaucracy has continuously progressed since the early 1980s. In the Democracy and Bureaucracy section, I elaborate on the three criteria. In The Bureaucracy in Focus section, I briefly describe the Ministry of Posts and Telecommunications (MPT), the ministry whose interactions with other policy actors I focus on in discussing reforms, explaining why it is suitable for this evaluation. In The Nakasone Reform, The Hashimoto Reform, and The Koizumi Reform sections, respectively, I provide a brief overview of the reform and evaluate the ministry's interactions with other policy actors with regard to responsiveness, accountability, and capability. In the Conclusion, I sum up and evaluate changes in the democratic quality of the Japanese bureaucracy.

Democracy and Bureaucracy

Unlike in autocracies where a political leader(s) and his or her staff rule society without being appointed by the people, democracy includes a mechanism (elections) by which the people choose power holders. The selection process must be free and fair so that no citizens are barred from participating in the process. Because excessive concentration of power in a political leader(s) is likely to make him or her less responsive to the people's interests, a democratic system includes several kinds of checks and balances such as a bicameral legislature, the separation of powers, and judicial review. Also, to prevent the abuse of power, the leader has to adhere to the rules of law. The locus of discussion about the fundamentals of democracy is in the procedures for the selection of power holders and their use of power. Despite its importance in democracy, the bureaucracy is not of central concern in many discussions of democracy. Although bureaucrats are essential to the use of power by political leaders, the procedures do not usually clarify the role of the bureaucracy. The ideal role of the bureaucracy needs to be inferred from fundamental features essential for democracy, in particular, responsiveness, accountability, and effectiveness. In the rest of this section, I discuss the relationship between the bureaucracy and each feature, and identify ways to measure the bureaucracy's consistency with democracy, which are pertinent to the policymaking process of each of the three reforms that this chapter deals with.

In democracy, government officials have to be responsive to the public. Government policy needs to accommodate or at least be consistent with citizens' interests. Since citizens have diverse and often contradictory interests, government officials may not serve the interests of the entire population, but they are expected to serve broad societal interests. Elections make politicians responsive to societal interests because politicians who appeal to the interests of the broader public are likely to gain more votes and therefore win elections. Electoral rules to ensure fairness are important in order for electoral outcomes to reflect the interest of the broader public. Defects in electoral rules, such as malapportionment and gerrymandering, may prevent election outcomes from accurately reflecting the interests of the broader public. Similarly, bureaucrats in democracies are civil servants of society as a whole. Theoretically, the responsiveness of the bureaucracy is straightforward, yet in reality it is very complex because the interests of a given society are not necessarily short term and economic but also ideological and normative. A policy that gives benefit or privilege to a segment of society is consistent with the principle of democracy if it serves society's general interest. For example, although affirmative action to improve racial equality in the United States targets a specific segment of the society, it is justifiable (albeit controversial) because racial equality is desirable from a broad social point of view.

Because of this complexity, strict measurement of the bureaucracy's responsiveness to society is difficult, but some criteria can be clearly defined. The bureaucracy's relationship to elected officials, particularly its leaders, is important in this respect. In the sense that support from a majority of citizens in elections puts a party in power, the party and its leader represent the interests of the broad public in a democracy. One way to measure the bureaucracy's responsiveness to the public is its responsiveness to political leaders, that is, the prime minister and Cabinet members in Japanese politics. When the leaders order bureaucrats to formulate and implement a policy based on a clear and coherent idea, bureaucrats need to follow the order unless it contradicts fundamental principles of democracy. In reality, however, the leaders' ideas are neither clear nor coherent, although they may have simple catchy slogans, such as "*zozei naki zaisei saiken*" (the restoration of fiscal austerity without tax increases) and "*kan kara min he*" (from a public sector–dominant to a private sector–based ecomony); bureaucrats determine a great deal of the content of policy. Instead of straightforward resistance, bureaucrats may alter policy content and orientation by inserting their ideas and preferences into policy. The responsiveness should be evaluated by how bureaucrats mix their own interests with reform leaders' intent in the policymaking process. Bureaucrats' pursuit of their ministry's interest, such as the expansion of jurisdiction, and the interest of social groups with which they maintain close connections, indicates a low degree of responsiveness.

Although elections are most important for the general direction of government policymaking, electing government officials is not the only way for citizens to express their preferences. As found in the House of Representatives (HR) elections in 2005 in which parties fought around the privatization of postal business, a single reform issue can be at the center of an electoral campaign (see Ellis S. Krauss and Robert Pekkanen in Chapter 2 of this volume). However, usually parties set out a long list of policy preferences, making it difficult to detect the strength of public support for specific campaign issues. Also, elections are held neither frequently nor timely enough for citizens to express their short-term preferences. As a result, government officials learn citizens' up-to-date preferences about specific policy issues from public opinion expressed in the news media (Manin, Przeworski, and Stokes 1999, 9). How bureaucrats react to a surge in public opinion on policy issues is an additional indicator of responsiveness.

Accountability is another fundamental feature of democracy. Essentially in democracy, both elected government officials and bureaucrats are accountable in that they are fundamentally responsible for the consequences of their actions and that they are subject to sanctions by the public when their actions negatively affect the public (Manin, Przeworski, and Stokes 1999, 9). In the case of elected officials, elections provide a mechanism to infuse accountability into policymaking. If citizens do not approve of policies that an elected official makes or supports, they can choose not to vote for him or her, possibly removing him or her from office. As discussed above, since elections involve various issues, citizens rarely evaluate candidates based on their actions on specific issues. However, considering that many politicians lose elections due to their misbehavior, they are ultimately subject to sanction from citizens. In contrast, bureaucrats are not directly accountable to the public. Instead, accountability is maintained through the appointment and dismissal of (senior) bureaucrats. Formally, the expansion of elected officials' authority to appoint bureaucrats indicates improvement in accountability but, if politicians appoint bureaucrats to senior positions based on lists provided by bureaucrats, this does not improve accountability. Their actual exercise of this authority is a more important indicator of accountability.

Appointment is certainly important in influencing the general direction of the bureaucracy's policymaking, but it does not clarify who—elected officials or bureaucrats—is responsible for what aspect of specific policy; this is particularly difficult when the government party or the bureaucracy lacks cohesion and when they share responsibilities for policymaking.[1] In the policymaking process, bureaucrats may significantly change the content of a policy from the one that elected officials have envisioned but, when the policy becomes unpopular among the public, elected officials may be blamed (and lose their jobs). Conversely, elected officials may blame bureaucrats for a policy failure, citing their inflexibility, slowness, unresponsiveness, and so forth, even when the officials' original policy intent is flawed and they are fundamentally responsible for the failure. In this regard, the use of law clarifies the bureaucracy's accountability toward elected officials. Although both elected officials (legislators) and bureaucrats participate in lawmaking, the former make the ultimate decision in the legislature. Clearer and more detailed laws differentiate, if not perfectly, policy outcomes attributable to elected officials from those that result from bureaucrats applying the laws. Since elected officials are the principals whereas bureaucrats are the agents in democracy, clearer and more detailed laws increase the importance of the former and are more consistent with democratic accountability (Aberbach and Rockman 2000, 14).

Because bureaucratic intervention into citizens' social activities restricts their freedom, bureaucratic intervention seems to decrease the bureaucracy's accountability. This perception is strongly held among the public with regard to economic activity, due to the prevalence of neoliberal economic ideology emphasizing the superiority of market mechanisms. Many regard bureaucratic intervention itself as undesirable and undemocratic because of its hindrance on free-market activities. However, the extent of bureaucratic intervention should not be the criterion of accountability.

As discussed below, the bureaucracy is an integral part of democracy, and its actions should not be regarded as inherently undemocratic. In dealing with specific policy issues, as long as the bureaucracy acts within the boundaries clearly defined in laws formulated through the democratic process, its actions are accountable, and therefore consistent with the principles of democracy, even if the actions impose severe restrictions on citizens' activities.

Responsiveness and accountability are commonly cited as the most important elements of democracy because they are important criteria in distinguishing between democratic and undemocratic systems. Since government capability is important for both systems, this aspect has often been left untouched in discussions of democracy. In particular, bureaucrats are not directly (democratically) elected by citizens, and restraining their power tends to be emphasized over letting them effectively govern. However, the bureaucracy is an integral component of democracy. In order for a democratic system to operate effectively, the bureaucracy needs to be capable and, if necessary for the maintenance of the system, to intervene into social activities. Particularly during the early stages of democratic consolidation, the government bureaucracy's ability to enforce laws, collect taxes, and regulate economic activities is very important for the stabilization of democracy. If government bureaucrats are incapable of effectively performing tasks assigned for the benefit of the general public, democratic rule becomes chaotic, and public issues are liable to be controlled by private interests, exemplified by the lack of adequate democratic rules and looting of public property such as petroleum resources controlled by oligarchs in post-Soviet Russia (Suleiman 2003).

Rather than as exercising power over society, the bureaucracy's capability needs to be evaluated in relationship to goals formulated through democratic processes. The major criteria of capability are effectiveness and efficiency. Effectiveness is measured by how close the bureaucracy brings policy outcomes to the situation envisioned in the policy formulation and lawmaking processes. For the bureaucracy to be effective, it needs to be equipped with legal authority to act on societal actors even in situations where they are unwilling to comply with bureaucrats' orders. Specific legal provisions that do not restrict bureaucrats' activities enable bureaucrats to strongly pursue policy goals. Similarly, though rarely done recently in Japan, the increased allocation of budgets can help bureaucrats enhance their effectiveness. Also, bureaucratic infighting among ministries forces bureaucrats to spend resources to deal with rival bureaucrats instead of societal actors and generates space for societal actors to manipulate bureaucrats. The clear and stable division of labor among ministries is essential for effective policymaking.

If the government implements a policy effectively but incurs large monetary or social costs in the policymaking process, the government cannot be deemed capable. Therefore, efficiency, as measured by value output per value input, is another criterion of bureaucracy capacity. Unlike private sector business where both input and output can be gauged in monetary terms, policy output and input can both take various forms such as citizens' satisfaction, fairness, and time, in addition to financial resources (Wilson 1989, 317). The contribution of reform to the improvement of the bureaucracy's efficiency needs to be evaluated in various ways. Although reformers tend to emphasize the reduction of budget allocation to the bureaucracy's policymaking and that of labor costs in government operation as indicators of efficiency, other political and social costs (such as the time and energy bureaucrats spend on political interactions) need to be considered in evaluating the bureaucracy's efficiency.

To evaluate improvements in the democratic quality of the Japanese bureaucracy through government reforms, we should examine changes in its responsiveness (whether the bureaucracy was more likely to incorporate the interests of the general public into policy outcomes), accountability (how elected officials exercise control over the bureaucracy), and capability (how effective and efficient the bureaucracy has become). Ideally, the bureaucracy in democracy should be highly responsive, accountable, and capable. However, the perfectly democratic bureaucracy that scores perfect points on all three measures does not exist because the three are not completely consistent with one another.[2] Flexibly applying laws in response to public reaction may improve on the bureaucracy's responsiveness, but it compromises on accountability when it deviates from the lawmakers' intent. Perfect adherence to accountability impinges on the bureaucracy's capability; forcing bureaucrats to strictly follow rules set by elected officials can waste time and resources, making them less capable of flexibly implementing policy. Because of trade-offs inherent between these three aspects, even when a reform improves one aspect of democracy, it is important to examine what, if anything, has been lost in another aspect(s).

The Bureaucracy in Focus: The Ministry of Posts and Telecommunications

In evaluating changes in the democratic quality of the Japanese bureaucracy through reforms, I focus on the MPT, which was incorporated into the Ministry of Public Management, Home Affairs, Posts and Telecommunications (MPHPT) in 2001 as a result of the Hashimoto reform.[3] Through the examination of the MPT's interactions with other policy actors, as well as policy outcomes that the interactions generated, I gauge changes in the bureaucracy's responsiveness, accountability, and capability. Three main reasons make the MPT particularly suitable for this evaluation. First, the MPT was one of the important actors in each of the three reforms. Each reform covered various areas of government policymaking and made significant changes in various aspects of government regulation and operation, but it included an issue(s) that reformers deemed central to the reform: the privatization of government corporations in the Nakasone reform, bureaucratic reorganization in the Hashimoto reform, and postal privatization in the Koizumi reform. Since the result of each issue was going to greatly affect (and possibly eliminate) the MPT, the MPT was actively involved in all three reforms, thereby allowing us to hold the focus of the analysis constant.

Second, the MPT is suitable for evaluation of the relationship between bureaucrats and elected officials because the MPT maintained close connections with LDP politicians, especially so-called *yusei zoku* (postal tribe) politicians, who are LDP Diet members mostly from rural districts. The basis of the connection between the MPT and *yusei zoku* politicians is the nationwide networks of *tokutei* (special) postmasters.[4] As Ellis S. Krauss and Robert Pekkanen describe in Chapter 2, *tokutei* postmasters actively support LDP politicians especially by campaigning for LDP candidates in elections. In return, *yusei zoku* politicians get involved in telecommunications and postal business policymaking and support the MPT in securing budget allocation, extending regulatory authority over telecommunications business, and protecting or expanding privileges given to postal business. MPT bureaucrats' interactions with *yusei zoku* and other politicians illuminate how and to what extent reform policy outcomes reflect the interest of the general public, as opposed to that of a narrow segment of society, such as MPT bureaucrats and *tokutei* postmasters, enabling us to evaluate the bureaucracy's responsiveness and accountability.

Third and finally, the MPT deals with significant economic issues, namely, telecommunications and postal savings, and its capability to effectively handle them has strong implications for the Japanese economy. In the 1980s, telecommunications was transformed from a mere public utility industry into a leading industry where market competition promotes its development. Since the 1990s, due to the development of the Internet, telecommunications has been becoming even more important. The development of telecommunications has been greatly affected by the MPT's regulatory policy that set rules of competition among telecommunications carriers. Similarly, postal savings has a strong presence in the economy. The postal savings fund is the world's largest consumer bank with a total deposit of about $2 trillion, or about one-third of total bank deposits in Japan. In both cases, due to the high stakes deriving from the MPT's policy, major business organizations, including major telecommunications carriers and banks, opposed or tried to influence the MPT, making MPT policy a very good subject for the evaluation of the bureaucracy's capability to pursue policy while dealing with strong societal actors.

The MPT became deeply involved in all three of the reforms, maintained close connections with LDP politicians, and dealt with important economic issues. The MPT is a good, if not the only, case suitable for the evaluation of the democratic quality of the bureaucracy. In the following three sections, focusing on the MPT's activities, I evaluate changes in the democratic quality of the Japanese bureaucracy through reforms. Each of these sections begins with a brief description of the political process of each reform, followed by the evaluation of its impact on changes in the bureaucracy's responsiveness, accountability, and capability.

The Nakasone Reform: The Origin of Government Reforms

Although the 1955 System was a rather stable system in that the LDP had been continuously in power and because drastic policy change deriving from government party change did not occur, some prime ministers embarked on major policy shifts. In the 1960s, Prime Minister Hayato Ikeda came to emphasize the importance of economic development, abandoning direct confrontation with the left. In the 1970s, Prime Minister Kakuei Tanaka shifted the goal of government policy from economic development to the improvement of social overhead capital through the expansion of government spending. Although each of their policies was important for changing the content of government policy, they were more like adjustments and did not seek to fundamentally change the format of government operation. In contrast, Prime Minister Nakasone tried to radically change the format, labeling his reform a comprehensive restructuring of the Sengo Seiji no Sokessan (post–World War II political regime). The Nakasone reform was a major reform during the 1955 System period, and it marked the beginning of a series of neoconservative government reforms in the 1990s and 2000s that sought to reduce the size (and influence) of the government.[5] It set a basic pattern of government reform in which the prime minister exercised leadership with support from his handpicked staff who were knowledgeable about reform issues, but bureaucrats still ultimately determined the content of reform measures.

The Nakasone reform began in 1980 when, as the director general of the Administrative Management Agency, Nakasone established Rinji Gyosei Chosakai (the Second Provisional Administrative Commission; hereafter, Rincho) and appointed Toshio Doko, the honorary chairman of the Federation of Economic Organizations, as the leader of Rincho. Gaining support from Prime Minister Zenko Suzuki, Rincho generated recommendations for government reform. In particular, Rincho set the privatization of

NTT, the telecommunications government monopoly, as a central item in the reform, and set the general direction for the realization of the privatization. Since Nakasone took over the prime ministership from Suzuki, Nakasone further pursued reform by pushing Rincho recommendations through the legislative process of NTT privatization.

Both NTT and MPT bureaucrats got involved in Rincho deliberation from relatively early stages, realizing the utility of NTT privatization. NTT officials thought that, if privatized, NTT would acquire managerial flexibility whereas the MPT hoped to take over NTT's regulatory functions and to assume charge of a leading industry in the upcoming information age. Both NTT and the MPT supported privatization, but their positions differed significantly over the format of telecommunications regulation after privatization. With the privatization of NTT, the telecommunications service market was going to be liberalized and new entrants would be allowed to operate along with the privatized NTT. NTT tried to keep its organizational cohesion intact and minimize restrictions on its business activities. The MPT, in contrast, wanted to weaken NTT through privatization to strengthen its position vis-à-vis the privatized NTT, while providing a leveling field for new entrants. For this, the MPT sought to break up NTT and acquire specific legal authority to regulate NTT's and new entrants' activities. In addition, the Ministry of International Trade and Industry (MITI), as a government ministry that promoted Japan's economic development, found in NTT privatization the chance to extend its jurisdiction into the telecommunications service market and vehemently opposed the MPT's attempt to obtain strong authority over the market so that the MITI would be able to influence telecommunications service through its close connections with telecommunications equipment manufacturers.

These bureaucratic actors fiercely fought each other around various issues related to NTT privatization. Due to conflicting interests, none of them were willing to compromise, making it difficult for the MPT to write legislative bills. In settling disputes among them, Hashimoto, then chair of the LDP's policy coordination organ, played an active role. By skillfully balancing each other, Hashimoto mediated among these actors and persuaded them to compromise.[6] After compromise induced by Hashimoto was reached, the bills were sent to the Diet in May 1984. Because of party politics, the bills were temporarily stalled in the Upper House, but they eventually passed in December, and NTT began to operate as a private sector company in April 1985.

Since NTT had a balanced budget and maintained stable labor relations, it was not an immediate reform target. However, reformers thought that NTT, as a government corporation, had potential to accumulate deficit and that its privatization would make its operation more efficient. Also, NTT privatization was necessary for the liberalization of the telecommunications service market, which would promote the development of the telecommunications service market by introducing competition that drove both NTT and new entrants to improve their businesses. In general, both reformers and bureaucrats intended to serve the public through NTT privatization, which did contribute to the development of telecommunications, benefiting citizens with the provision of diverse services at relatively low service charges.

NTT privatization definitely was not a cosmetic adjustment whereby NTT maintained its monopoly status, minimizing the possibility of new telecommunications carriers entering into the telecommunications service market. Nonetheless, it was not a perfect reform where the idea of liberalization was realized to the fullest extent because bureaucrats inserted their narrow interests into policy in the bill-making process. Rincho members recommended the breakup of NTT so that it would not preserve unfair advantage over new entrants, but NTT avoided its breakup while preserving its privileges. Also, the MPT and MITI set up an arbitrary division between telecommunications service and equipment industries. This made telecommunications more complicated than necessary, while reducing the bureaucracy's capability to handle issues in telecommunications, because a great deal of time and energy had to be spent on bureaucratic infighting. Thus, the reform process and outcome shows the bureaucracy's rather mediocre level of responsiveness to the public.

Similarly, the MPT's policy was generally accountable to the public in that MPT bureaucrats followed the general direction set by elected officials and that they specified general policy content in laws. Prime Minister Nakasone and other LDP leaders took up NTT privatization as a central reform agenda, and MPT and other bureaucrats worked for its realization. MPT bureaucrats were influential in determining the content of bills for NTT privatization and telecommunications market liberalization, but legislators made the bills law through the legislative process. In implementing NTT privatization and the liberalization of telecommunications service, the MPT exercised detailed control over telecommunications. The MPT's policy was so intrusive that both NTT and new entrants complained about it, but it was generally based on specific provisions included in laws related to NTT privatization. Although the MPT used discretion in pursuing some policy goals, including the breakup of NTT, which was not specified in the laws, the bureaucracy was generally accountable.

Aided by the specific provisions that authorized the MPT to take strong actions, the MPT's policy was generally effective in transforming the telecommunications service market. After the privatization through the 1990s, the MPT was a target of various criticisms. Some argued that the MPT obstructed the development of new entrants in favor of NTT, while others criticized the MPT for exercising unnecessarily detailed control over NTT. However, in dealing with a market condition where a gigantic incumbent carrier and novice new entrants competed, the MPT succeeded in developing competition, particularly in long-distance and mobile telephone service markets in a reasonable period of time. Generally, the reform process furnished the MPT with tools to pursue its policy goal effectively and efficiently. However, this was not always the case. Although Rincho reformers suggested the breakup of NTT through privatization and the MPT supported it, NTT's vehement opposition prevented LDP leaders from making a definite decision on NTT breakup. The tug of war between the MPT and NTT continued until NTT was finally reorganized into a group of NTT carriers under the leadership of a shareholding company (Kawabata 2001, 414–418). Not only the MPT and NTT, but also LDP politicians and business leaders, got involved in this dispute, forcing them to waste a lot of time and energy. This conflict stalled some aspects of the development of Japan's telecommunications business, exemplified by delays in NTT's entrance into the international market. The indecisiveness among the elected officials during the reform period resulted in decrease in efficiency of the bureaucracy.

The Nakasone reform occurred in the early to mid-1980s, before the reform period of the 1990s and 2000s. The analysis of this reform in the prereform period shows that Japan was not a bureaucratic kingdom in which the bureaucracy exercised total control of the society. The Japanese bureaucracy is far from being perfectly democratic but, similar to the bureaucracy of other advanced industrial countries, it had a reasonable level of democratic quality. It was generally responsive, accountable, and capable despite the fact that some defects existed in each category.

The Hashimoto Reform:
Reorganization of the Central Bureaucracies in the 1990s

In the mid-1990s, the bureaucracy became the major target of reform because the public was outraged by a series of scandals and misbehavior involving bureaucrats. After the 1995 Kobe earthquake, government bureaucracies were not able to engage in rescue and recovery operations due to bureaucratic red tape. The Ministry of Health, Labor and Welfare's mishandling of imported blood that resulted in the spread of AIDS to hemophiliacs became a national issue as well as bribery scandals involving bureaucrats. Momentum was rapidly rising for government reform when Hashimoto became prime minister in January 1996, following the resignation of the SDPJ prime minister. In fact, government reform was a primary campaign issue in the HR elections in fall 1996. Responding to the growth of public support for reform, Hashimoto, an expert on government reform who had played a major role in the Nakasone reform, actively pursued reform. Similar to Nakasone, Hashimoto utilized his advisory council, but he played a more direct role in the reform policymaking process by participating in the discussion in the advisory council. Although his pursuit of bureaucratic reorganization was watered down due to fierce resistance from bureaucrats and *zoku* politicians, he strengthened the leadership of the prime minister by expanding the Cabinet Office. Hashimoto's reform changed the balance of power between politicians and bureaucrats in policymaking by making it easier for the former to intervene into the latter's activities.

In fall 1996, Hashimoto set up the Administrative Reform Council (ARC) as an organization to formulate reform measures. Similar to Rincho, the ARC consisted of business and labor leaders as well as academics and its secretariats were bureaucrats sent from major ministries. Whereas Nakasone and other politicians did not directly participate in Rincho deliberation and let its members set the general direction of reform, Hashimoto and reformist politicians were deeply involved in the reform discussion in the ARC, which was headed by Hashimoto himself. In the early stages of ARC deliberation, Hashimoto kept a low profile but, in the formulation of the ARC's interim report that identified specific reform measures along with general direction, Hashimoto's involvement was crucial. During the deliberation session held in summer 1997, Hashimoto not only mediated among ARC members' opinions, but also led the discussion and provided concrete ideas about government reform.

The ARC interim report recommended drastic government reform measures that were designed to rectify problems associated with the bureaucracy. To strengthen political leadership over the bureaucracy, the report suggested the expansion of the prime minister's policymaking capability by assigning more functions to the Cabinet Office and an increase in the number of political appointees in each ministry. To downsize the government, it proposed the reduction of the number of ministries and agencies by merging two or more ministries and agencies into one. Also, to rectify the bureaucracy's excessive intervention in the economy, the report recommended the privatization of government operations and deregulation (Kawabata 2004, 27–28). Since the report intended to weaken the bureaucracy's influence in policymaking, it resulted in a controversy involving *zoku* politicians and bureaucrats.

Some of the recommendations were devastating to a number of government ministries, and particularly affected the MPT in two ways. On the one hand, the report recommended the division of the MPT's telecommunications policymaking organ into an independent regulatory commission in charge of telecommunications regulation and a bureau for the promotion of telecommunications, which would be incorporated into the MITI, the MPT's nemesis. In essence, this would abolish the MPT's telecommunications policymaking organ. On the other hand, the report sought to implement major changes in the MPT's postal business operation, supporting the privatization of postal life insurance and calling for the discussion of the privatization of the postal savings fund (Kawabata 2004, 28). The privatization would be a major blow to *tokutei* postmasters. Because most of them operated in sparsely populated areas, if privatized, it would be impossible for *tokutei* post offices to generate profit and many of them were likely to be forced out of business. Since *tokutei* postmasters provided *yusei zoku* politicians with invaluable electoral support, the privatization was a crucial issue for the politicians as well.

Given that the report had strong support from the prime minister, it was impossible for the MPT and other ministries to ignore the report and completely abort the reform. The MPT along with other ministries explored ways to minimize the impact of the reform. The MPT sought to merge with another ministry(ies) while keeping telecommunications and postal business policymaking mechanisms intact and avoid the privatization of (any part of) the postal business since the preservation of the MPT's policymaking format, especially the government operation of postal business, was important for *yusei zoku* politicians. While *yusei zoku* politicians actively lobbied in support of the MPT, *zoku* politicians who were affiliated with other ministries (such as the Ministries of Construction and Transportation) fought against reform measures and tried to alter them, significantly weakening Prime Minister Hashimoto's leadership with the LDP. In the ARC's final report, many of the reform measures were modified to appease *zoku* politicians. Eventually, the MPT was incorporated into the MPHPT and continued to operate the postal business with a newly established government corporation, called Japan Post. Since the final report was satisfactory to both Hashimoto and LDP *zoku* politicians, legislative bills based on the report passed the Diet in 1998, and reform measures were implemented in 2001.

Although Hashimoto was not able to enact all the reform measures that he and reformers formulated, his reform brought about significant changes in the bureaucracy. He reduced the number of ministries and made it easier for bureaucrats to communicate and coordinate. He also expanded the power of the Cabinet Office. The prime minister was able to appoint the ministers of state in charge of important policy issues (such as economic and fiscal policy, administrative reform, and depopulation) who could flexibly pursue policymaking without being constrained by existing bureaucratic boundaries. In this sense, the Hashimoto reform was responsive to the general public that called for changes in the inflexibility of the bureaucracy. However, narrow interests of ministries and *zoku* politicians wielded a great deal of influence on setting up the details of reform, significantly reducing the Hashimoto reform's responsiveness to the general public.

The *zoku* politicians' involvement blurred the line of accountability of the reform process. Since the reform's main target was government organizations, reform measures were written in the laws that had been made by the Diet. However, most of the modifications were made through the interactions among LDP leaders and *zoku* politicians. Unlike in the legislative process, the interactions mainly occurred in informal settings, making it difficult for the public to find out how politicians and bureaucrats act for what purpose and greatly decreased the transparency of the reform policymaking process. Despite problems with the process, the Hashimoto reform resulted in the improvement of the accountability of the bureaucracy through the expansion of the power of the Cabinet Office. Because many of the office's secretariats are still sent from other ministries, bureaucrats play an important role in the office. However, different from the previous format whereby political leaders had to let bureaucrats decide most details of legislative bills, appointed ministers have more direct oversight over the legislative bill-writing process.

The expansion of the Cabinet Office also enhanced the capability of the bureaucracy. Since the bureaucracy generally operates based on precedents, emphasizing continuity, the bureaucracy is unskilled at making drastic changes in a timely manner. In contrast, politicians are less constrained by precedents, and political leaders need to make changes, if necessary, to gain support from the public. The expansion increased the possibility for political leaders, especially the prime minister, to force the bureaucracy to quickly change policy in accordance with social change. In this regard, the reform made the bureaucracy more effective, but it did not significantly improve its efficiency despite Hashimoto and other reformers' original intention to do so through bureaucratic reorganization. Although the number of ministries was reduced, the overall size of the bureaucracy stayed the same. As shown in the continued sharing of jurisdiction over telecommunications, one of the most important industries, between the MPT and MITI, the reform did not succeed in the rationalization of the bureaucracy's policymaking through the elimination of jurisdictional overlaps.

When Hashimoto lost his position in 1998 due to the LDP's loss in the House of Councilors (HC) elections, he was not able to further pursue government reform. Also Hashimoto was a senior member of the LDP's major faction known for its resistance to reform for the protection of vested interests (and later became its leader); he was vulnerable to resistance from antireform politicians and made a number of compromises. Therefore, Hashimoto was not known as a reformer, but the Hashimoto reform made significant changes through bureaucratic reorganization, contributing to the quality of democracy. In particular, the enhancement of the prime minister's power through the expansion of the Cabinet Office improved the bureaucracy's responsiveness, accountability, and capability.

The Koizumi Reform: The Beginning of New Reform Politics?

After the departure of Hashimoto, the public dissatisfaction with the government continued to grow. The Japanese economy had been depressed since the bubble economy burst in the early 1990s, and showed no sign of recovery when the new decade (century) began. The public rightly or wrongly blamed the government for not effectively dealing with economic problems. Nonetheless, the two prime ministers who succeeded Hashimoto in turn did not seem to have the sense of urgency and were not willing to exercise strong leadership to get Japan out of trouble. This public frustration led a maverick LDP politician, Koizumi, to become the prime minister in April 2001. Under the slogan, *"kozo kaikaku nakushite keiki kaifuku nashi"* (no economic recovery without structural reform), Koizumi embarked on government reform as soon as he took office. He fully utilized the expanded Cabinet Office and kept the policymaking process under his control, preventing bureaucrats from stalling reform. In dealing with *zoku* politicians, Koizumi minimized the use of backstage negotiations and ultimately achieved his reform goal by defeating his opponents in elections, making his bureaucratic reform highly responsive and accountable (probably at the expense of the bureaucracy's capability).

For Koizumi and reformers, the postal business symbolized excessive government intrusion into private sector business and the inefficiency of government operations. Taking advantage of its status as a government operation, postal savings, postal life insurance, and postal (mail) service took away business chances from their competitors from the private sector such as consumer banks, insurance companies, and package delivery carriers. Most of the postal savings' vast amount of funds ended up financing costly and inefficient pork barrel projects. Also, since profit maximization was not its goal, postal business operation was inefficient, as evidenced in the maintenance of a large number of *tokutei* post offices in rural areas. The postal business was not particularly unpopular among the public but, citing these problems, Koizumi pursued the privatization of the postal business.

As a result of the Hashimoto reform, Japan Post was established as a government corporation in April 2003. Critics of Koizumi's postal reform claimed that it was too early to further change the postal business operation, but Koizumi was determined to pursue postal business privatization. In his reelection campaign for the LDP presidential elections in September 2003, he promised to privatize Japan Post and won, enabling him to remain prime minister. In electoral campaigns for the HR elections held in November 2003, Koizumi emphasized Japan Post privatization as the central campaign issue. Since the LDP won the majority of HR seats, albeit with a slim margin over opposition parties, Koizumi asserted that he had won public support for the privatization. He appointed Minister of State for Economic and

Fiscal Policy Heizo Takenaka, an economist who advocated radical economic reforms, to be in charge of the formulation of privatization plans, minimizing the influence of MPHPT bureaucrats and *yusei zoku* politicians. In August 2004, Takenaka and his advisory council disclosed a basic plan for Japan Post privatization, which proposed the breakup of Japan Post into a shareholding company with four separate companies for postal service, postal savings, postal life insurance, and post office service networks in 2007 with a ten-year transition period for the completion of the privatization plan. After Koizumi adopted the plan at a Cabinet meeting, he created the position of minister of state for privatization of the postal services, to which Takenaka was assigned. Instead of MPHPT bureaucrats, Takenaka and his staff exercised leadership in writing legislative bills for Japan Post privatization.

Unlike MPT bureaucrats who were in charge of writing NTT privatization bills, MPHPT bureaucrats did not have much leeway to alter the content of the bills for Japan Post privatization, leading *yusei zoku* politicians to fight against the privatization. Since most of LDP Diet members were against, or at least skeptical of, the privatization, pro-Koizumi LDP leaders actively negotiated with the members to increase support while asking Koizumi to make some concessions. Due to a series of minor concessions given by Takenaka, more and more LDP members changed their positions and supported the privatization. As Krauss and Pekkanen describe in Chapter 2, a significant number of LDP Diet members, along with Diet members from opposition parties, opposed the bills, making the possibility of their passage uncertain particularly at the HC where the LDP and its coalition partner had a smaller margin of seats over opposition parties. Conceding to Koizumi's threat to dissolve the HR if the bills did not pass either the HR or HC, most LDP Diet members, except hard-core *yusei zoku* politicians, decided to support the bills and the bills narrowly passed the HR. However, due to defections of LDP HC members, the bills were defeated in the HC in August 2005.

As promised, Koizumi promptly dissolved the HR and made postal privatization the central campaign issue. This strategy resulted in overwhelming victory and the Japan Post privatization bills quickly passed both houses of the Diet when legislative sessions resumed following the HR election. Japan Post would be broken up and the privatization process would begin in October 2007 (see Krauss and Pekkanen in Chapter 2).

Among Koizumi's reforms, the privatization of Japan Post was an extreme case. Since the 1990s, Koizumi had been advocating the issue and made it the most important campaign issue in his quest for the prime ministership in 2001. He consistently oversaw policy development, actively intervened when necessary, and resorted to a political gamble of HR dissolution to overcome resistance from his own party. His commitment was less direct and less extensive, if not negligible, in the policymaking of other reforms such as the privatization of public highway corporations and fiscal decentralization. However, Koizumi pursued postal privatization and other reform measures, whose major targets were bureaucracies, in response to the public's frustration with the government bureaucracy's seeming aloofness to problems in Japanese society, In general, however, Koizumi's reforms were highly responsive to the interests of the general public. As shown in postal privatization, neither the MPHPT nor business organizations (such as big banks) could insert their specific preference into the policy outcome, although many small compromises were made in response to LDP Diet members' concerns, making the policy outcome largely consistent with the general public's interest. It is still too early to tell if the Koizumi reform has made the bureaucracy more responsive, but it seems reasonable to predict that the privatized postal business companies will be responsive to citizens as customers.

Similarly, the Koizumi reform scores high on accountability. As a result of the Hashimoto reform, the prime minister came to have more resources, and Koizumi took full advantage of this change. Appointing reformist politicians, academics, and business leaders to positions essential for the promotion of reform, he was much less dependent on bureaucrats than Nakasone and Hashimoto had been and increased the relative importance of elected officials in reform policymaking. In dealing with LDP politicians, Koizumi did not directly or indirectly engage in backstage negotiations, making the interaction between reformers and antireformers highly visible. Ultimately in the privatization of Japan Post, he dissolved the HR and made the elections a referendum on it, making his action accountable to the public. Given that there will be a ten-year transition period to complete Japan Post privatization, long-term implications are not so clear, but Koizumi made the (MPHPT) bureaucracy highly accountable in the short term.

Unlike the Koizumi reform's high levels of responsiveness and accountability, the reform's contribution to improvement in the bureaucracy's capability is ambiguous at best. After privatization, the postal business is highly likely to improve operational efficiency. Using private sector accounting methods, it will recognize internal inefficiency and work hard to survive market competition. However, the privatization's contribution to the improvement of the effectiveness of the bureaucracy is unclear, considering its original goal, which, as discussed above, had two major components. One major component was to stop market dominance by postal savings and postal life insurance while the other was to cut off the flow of funds from postal savings to inefficient government spending. As critics suggest, Koizumi's postal privatization did not clarify paths to achieve these goals.[7] Japan Post would be broken up into four operational companies and a shareholding company, but Koizumi left it possible for these companies to maintain affiliation through cross-sharing as well as de facto government guarantees. Keeping most of the current advantages, the privatized savings bank (and the privatized postal insurance company) might continue to dominate the market. Should the link between the government and the postal companies persist, it is likely that the postal savings bank would continue to provide funds to the government through the purchase of government bonds, which was basically the way funds had been handled since 2001 (Minshuto Yusei Kaikaku Chosakai 2005, 2–5). The effectiveness of Koizumi's postal privatization is therefore highly questionable because he did not arrange the bureaucracy to strongly pursue a reform goal to lessen government intervention in the economy.

The problems with postal privatization point to a fundamental problem with reforms through the reduction of government involvement. As the government transforms a public organization into a private sector entity, the former loses leverage to pursue public goals. If the government imposes detailed restrictions on the privatized entity, the former has the latter pursue public goals. However, since doing so fundamentally contradicts the purpose of privatization, reformers tend to be ambiguous about this trade-off, compromising the effectiveness of the government (bureaucracy) while pursuing public goals. Because Koizumi's other reform measures emphasized the use of private sector vitality, they seem to have this problem. Nonetheless, it must be reiterated that his reform had high-level responsiveness and accountability.

Conclusion

Koizumi brought about dramatic changes in the government bureaucracy, exemplified by the privatization of Japan Post, and this contradicts a prevalent image of Japanese politics—nothing changes in Japanese politics because it is dominated by a strong bureaucracy that is resistant to change. However, the magnitude of the Koizumi reform's impact on the bureaucracy should not be overemphasized for the following two reasons. On the one hand, as shown by NTT privatization in the Nakasone reform, the bureaucracy did change and was susceptible to social and political pressure in the 1955 System, and Koizumi did not induce a quantum leap of the bureaucracy from an autonomous bureaucracy into a docile one. On the other hand, it must be noted that Koizumi pursued reform based on the results from the previous reforms. Nakasone brought the bureaucracy to the center of government reform, setting the general direction of reforms that developed since the 1990s. The Hashimoto reform changed the format of the government organization and laid the basis for the strong pursuit of government reform by reformist prime ministers, such as Koizumi. Thus, the bureaucracy evolved through these reforms.

The Koizumi reform should not be seen as a radical departure from other reforms. Koizumi himself developed his strategy of bureaucratic reform in his political activities during the past two decades when the reform was consistently one of the primary political agendas. Koizumi took advantage of structural changes that Hashimoto set up, particularly the strengthening of the Cabinet Office. Of course, Koizumi's determination to pursue reform and his political skills were important. However, without these ideological shifts and institutional changes that his predecessors had enacted, Koizumi's reform would not have been possible. In this sense, the Koizumi reform is an extension of other reforms. We may not see another strong leader like Koizumi in the near future, but the policy environment is accommodating to reformist leaders. In addition to the accumulation of reform results from pre-Koizumi days, Koizumi set an example of successful reform. Future leaders may still face difficulties, but they would be in a better position to achieve reform goals than the three prime ministers discussed in this chapter.

This evolution of the bureaucracy changed the democratic quality of the bureaucracy regarding responsiveness, accountability, and capability. In general, the reforms were responsive to the general public's frustration with the government bureaucracy's apparent rigidity, intrusiveness, and inefficiency. Also, in the legislative process for the enactment of reform measures, each reformist prime minister had to make compromises to bureaucrats and politicians who worked to protect their narrow interests. Yet Koizumi made fewer and smaller compromises than Nakasone and Hashimoto did, taking advantage of the expanded function of the Cabinet Office, suggesting improvement in responsiveness. Similarly, the bureaucracy has become a little more accountable. Although a great deal of political interactions continued to be held in the rather informal domain and reform laws remained vague about certain specifics of reform measures, elected officials' influence on policymaking increased, particularly in the reform policy formulation process as shown in Takenaka's control over the bill-writing process of postal privatization.

Nonetheless, these improvements were made without significantly improving the capability of the bureaucracy. The reforms introduced efficiency to the bureaucracy's operation, especially through privatization, but they did not intend to make the bureaucracy more effective in pursuing public goals. Although they did not make any fatal changes to the bureaucracy, the long-term consequences on the effectiveness need to be examined in the future. Significant improvements were made on the bureaucracy by Nakasone, Hashimoto, and Koizumi. And despite some ambiguities, one should answer a qualified yes to the question, Have the reforms made the Japanese bureaucracy more democratic?

Notes

1. According to G. Bingham Powell Jr. and Guy Whitten, "the lack of voting cohesion of the major government party" and "a participatory and inclusive committee system in the legislature" obscure the clarity of responsibility of the incumbent government party (1993, 399–400).

2. It must be noted that contradiction is inherent to democracy, exemplified by majority rule and minority right. This inconsistency is not special to the discussion of democracy and bureaucracy.

3. In this chapter, the acronym MPHPT will be used to identify the government agency in charge of posts and telecommunications when its activities occurred mainly after 2001. Otherwise, the acronym MPT will be used.

4. About three-fourths of the 24,000 post offices in Japan are *tokutei*. Although *tokutei* postmasters are government employees, their position is transferred mainly through inheritance. After World War II, Kakuei Tanaka organized *tokutei* postmasters into an important LDP support group. For an extensive analysis of *tokutei* postmasters, see Patricia L. Maclachlan (2004).

5. For more extensive analyses of the Nakasone reform and the MPT, see Chalmers Johnson (1989b), Steven K. Vogel (1996), and Jun Iio (1993).

6. For example, using the MPT-MITI rivalry, Hashimoto prevented the MPT from gaining excessive control over the privatized NTT. He persuaded the MPT to concede by indicating that its persistence on excessive control would lead him to give jurisdiction over telecommunications to the MITI.

7. The Democratic Party of Japan, the largest opposition party, supported the idea of postal privatization, but opposed Koizumi's postal privatization proposal, arguing that it would not eliminate problems that were inherent to the existing format of the postal business. See Minshuto Yusei Kaikaku Chosakai (2005).

PART 2
The Local Level

CHAPTER 7

Keeping Women in Their Place: Penetrating Male-dominated Urban and Rural Assemblies

Sherry L. Martin

THE EXTENT OF WOMEN'S UNDERREPRESENTATION IN ELECTED offices makes Japan an outlier in comparative studies of women and politics. Japan is atypical on several counts if, and when, it is compared to primarily Western nations that have experienced a similarly long period of uninterrupted democratic rule and that rank high on global indicators of economic and human development. Women currently hold 14.5 percent of seats in the House of Councilors and 9.4 percent of seats in the more powerful House of Representatives.[1] Contrary to studies of other democracies that find that women's representation is higher in elected assemblies at lower levels of government where the issues are most proximate to their everyday lives, Japanese women have traditionally fared worse in achieving representation on elected assemblies at the subnational level (Bochel and Bochel 2005; Jaquette 2001). Women hold approximately 7.5 percent of prefectural assembly seats and 8.4 percent of 5,625 seats in town and village assemblies.[2] This is worrisome because local politics is a training ground for high-level office; fewer women in the "pipeline" results in negative forecasts about the prospects for future advancement in national officeholding (Vengroff et al. 2003). The small percentage that summarizes the current state of Japanese women in local elected office fails to capture a surprising increase in the number of women elected to local assemblies[3] since the early 1990s, and understates the gains women have achieved in a relatively short period of time.

In the four decades following the end of the Allied occupation, women's representation across subnational assemblies held steady at approximately 2 percent of total seats.[4] Over the past decade, women's representation has increased across all subnational assemblies and this is all the more striking when we control for level of government and whether the assemblies represent primarily rural or urban districts. In some Tokyo ward assemblies, women have increased their share of seats from single-digit representation to near parity in less than two decades. Even though the focus here is on women in elected office, women's representation on *shingikai* (national advisory councils), decisionmaking bodies that inform national policymaking processes, has doubled in a decade—rising from 16.1 percent to 31.3 percent between 1996 and 2006 (Gender Equality Bureau 2007, 17). These achievements reflect a trend worthy of closer examination (see Figure 7.1).[5]

This chapter examines patterns in women's subnational representation to bring the combined effects of electoral reform, administrative reform, and demographic change into focus. Assessments of the success of national reforms in disrupting the local support bases of male political bosses and channels of patronage politics constitute one means of determining whether channels of interest articulation are shifting to allow expression of margin-

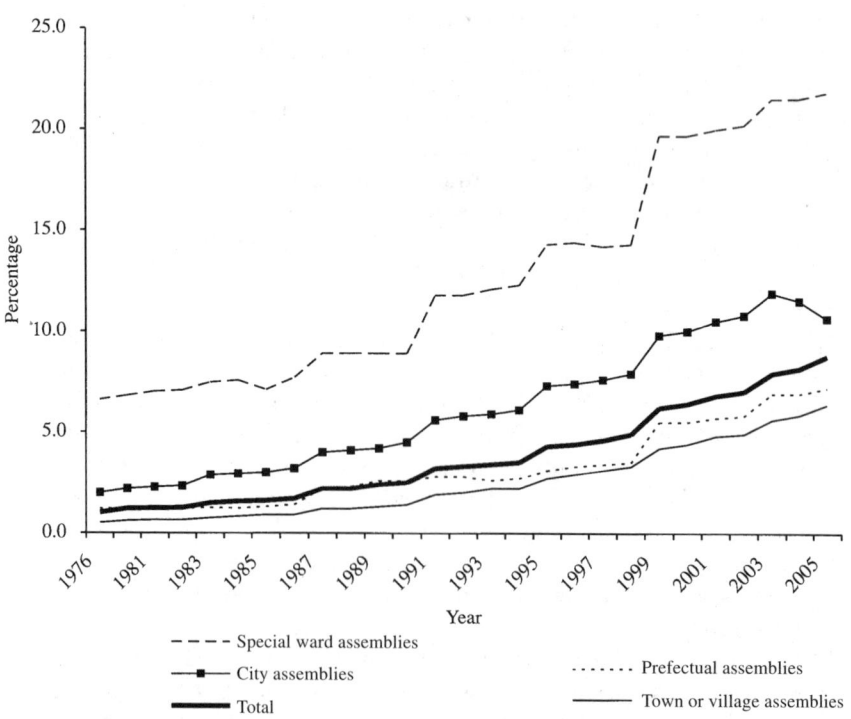

Figure 7.1 Women's Representation on Subnational Assemblies

Source: Ministry of Internal Affairs and Communications (2005a).

alized groups such as "the white-collar middle class, youth, and urban housewives" (Otake 2000, 130). Here, I focus on women's experiences on local assemblies as an indicator of whether politics is becoming more descriptively representative. Electoral and administrative changes are correlated with the recent, and sometimes dramatic, increase in women assembly members in local politics.

Below, I situate this chapter at the intersection of two literatures in Japanese politics—work on women's political participation and the experiences of opposition parties in this one-party-dominant democracy. As political outsiders, the fates of Japanese women and opposition parties have been tightly linked, their electoral outcomes rising and falling in tandem. In fact, the inroads that women have made in electoral politics over the course of the postwar period have been attributed to opposition parties that traditionally have been more likely to support women as candidates (Ogai 2001).[6] I then discuss changing institutional factors that promise to benefit women candidates, and present data that delves under aggregate trends in women's officeholding to provide a closer look at patterns of women's representation in rural and urban Japan, and in national and subnational assemblies. I test conventional wisdom that predicts that women as political outsiders enjoy greater electoral success in urban districts than rural districts. I conclude this chapter with some thoughts on how the experience of women and opposition parties diverge, with the latter standing to gain from observing the behavior of women as traditional outsiders to Japanese politics.

Women and Subnational Officeholding: Setting the Inverted Pyramid Right Side Up

Aggregate statistics disguise important variation in women's representation across Japan. Chronic underrepresentation of women in the Diet and a steady decline in overall percentages as we move to lower levels of government conceals women's rapid gains in representation on subnational assemblies in recent years. In the April 2007 unified local elections, 190 women won seats on forty-four prefectural assemblies and set a new record for successful women candidates for the sixth consecutive election.[7] Women comprised 14 percent of all winning candidates vying for a total of 8,024 municipal assembly seats in 310 cities; an increase over the 12 percent of seats that women won in the 2003 unified local elections. Since the late 1990s, women's groups have mounted an ongoing and highly publicized, nationwide campaign to reduce the number of local assemblies with no elected women. Thus, many would be surprised to learn that, during this same period, women already constituted upwards of 30 percent of some Tokyo ward assemblies. Thirty percent constitutes a "critical mass," the proportion identified by feminist researchers as necessary for women to shift legislative norms and successfully advocate for legislation beneficial to women (Grey 2006, 494).[8]

On average, women achieve higher levels of representation in urban districts than rural districts, and this is true for elected decisionmaking bodies at the national and local level. This finding is consistent with the argument that Japan should be viewed as one nation with two parallel party systems with their own internal logics; one party system is rural and dominated by the conservative Liberal Democratic Party (LDP), and the other is urban and competitive (Scheiner 2006, 5). Opposition parties and political outsiders perform better in urban districts, in part because large populations weaken the dense social networks that help incumbents to establish personal ties to mobilize voters; larger tax bases make programmatic appeals by the opposition more credible. The threshold for victory also lowers with larger assemblies. Urban voters are also more educated, exhibit more elite-challenging attitudes and behaviors, and are more supportive of gender equality—all qualities that are associated with greater tolerance of political outsiders (Flanagan 1991). For these reasons, it should follow that women, like opposition party candidates, should achieve higher levels of representation as population size and density also increase (Mabuchi 2001).

Increasingly, local assemblies do not follow a pattern where women are more likely to be elected to urban assemblies than rural ones. More and more assemblies outside of the most densely populated metropolitan districts are nearing parity. Voters in Shimamoto, a commuter town of 30,000 residents that is located in Osaka Prefecture, broke records when it elected eight of nine women candidates to seats in its eighteen-seat local assembly in April 2001.[9] At 44.4 percent of the town assembly, Shimamoto had the highest proportion of women representatives in all of Japan. The Awaji town assembly in Hyogo Prefecture trailed behind, having elected five women to its twelve-seat assembly to achieve a proportion of 41.6 percent ("Record High Proportion of Women Wins Seats in Local Assembly" 2001). Awaji is home to less than 7,000 residents. These two assemblies are interesting for two reasons. First, they deviate from the pattern of more women in urban assemblies. Second, there is something else going on that has helped women to penetrate the local political arena. News reports indicated that the women in Shimamoto were more politically active than is typical thanks in part to 50 Net, an Osaka-based nonprofit organization (NPO) that runs a school that trains women candidates (Murakami 2001). Two of the successful women candidates had attended the school to learn about campaigning, legislative behavior, and policymaking.[10] In the aftermath of the Great Hanshin-Awaji Earthquake that struck Kobe in 1995, the unprecedented number of volunteers that stepped in to provide services to residents sharply contrasted with the inefficiencies of the state's response at every level of government. As noted by Yuko Kawato and Robert Pekkanen in Chapter 10, this experience heightened interest in voluntarism across Japan and the benefits of state-society partnerships in social service provision. The long-term repercussions of this civic mobilization on participation in local governance in Kobe and surrounding communities such as Awaji are still emerging.

Even as opposition parties perform best in urban districts, the overall distribution of opposition strength across national and subnational levels of government looks likes an "inverted pyramid": strong at the national level, but steadily declining at the prefectural, municipal, and town and village levels (Flanagan 1980, 149). The opposite is true for women's representation on national assemblies. A closer examination of where women are elected to politics hints at a rapidly expanding base at the local level from which women will be able to train and launch campaigns for higher offices. Why, and how, have women been able to rapidly set the pyramid right side up? The expanding base of women elected to subnational assemblies, including those outside of urban areas, indicates that new resources are being brought to bear to overcome traditional barriers to women's candidacies and successful campaigns at the subnational level.

Women and Opposition Parties: Traditional Barriers

Studies of Japanese women and politics commonly note that women are disadvantaged because they lack *kaban* (money), *kanban* (name recognition), and *jiban* (support base), all resources necessary for overcoming the institutional hurdles that Japanese-style pork barrel politics present (Ogai 2001). Even as women attain resources typically associated with higher levels of political engagement (e.g., education, workforce participation, income, leisure time), they remain unable to convert these resources into political clout. Cultural and structural factors continue to present significant challenges to women who seek political involvement beyond the act of voting. For example, the belief that women are the best-suited primary caregivers leads to the interruption of women's career paths and access to resources, experiences, and networks that can be transferred to the political arena (Ogai 2001, 209).

Women, like opposition party candidates, must struggle with LDP dominance as traditional political outsiders. Scheiner (2006), puzzled by enduring opposition party failure given widespread unpopularity of the LDP, argues that clientelism and fiscal centralization are the powerful forces that have sustained LDP dominance over the postwar era. Local politicians rely on the central government for locally distributed goods and services (pork) that support their reelection. Voters thus have an incentive to elect political insiders with tight ties to the pipeline connecting local government to Tokyo to guarantee continued access to resources (pork). Under these conditions, political outsiders can gain a foothold in the system only if the local tax base is large enough for them to enact their proposed policies independently of the central government. Consequently, the LDP is strong in rural districts that rely heavily on the redistribution of funds from the central government; political outsiders are stronger in urban districts with a tax base large enough to enact programs independently of the state. The LDP is difficult to dislodge because it captured state resources during the early postwar period to achieve "firstcomer" status. The party has retained power after 1994 because it was already positioned to further its own interests via democratic institutions and reform processes.

The LDP dominance at the national level depresses competition for political offices in subnational politics (see Robert J. Weiner in Chapter 8 of this volume). Some towns and villages have not held elections because local notables are so firmly entrenched that new candidates are discouraged from running (Gotoda 1985, 46). Opposition parties and the minority perspectives that they represent have little chance of capturing the national government to rule from the top down when they are unable to infiltrate the LDP's local and predominantly rural strongholds from the bottom up.

Scott C. Flanagan (1980), building on work by Robert Dahl and Edward Tufte, predicted that urbanization in Japan increases population density and disrupts traditional social networks by providing associational opportunities for minority interests. Disruption of occupational and other types of associations diminishes the utility of personal connections in everyday life. At the same time, increased contact with diverse perspectives also increases the chances of encountering like-minded individuals and reduces the cost of fomenting dissent. The end result is an increase in political competition in electoral races in urban districts (see also Steiner 1965, 391). Flanagan used the changes that accompany the urbanization process to explain the gains by opposition parties at the subnational level in the 1970s. The most recent round of municipal mergers reduced the number of administrative units below the prefectural level from approximately 3,232 units and assemblies in 1999 to 1,820 units and assemblies in 2006. An immediate consequence has been an increase in the average size and density of districts.[11] If larger districts are correlated with increased competition, we should see an increase in elected women in large urban districts as opposed to smaller rural districts.

Women and Opposition Parties: New Opportunities

In this section, I discuss existing literature on subnational politics and institutional change that, when combined, fuel predictions about local political change in Japan that implicitly encompass women's experiences. Electoral and administrative reforms promise to disrupt the stagnancy of local politics, providing new opportunities for political outsiders seeking to upset the base of LDP politics. The impact of electoral and administrative reforms, however, will not be straightforward as past evidence suggests that trends produced by one set of reforms will be counterbalanced by another. Still, women are well situated to take advantage of new opportunities. From consumer activism to efforts to train and raise money for women candidates, many strategies that women evolved to circumnavigate former institutional constraints as women may prove advantageous as Japanese politics approaches a new equilibrium.

An important thread coloring discourse around electoral and administrative reforms calls attention to the relationship between deeper civic engagement, increased responsiveness and accountability among elected officials, and higher faith and engagement in politics. As noted by Gill Steel in Chapter 5 of this volume, reestablishing the electoral connection has become a focal point in reengaging Japanese voters. Given that the long-term decline in faith in politics is less pronounced at the local level than in national-level politics, local politics assumes renewed importance (Foljanty-Jost and Schmidt 2006). Reports of higher faith and engagement among voters in local politics increasingly support positions that view the local political arena as a reservoir that can be tapped into for the purpose of renewing faith in national politics. Deepening citizen engagement with democracy at the local level is expected to generate resources transferable to the national level (Foljanty-Jost and Schmidt 2006).

If higher voter turnout is correlated with deeper political engagement, evidence for deeper engagement in local politics is already present in higher voter turnout rates in subnational elections than national elections. Yusaku Horiuchi (2005) argues that citizens are "rational" voters who turn out to vote at the local level because their individual vote can make a tremendous difference. As representatives per capita increase and population decreases, the difference between the last winner and the top loser narrows in the at-large single nontransferable vote electoral systems used to elect local assemblies throughout Japan; a handful of voters often make the difference between winning and losing. This does not hold true for local urban politics. As district size increases and the number of representatives per capita decreases, turnout similarly declines as citizens realize that any individual vote makes less of a difference. These conditions raise questions about the utility of municipal amalgamations and a corresponding increase in district size in fostering deeper political engagement.[12]

At the same time, expanding tax bases and the devolution of fiscal and social welfare responsibilities due to the Local Autonomy Law Amendment (1999) increase opportunities for political entrepreneurship, beneficial to opposition parties and traditional political outsiders in the past (Scheiner 2006). Misako Iwamoto suggests that the impact of administrative reforms on local budgets was felt as early as the 1980s, and "cutbacks galvanized women into action" (2001, 225). In the aftermath of the 2003 unified local elections, the *Asahi Shimbun* reported that candidates unaffiliated with political parties or business organizations and many women and young candidates succeeded in winning assembly seats ("Make Your Vote Count in Shaping Communities" 2003). Voters are more likely to elect nontraditional candidates unconnected with the central government and the party in power when they are less reliant on them for financial survival. Prior to the 2007 unified local elections, polls indicated that voters were following campaigns with avid interest because highly publicized local government bankruptcies raised consciousness about the importance of electing local officials who could be entrusted with revitalizing local economies. Many voters might deepen their engagement with politics as decisionmaking about finances and social programs occurs closer to home.

Decentralization entails revisiting debates about the trade-off between assembly size and quality of representation; smaller size fosters deliberation and consensus, but larger size gives voice to a wide range of competing viewpoints (Flanagan 1980). Local residents concerned about assuming fiscal responsibility see new opportunities for involvement in the new freedom-of-information laws. For example, more and more citizens are monitoring local elected officials' expenditure of public funds and are attentive to assembly proceedings.[13] Bringing more citizens into local politics has also been touted as necessary to rooting out local government inefficiencies generated by close ties between LDP politicians, bureaucrats, and business interests, and the creation of greater efficiency through state-society partnerships in local governance.

As discussed at length by Kawato and Pekkanen in Chapter 10, administrative decentralization has been accompanied by a proliferation of partnerships between NPOs and local governments to provide local services. Such partnerships are viewed as a means of harnessing the energies of citizens across Japan, and bringing them into political decisionmaking processes. Echoing Kawato and Pekkanen, Gesine Foljanty-Jost and Carmen Schmidt (2006) find that a proliferation of NPOs draws increasing numbers of local residents into new channels of political participation as NPOs seek to influence local government in pursuit of its defined social mission. The NPOs are most active where rates of volunteerism are highest—in cities with over 1 million inhabitants (Foljanty-Jost and Schmidt 2006, 388).

Women are well situated to take advantage of new openings in the political opportunity structure at the local level. First, women have a head start in building up a reputation for expertise in local governance in advance of administrative reforms. Women have a history of effectively launching campaigns that capitalize on their expertise with issues rooted in their everyday experiences as housewives and mothers. Sanitation and public health, roads and traffic safety, environmentalism, and safe consumer goods and fair pricing have been among the concerns that have animated women's candidacies. Women have pursued these goals through the political arm of the Seikatsu Club Consumer Cooperative Union, the Seikatsusha Nettowaku (Citizen's Network) (see LeBlanc 1999). The Citizen's Network has expanded beyond its origins and stronghold in Tokyo's Setagaya Ward and Kanagawa Prefecture, and is now active in approximately fifteen prefectures. Its number of sponsored candidates and successful campaigns has increased in each election cycle. All 153 Netto (a political network that advocates for social policies while "escaping" ideological constraints of the Japan Communist Party [JCP] and the Social Democratic Party of Japan [SDPJ]) candidates elected to prefectural and local assemblies in 2003 were women.

Second, the Basic Law for Gender Equality (1999) encouraged widespread adoption of local ordinances detailing plans for, and a commitment to, achieving parity on decisionmaking bodies across all administrative levels (Otsuru 2004; Osawa 2000). Concurrent with these efforts, in the late 1990s activist women launched nationwide campaigns to elect women to the more than 50 percent of assemblies that still had no women representatives. Their goal was not only to elect women to all assemblies throughout Japan, but to increase women's share of seats to 30 percent of each elected assembly (Mitsui 2003).

Finally, activist women established an infrastructure to support these goals. Recognizing that increasing the numbers of quality women candidates available during the recruitment process is central to increasing the proportion of elected women, activists constructed alternative avenues to providing women with the resources needed to make up the deficit between themselves and quality male candidates (see Bochel and Bochel 2005). Women began to run backup schools and model assemblies where participants learned about legislative decisionmaking through simulations (Ogai 2004). Women candidates gained further support through the efforts of WINWIN, an organization modeled after EMILY's List, to raise funds to narrow the gap between women candidates and their better-financed male counterparts. Each of these innovations is important because they are strategies that, while specific to women, are crucial to any potentially successful candidate in a democratically elected system.

Women in Subnational Offices in Urban and Rural Japan: Data and Findings

Assuming that women as political outsiders face institutional constraints similar to those encountered by opposition party candidates seeking entry to the two parallel party systems, women should attain higher levels of representation on subnational assemblies in more densely inhabited (i.e., urban) districts. By extension, we might predict that municipal amalgamation may lead to some "natural" rate of increase. Finally, nearly one-half of Diet women (re)elected in the 2005 Lower House elections, in both the proportional representation and single-member districts, were elected from urban districts in the Kinki, Tokyo, and Kitakanto regions, which are home to Tokyo, Osaka, and Nagoya and nearly half of the nation's population. We can expect patterns of women's officeholding at the national level to be replicated at the local level if urban local assemblies serve as training grounds for advancement to national office. If the correlation between women's officeholding and population density is not strong, however, this might suggest that electoral and administrative reforms as well as grassroots efforts to increase women's representation are significant contributors to the increase. In short, there should be more locales that resemble Awaji and Shimamoto.

Below, I use data compiled by Ichikawa Fusae Kinenkai and published in hard copy in *Local Assemblies, Handbook of Data on Japanese Women in Political Life, 2003* to provide a closer look at women's subnational officeholding as a barometer of the increasing rate of success of women candidates in rural and urban districts across Japan. If the parallel party systems thesis holds true, the data should reveal higher proportions of elected women in urban districts at the subnational level. If electoral and administrative reforms matter, we should find a weak correlation between women's officeholding and population density. How much of the observed pattern in women's officeholding can be attributed to the impact of national reforms on (1) the balance of resources available to women and (2) changing attitudes about women and politics at the grassroots level remains speculative and worthy of further examination.

Unfortunately, subnational elections do not attract as much attention as national elections and their salience declines further as the size of the population represented dwindles. Consequently, several data limitations preclude answering some of the more salient questions raised by the current work. While the current analysis is suggestive of whether reforms matter, how much reforms matter relative to other factors such as women's activism warrants closer attention. The need for a considerable amount of data collection for district-specific indicators over time remains. Data from local election cycles preceding electoral and administrative reforms as well as future elections will help to disentangle the combined effects of institutional and structural factors in lowering the barriers to women's entry to subnational politics. The most comprehensive and available data, while recent, are cross-sectional. Data on women's officeholding at the subnational level in 2003 do not permit controls for the rate of change in women's representation in different types of assemblies over time. This is disappointing because aggregate-level statistics show us trends that suggest when women's representation began to increase significantly across different administrative levels, but missing subnational data do not allow us to delve beneath the aggregate statistics to calculate the rate of change in city councils and ward assemblies compared to town and village assemblies. Calculating the rate of change is further complicated by municipal mergers of the past decade. While the overall number of seats may remain the same across all local assemblies, the absolute size of any given assembly relative to the population it represents has been in flux. Most significantly, the data are not comparative; we do not have comparable statistics on male officeholders (e.g., times reelected, party support, average age, hereditary seat).

In Table 7.1, prefectures appear according to size of population in 2000 and a corresponding proportion of seats held by women in the prefectural assembly in 2003. Columns 4 and 5 reflect the percentage of city councils and ward assemblies, and town and village assemblies, in each prefecture that achieve a 1 in 5 threshold (20 percent women) for the proportion of elected women relative to men. If high population density is correlated with an increase in officeholding by women, we should expect to observe a monotonic decline in the women's representation as prefectures become increasingly rural.[14] I will first examine the proportion of women in the prefectural assemblies.

Tokyo tops the list with women holding 15 percent of seats on the metropolitan assembly (equivalent to prefectural assemblies elsewhere). Seven of the top ten most populous prefectures exceed the national average of 7.2 percent of prefectural assembly seats held by women. Rural Tottori Prefecture, which ranked last in overall population size, also exceeds the national average with 7.9 percent of seats held by women. The pattern of women's officeholding across prefectures is diffuse, and the correlation between population size and percentage of women elected to the prefectural assembly is weak (Pearson coefficient = 0.395). Comparably rural prefectures not only have exceeded the national average, but have elected women to a proportion of assembly seats in excess of that observed in all of the top ten most populous prefectures with the exception of Tokyo. Women comprise 14.9 percent of the Shiga Prefectural Assembly, 13.8 percent of the Nagano Prefectural Assembly, 11.9 percent of the Yamanashi Prefectural Assembly, and 10.4 percent of the Nara Prefectural Assembly. These less populous prefectures achieve higher levels of women's representation on prefectural assemblies than any of the top nine most populous prefectures after Tokyo.

Though 30 percent is cited as the commonly agreed-on proportion of women needed to attain a critical mass on a decisionmaking body, I highlight those prefectures with the highest overall proportion of local assem-

Table 7.1 Women's Representation on Subnational Assemblies, by Prefecture

Prefecture	Population, 2000	Percentage of Seats Held by Women in the Prefectural Assembly, 2003	Percentage of City Councils Achieving 1:5 Threshold	Percentage of Town/Village Assemblies Achieving 1:5 Threshhold
Tokyo	12,064	15	57.6	7.6
Osaka	8,805	6.3	27.3	27.2
Kanagawa	8,490	9.3	47.7	33.3
Aichi	7,043	4.7	6.4	5.2
Saitama	6,938	9.6	39	10.2
Chiba	5,926	8.2	21.2	0
Hokkaido	5,683	7.3	8	0.5
Hyogo	5,551	13	0	6
Fukuoka	5,016	4.5	12.5	5.5
Shizuoka	3,767	9	0	0
Ibaraki	2,986	6.2	4.5	1.6
Hiroshima	2,879	4.3	7.6	4.5
Kyoto	2,644	8.1	25	12.5
Niigata	2,476	4.9	0	1
Miyagi	2,365	2.2	0	3
Nagano	2,215	13.8	5.8	4.8
Fukushima	2,127	5.2	0	0
Gifu	2,108	6.1	0	1.25
Gumma	2,025	1.8	0	0
Tochigi	2,005	5.6	16.6	2.7
Okayama	1,951	8.9	0	8.8
Kumamoto	1,859	1.8	0	0
Mie	1,857	3.9	7.6	5
Kagoshima	1,786	3.7	0	0
Yamaguchi	1,528	7.5	7.6	0
Nagasaki	1,517	2	0	1.3
Ehime	1,493	6	8.3	3.5
Aomori	1,476	2	0	0
Nara	1,443	10.4	0	6.3
Iwate	1,416	7.8	0	0
Shiga	1,343	14.9	12.5	9.5
Okinawa	1,318	8.3	0	0
Yamagata	1,244	2.2	0	0
Oita	1,221	6.5	0	0
Akita	1,189	6.3	0	0
Ishikawa	1,181	6.5	0	0
Miyazaki	1,170	2.2	0	0
Toyama	1,121	4.4	0	0
Wakayama	1,070	2.2	0	0
Kagawa	1,023	4.4	0	0
Yamanashi	888	11.9	0	0
Saga	877	2.4	0	2.3
Fukui	829	0	0	0
Tokushima	824	9.5	0	0
Kochi	814	2.4	0	2.2
Shimane	762	0	0	3.9
Tottori	613	7.9	25	0

Source: Ichikawa Fusae Kinenkai (2003).

blies in which women hold 20 percent or more of assembly seats because this is the government-specified target for 2000 (Hashimoto 2001). Statements by members of the government's Council for Gender Equality suggest that the 20 percent target for 2000 represented a midterm goal on the way to achieving a numerical target of 30 percent.[15] A minimum of 20 percent for women's representation on all elected decisionmaking bodies is the national goal that local governments have been encouraged to meet. I use this summary statistic to foster comparison across assemblies that vary in size; the number of city councils per prefecture ranges from seven to over thirty, and town and village assemblies per prefecture range from approximately ten to over 100. I divide the absolute number of assemblies that achieve or exceed the 20 percent target in each prefecture by the total number of assemblies in that prefecture to calculate a proportion that facilitates comparison of women in elected office across prefectures.[16]

On average, women seem to do better in urban districts across the board. In Tokyo, Osaka, Kanagawa, Kyoto, Saitama, and Chiba—all areas that lie within Japan's densely populated Pacific belt—women are represented on city councils with spillover effects into town and village assemblies. This pattern of diffusion from inner-city districts to more rural areas in the same prefecture is uneven and perhaps reflects similarly uneven patterns of development and demographic change at the grassroots level. While Tokyo tops the list in electing at least 20 percent or more women to over one-half (57.6 percent) of its ward assemblies, it has only achieved similar representation on 7.6 percent of its assemblies at the town and village level. In contrast, Kanagawa Prefecture meets the 20 percent target on nearly half (47.7 percent) of its city councils and one-third of its town and village assemblies. In Chiba Prefecture, women held 8.2 percent of prefectural assembly seats and over 20 percent of city council seats in one-fifth of its city councils in 2003. Yet, Chiba was unable to attain similar results on town and village assemblies; none had reached the 20 percent target. Why? It may be significant that Chiba Prefecture was unable to pass its ordinance for gender equal participation (Funabashi 2004, 31). As we move down the prefectural list, from most to least populous, most have failed to meet the 20 percent target for assemblies below the prefectural level. This is unsurprising given that one-half of local assemblies had yet to elect women at the turn of the decade. Still, that rural prefectures at the bottom of the list such as Tottori, Shimane, and Kochi have been able to achieve the 20 percent target on some assemblies—surpassing some urban prefectures such as Shizuoka and other more densely populated prefectures—suggests that the rural areas are not an insignificant part of the increase in women elected to subnational assemblies across Japan.

Paradoxically, Japanese women are latecomers to local electoral success given that local assemblies are selected using electoral rules that should have worked to their advantage; at-large elections (where the district magnitude is equal to the number of seats) relax barriers to entry for underrepresented interests because candidates can be elected with small percentages of the vote (MacDougall 2001). The aggregate increase in women elected to local assemblies coincides with the introduction of national-level electoral reforms and decentralization; both efforts presumably would make it easier for political outsiders to break into the system. Both electoral reform and decentralization were expected to decrease incentives for voters to support well-connected political insiders at every level of government. Increase in average district size, as past evidence suggests, could also be expected to work to the advantage of previously marginalized interests (Mabuchi 2001; Flanagan 1980; Steiner 1965). Additionally, institutional changes coincide with (and, to some extent, have provoked) activism and volunteerism around gender equality and other issues at the grassroots level, as aptly described by Robin M. LeBlanc in Chapter 9 and Kawato and Pekkanen in Chapter 10. Disparate patterns of increase across the urban-rural divide suggest again a more complex, potentially exciting, underlying story because women are enjoying success under different electoral systems that are operative in electoral contests at various levels of government across Japan.

In the next section, I once again compare the experience of women and opposition parties under different electoral rules in national politics to draw some inferences about how Japanese women's experiences "talk back" to conventional wisdom on electoral rules and the representation of minority interests. If women are increasing their proportion of seats on assemblies across Japan under different electoral rules while opposition parties continue to encounter constraints, this might suggest that women are evolving strategies that supplant, rather than operate within, the confines of electoral rules.

Rural and Urban Women Bridging the Subnational-National Divide in the Postreform Era

There is a strong consensus among elections researchers examining Japan that multimember districts combined with single nontransferable vote systems have been detrimental to politically underrepresented groups seeking entry to electoral politics, especially women (Funabsahi 2004; Ogai 2001; Christensen 2000b; Hickman 1997; Darcy and Nixon 1996). When electoral reforms were instituted in 1994, women and opposition parties were expected to fare better in proportional representation races where the focus would be on party labels rather than individual candidates. In contrast, women and opposition parties feared that they would be worse off than before in the single-member districts where the same incentives for candidates to cultivate their personal vote would persist as under the multimember district/single nontransferable vote system. Outsiders to the field might be somewhat surprised by the unfavorable view of multimember districts in the Japanese literature because it contrasts sharply with research outside of the Japan field that holds favorable views of descriptive representation achieved under multimember district systems. Representative of this view, R. Darcy, Charles D. Hadley, and Jason R. Kirksey (1993) found that, where multimember districts were used to elect US legislatures at the local or state levels, women's electoral success improved.[17] Thus, Japanese women's experiences under different electoral systems locally and nationally promise to deepen our understanding of how the relationship between electoral rules and representation of underrepresented interests in elite politics evolves over time.

Tables 7.2 and 7.3 present trends in the share of seats held by opposition parties and women in the House of Representatives and the House of Councilors respectively. Opposition parties included all parties other than the LDP prior to 1993, and parties excluded from the governing coalition afterward.[18] The two trends are not independent of one another as opposition party support has been an important resource for women seeking office over the postwar era; the JCP, the SDPJ, and Komeito have all been more likely than the LDP to support women. I did not separate the women out from opposition party strength (and vice versa) because their low numbers do not impact the overall trend for opposition party strength in the Diet. Further, it was generally anticipated that the decrease in the strength of the traditional opposition in the aftermath of reform would hurt women's success in national races for the Lower House. If so, both trends should move in the same direction.

The first two rows in each of Tables 7.2 and 7.3 are the total proportion of seats held by opposition parties and women in each house; the bottom four rows disaggregate the proportion of seats won by opposition parties and women under the parallel systems used to elect members of each house. Existing literature finds strong relationships between electoral system (single-member district, multimember district, proportional representation), ballot structure (open- or closed-list, single nontransferable vote, party vote vs. candidate vote), district magnitude (number of seats per district), party competition, and the representation of women and underrepresented interests (see Norris and Inglehart 2005; Hasunuma 2002; Rule 1994; Darcy, Hadley, and Kirksey 1993). Generally, women gain more elected seats in proportional representation systems with large district magnitudes than in single-member district systems. The Upper House is elected in two tiers, a national tier in which ninety-six seats are elected using proportional representation and an open-list system, and a local tier in which 146 seats are

Table 7.2 Percentage of Seats Won by Opposition Parties vs. Women in the House of Representatives

	Prereform: Multimember District and Single Nontransferable Vote												Postreform				
	1958	1960	1963	1967	1969	1972	1976	1979	1980	1983	1986	1990	1993	1996	2000	2003	2005
Opposition party members	38.5	36.6	39.4	45.1	40.7	44.8	51.3	51.5	44.4	51.1	41.4	46.2	56.3	48.8	61.1	34.1	50.4
Women	2.4	1.5	1.5	1.4	1.6	1.4	1.2	2.2	1.8	1.6	1.4	2.3	2.7	4.6	15.9	14.9	12.4
Opposition party members elected by proportional representation														59.5	44.4	47.7	44.4
Women elected by proportional representation														8	12.2	11.1	13.3
Opposition party members elected in single-member districts														41.7	36.3	41	24.3
Women elected in single-member districts														2.3	4.3	4.7	6.8

Sources: Ministry of Internal Affairs and Communications (2005b, 2005c); and FairVote.org.
Notes: Success rates for women candidates are higher in the proportional representation districts, but there are fewer seats. Lower success rates in the single-member districts yield a roughly equivalent absolute number of seats in the House of Representatives.

Table 7.3 Percentage of Seats Won by Opposition Parties vs. Women in the House of Councilors

	1956	1959	1962	1965	1968	1971	1974	1977	1980	1983	1986	1989	1992	1995	1998	2001	2004
Opposition party members	51.9	44	45.6	44	45.2	50.4	52.3	50	45.2	46	42.8	71.4	46.8	48.4	61.1	34.1	50.4
Women	3.9	6.3	6.3	7.1	4	6.4	6.2	6.3	7.1	7.1	7.9	17.5	10.3	16.7	15.9	14.9	12.4
			Single Nontransferable Vote									Closed List				Open List	
Opposition party members elected by proportional representation	63.4	57.6	58.8	51.9	58.8	58	64.8	64	58	62	56	70	62	48	64	39.5	52
Women elected by proportional representation	5.8	9.6	11.8	13.5	7.8	10	9.3	12	12	12	10	24	12	26	20	22.9	16.7
												Single Nontransferable Vote					
Opposition party members elected in multimember districts	44	34.6	36.8	38.6	36	45.3	43.4	40.7	36.8	35.5	34.2	72.3	36.8	48.6	59.2	32.8	49.3
Women elected in multimember districts	2.7	4	2.6	2.7	1.3	4	3.9	2.6	3.9	3.9	6.6	13.2	9.2	10.5	13.2	9.6	9.6

Sources: Ministry of Internal Affairs and Communications (2005b, 2005c).

elected using single nontransferable vote systems in forty-seven prefectural districts that range between one and four seats.[19] Local tier elections for the Upper House resemble the multimember district/single nontransferable vote system used to elect the Lower House prior to 1996 (see Chapter 2 by Ellis S. Krauss and Robert Pekkanen). National tier elections for the Upper House employed the single nontransferable vote system until 1980 when the system was reformed and a closed-list proportional representation system was instituted in 1983. The system was reformed once again, and the open-list system was used in the 2001 election cycle.

Women's electoral experiences do not adhere strictly to the same patterns observed among the traditional opposition parties. The percentage of seats held by women and opposition parties do not rise and fall in tandem. Women have been able to increase their share of seats independently of opposition parties. On average, the conventional wisdom holds; women and opposition parties gain more seats in proportional representation races for the Lower House and across all balloting systems for the national (proportional representation) tier of the Upper House. However, closer examination reveals interesting trends emergent over the past decade. First, women's officeholding has risen faster in the period after reform than in the three preceding decades. Second, even though women tend to perform better in the proportional representation races, the proportion of seats held by women has also been increasing in the single-member district round of Lower House elections despite higher barriers for women's entry to politics in single-member districts. Conversely, opposition parties' experiences in both rounds have been mixed, seeming to vary according to the dynamics of particular election cycles. Even when opposition parties experienced electoral defeats, women's share of seats increased (e.g., in 2000 and 2005) over the share gained in the preceding electoral cycles. One might be tempted to go as far as to say that women have gained seats in the House of Representatives since reform while opposition parties have experienced a steady erosion; opposition parties netted fewer seats in both rounds of every House of Representatives election cycle since 1996. In short, a closer look at how women relative to opposition parties fare in single-member districts versus proportional representation districts reveals that, since electoral reform, women have increased their share of seats in both segments of the electoral system while opposition parties have actually lost.

Turning to examine the experiences of women and opposition parties in the House of Councilors, there also have been some notable changes emergent there over the course of the past two decades (see Table 7.3; Figures 7.2 and 7.3). First, both women and opposition parties gained during the highly controversial 1989 Upper House election when voters turned out to penalize the LDP amid broken promises and corruption scandals (see Iwamoto 2001). A record number of women candidates ran and were elected during this election cycle, dubbed the "Madonna Boom." Even though women lost some ground in the following election cycles, unlike opposition parties women's share of seats did not return to their pre–Madonna Boom rates. Second, like House of Representatives elections, women's overall share of seats has trended upward over time and gains are concentrated over the course of the past two decades; opposition parties' success rises and falls depending on the dynamics of the election cycle. Third, notwithstanding the slight dip in 2004, women's success rates have been trending upward in both the national (proportional representation) and local (multimember district) tiers of House of Councilors elections. In contrast, opposition parties' electoral fortunes have converged; opposition parties in 2004 performed, on average, worse in the national tier and better in the local tiers of the House of Councilors.

Observed outcomes for political outsiders—opposition parties and women—are not as clear-cut as conventional wisdom would predict. While political outsiders in Japan fare better under proportional representation systems, the difference in the proportion of seats gained between these sys-

Figure 7.2 Women Elected by Proportional Representation vs. Multimember Districts in the House of Councilors

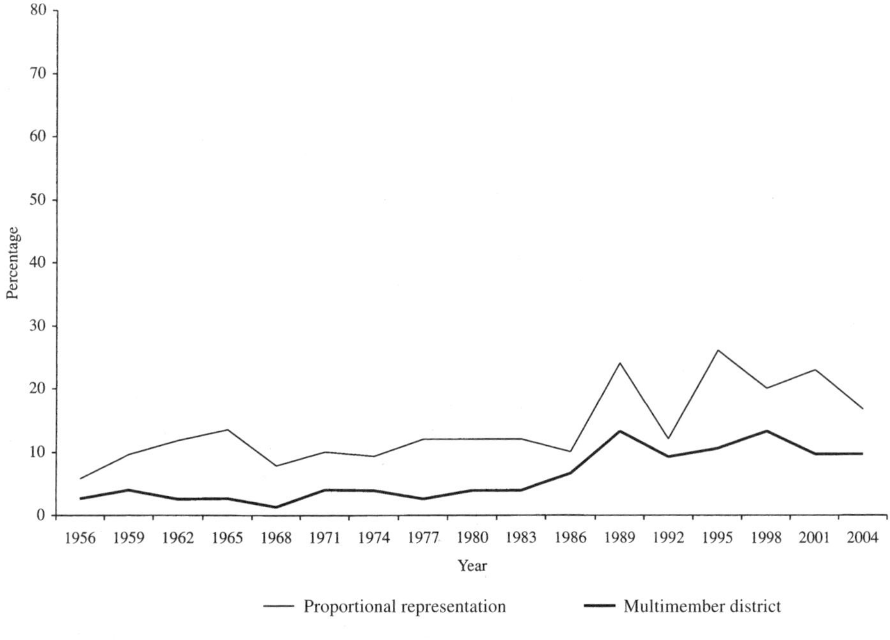

Sources: Ministry of Internal Affairs and Communications (2005b, 2005c).

Figure 7.3 Opposition Party Victories by Proportional Representation vs. Multimember Districts in the House of Councilors

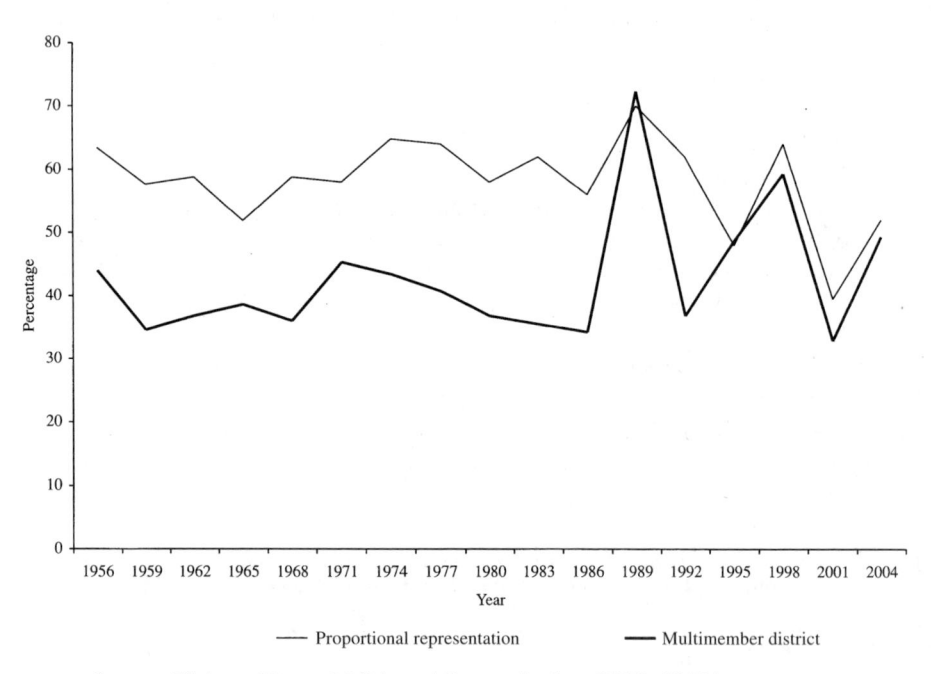

Sources: Ministry of Internal Affairs and Communications (2005b, 2005c).

tems—proportional representation, single-member districts, and multimember districts nationally, and at-large systems locally—have generally been small; these groups have constituted the perpetual opposition. That said, the increase in success for women in the postreform period is notable because (1) the rate of increase has been higher in the postreform period than in preceding decades; (2) women are increasing their proportion of seats on assemblies across Japan; (3) though rates of women's officeholding are lower in lower-level assemblies, there is an unmistakable upward trend in women's success observable under all electoral systems that are operative in national and subnational government; and (4) women are enjoying success even when opposition parties are not. Finally, even though one-half of women elected to the Diet are from urban districts where they are also more likely to hold more local assembly seats, diffuse patterns of representation throughout rural Japan suggest that grassroots efforts play important roles in helping women to overcome electoral hurdles—institutional, structural, and cultural. Women's grassroots' activities merit further investigation. While there is a growing body of ethnographic work that gives voice to new trends on the ground (see LeBlanc 1999, and Chapter 9 of this volume), the tremendous variation in strategies—where, when, how, and by whom strategies are adopted—calls for further research that will assemble these rich data to tease out patterns that yield significant changes in women's electoral fortunes.

Conclusion

This chapter has examined women's representation on elected assemblies across Japan. Japanese women are underrepresented at all levels of elected office, making Japan an outlier in comparative studies of women in politics in advanced industrialized nations. To date, women's officeholding at the national level has gained the bulk of scholarly attention, a focus reinforced by even lower levels of representation on subnational assemblies. In other nations, women's representation increases at the local level, where politics is closest to home; the exact opposite is true of Japan. Surprisingly, over the past couple of decades, women began to experience a rapid increase in their share of seats on local assemblies across Japan. Women hold upward of 30 percent of seats on some ward assemblies in urban Japan; a proportion that constitutes a critical mass. This period of increase corresponds with the adoption of electoral and administrative reforms; as the reform effort gained momentum, women experienced a corresponding growth in the proportion of seats that they held.

The proportion of women and other underrepresented groups in elected office is one measure of norms of equality, fairness, and representativeness in a democratic system. While it is commonly recognized that cultural norms and structural barriers in private and public life are as significant as electoral and other institutional factors in disadvantaging underrepresented groups, institutional reforms such as quota systems are increasingly promoted as an effective means of speeding up the rate of change (Dahlerup 2006). Japanese women are increasing their share of seats in the absence of quota systems, but in tandem with the institution of electoral and administrative reforms aimed at shifting the channels of interest articulation that connect masses to elites. Can we attribute the increase in women's representation on local assemblies to the reforms' success in disrupting patterns of politics that have benefited men at the political base, the local level? Or, are there other mitigating factors such as women's activism at the grassroots?

This chapter tries to weigh the institutional factors against "other" factors by comparing the experiences of opposition parties and women. Conventional wisdom holds that, under Japan's parallel party systems, opposition parties enjoy higher levels of success in urban districts where the barriers to entry are lower than in the LDP's rural strongholds. Social networks are weaker, the electorate is more progressive and elite challenging, and races are more competitive (Scheiner 2006; Flanagan 1991, 1980; Steiner 1965). Further, opposition parties have been a primary vehicle by which women have gained electoral office over the postwar era; the JCP, the former Japan Socialist Party (now the SDPJ), and Komeito have all been more likely than the LDP to support women candidates. Thus, we would expect to find that the fate of opposition party members and women would be tightly linked. Women, like opposition party members, should hold a higher proportion of assembly seats in urban districts than in rural districts. Additionally, both women and opposition parties should perform better under proportional representation than multimember districts/single nontransferable vote or single-member districts.

The distribution of seats held by women, compared to opposition parties, across the rural-urban divide and under different electoral incentives suggests that other factors aside from institutional reforms are operative. While not discounting the impact of the reform process, it is still unclear how much of an added benefit women gain from reforms. What is clear is that women are increasing their share of seats in parts of the electoral system where conventional wisdom holds that they are least likely to succeed, and their pattern of success looks different from that of opposition parties at the national level. While the fate of women and opposition party candidates might have been strongly linked in the prereform period (i.e., women gained seats because they were supported by the opposition party), patterns of electoral success deviate from the 1990s onward. Significantly, women are making inroads in local politics in rural Japan where most elections are competitions between nonpartisan conservatives. Women are becoming a stronger local presence in rural Japan and their experiences strike a sharp contrast to that of opposition parties.

Other factors contributing to the increase in women's officeholding on subnational assemblies include grassroots activism, training schools for aspiring women candidates, citizen's parties, and activities that evolve around local women's centers—all of which appear in different forms from one locale to the next. While opposition parties continue to run campaigns using traditional strategies that work as well after reform as they did before (see Dyron Dabney in Chapter 3 of this volume), women have had to evolve new strategies that circumnavigate rules that never advantaged their candidacies, pre- or postreform. The Seikatsu Club Citizen's Network, WINWIN, backup schools, the women's simulated assembly movement, and local gender equality ordinances all make a difference in increasing women's representation on local assemblies. Further work is required to help us to measure (1) the multiple strategies that women have advanced to break into the political realm, (2) how these strategies evolve at the grassroots level, (3) how much of a difference they make, and (4) how they interact with national reform initiatives.

Women seem to be making inroads to electoral politics at the subnational level independently of specific electoral reforms, that is, women are gaining seats in areas of the electorate where barriers remain high while experiencing smaller order increases where the barriers are lower. However, this does not mean that electoral and administrative changes have been ineffective in lowering barriers to political participation while shifting channels of interest articulation. As noted by LeBlanc in Chapter 9 of this volume, much of the change might be in consciousness about and orientation toward politics that is occurring on the ground level. Reforms have shifted public expectations about democracy and the role of everyday people within it, with repercussions for political outcomes. Traditional opposition parties are being displaced by organizations such as Netto. Voters across Japan are tuning into local politics after witnessing local governments go bankrupt, and with dawning realization of the fiscal responsibilities that accompany decentralization ("Campaigning Begins for Hundreds of Mayoral, Assembly Races" 2007). Two decades worth of reform effects have thus produced changes that are not uniform or linear, and may be more indirect than expected.

Notes

1. These percentages are seats held by women following the July 2004 House of Councilors election and the September 2005 House of Representatives election, as reported by the Inter-Parliamentary Union (2007).

2. This percentage fluctuates based on the method of calculation. Reports in the aftermath of the April 2004 unified local elections indicate that women won 190 of 2,544 seats in forty-four prefectural assemblies (excluding Tokyo, Ibaraki, and Okinawa); this constitutes 7.5 percent of these total seats (Foreign Press Center Japan 2007; Kyodo Tsushinsha 2007). This percentage increases if we include the cities in the three remaining prefectures. The percentage for local assemblies should be viewed with similar caution, though the margin of error is not great. This number reflects the percentage of village and town assembly seats won by women in the 2007 unified local elections. As all assemblies did not hold elections during this period, this number might decline somewhat if we include all assemblies. Further, municipal mergers have been ongoing since March 1999. The number of municipalities has been reduced from 3,230 in 1999 to 1,820 as of May 2006 (see Nomoto 2006).

3. I use the term "local assemblies" throughout this chapter when referring to all assemblies elected at the prefectural level and each administrative level below: Tokyo's ward assemblies, city councils, and village and town assemblies. Otherwise, I refer to specific ward assemblies or town or village assemblies.

4. As in elections for the Diet, women candidates were very successful in local elections in 1947, the first election cycle after World War II. Women won 793 seats in subnational assemblies; 677 of those seats were on town and village assemblies. Though women were able to maintain and slightly increase their small proportion of seats on prefectural and city and ward assemblies, they lost ground in local assem-

blies after the 1951 election cycle. By 1975, the number of seats held by women on national assemblies had dropped to 109. Women did not exceed the number of seats that they held on local assemblies in 1951 ($N = 775$) until 1999 when they won 867 seats (Ichikawa Fusae Kinenkai 2003). Funabashi (2004) draws attention to this often overlooked trend. Women's early electoral success in national and subnational politics has been attributed to (1) the large constituency system in the House of Representatives, (2) popular sentiment that women were attractive candidates because they were unaffiliated with the wartime leadership, (3) many men were lost during the war, and (4) voters thought that they had to vote for a man and a woman under the new democratic regime (see Ogai 2001).

5. Even though women have long achieved higher levels of representation on ward assemblies, and Figure 7.1 suggests that representation on these assemblies increased significantly prior to the introduction of electoral reforms for the Lower House of the Diet, absolute numbers of women have continued to increase across subnational assemblies since 1994. Prior to 1994, a 20 percent, 30 percent, or 40 percent increase was due to the election of a handful of additional women. After 1994, the baseline of women had expanded such that larger numbers of women were needed to achieve similar or higher rates of change.

6. Even though I draw a parallel between the experience of women and opposition parties, I do not focus here on the experience of women in opposition parties—a primary vehicle through which women have been elected to office over the postwar period. My reason is that these two factors—gender and party membership—should not be conflated. Recent elections suggest that men who are opposition party candidates may face as many barriers as women; both are equally likely to fail in overcoming the hurdles of running as an opposition party candidate. That women in local elections increasingly succeed by throwing off the constraints of party affiliation suggests that we need to consider how opposition party candidates and women candidates face differing constraints with some overlap.

7. Half of local assemblies and most prefectural assemblies hold "unified" elections every four years; the remaining hold elections on off years.

8. The critical mass debate, initiated by the work of Rosabeth Moss Kanter (1977), remains contentious with disagreement over minimum and maximum thresholds in the proportions of women needed to influence norms and culture in decisionmaking (see Grey 2006, Dahlerup 2006, and Childs and Krook 2006).

9. Parity is easier to achieve with a lower numerical threshold (i.e., one-half of eight seats is easier than half of eighty). However, gender parity on any local assembly is significant given that over 50 percent of all local assemblies have no elected women.

10. See profile of the Managing Director for 50 Net at http://fpcj.jp/old/e/mres/peopleinthenews/pin_36.html.

11. In 1999, there were 1,537 local governments administering populations numbering under 10,000 persons. This number declined to 504 by 2006. During this same period, the average population of local administrative units increased from 36,387 to 65,499. The smallest unit administers 509 people.

12. *Asahi Shimbun* reporters commenting on the 2003 unified local elections noted that low turnout nationwide and uncontested mayoral elections suggested that "interest is fading in politics at the local level" (see "Citizens and Elected Officials Can Work Together" 2003).

13. Residents of Tama City formed an association that recorded and reported on municipal assembly proceedings in the period prior to the 2003 unified local elections. Eight hundred copies of their account of the frequency of questions asked

by assembly members, their fulfillment of campaign promises, and efficiency of time usage were published and distributed community-wide ("Citizens and Elected Officials Can Work Together" 2003).

14. Population density is the commonly used measure of "urbanness." Though population density is not reported in Table 7.1, the correlation between population size and density is high (Pearson coefficient = 0.876). Reliance on population size/density is not without complications as most prefectures are a combination of rural and urban districts.

15. This remains a bit ambiguous as various documents state "councils," "decision-making bodies," "assemblies," and "elected assemblies." "Councils" and "decision-making bodies" can be interpreted as referring to appointed councils such as *shingikai* (see Sumiko Iwao's Keynote Speech, "The Challenge and Strategies for Gender Quality in Japan," at http://www.gender.go.jp/grobal/gb01-k1.pdf).

16. Another way of summarizing my findings would have been to look at the proportion of subnational assemblies that exceeded the national average for women's representation. In that case, I would calculate the percentage of assemblies for each prefecture that had more than 6.2 percent women in the prefectural assembly, more than 13.1 percent on city councils, and more than 5.9 percent on town and village assemblies. A 20 percent threshold represents a more stringent test.

17. A significant difference between multimember districts used to elect some US state legislatures, and that observed in the Japanese system, is that voters in the former had several votes while Japan has used the single nontransferable vote system. Voters are more likely to support women candidates if they are using one of several votes, and can select several candidates, than if they are using a single vote; in the latter instance, voters are more likely to see a single vote for a nontraditional candidate as wasted (see Rule 1994).

18. The LDP briefly lost control of the Upper House in 1989 and the Lower House in 1993.

19. Turnover is staggered. Councilors serve six-year terms and one-half of the seats in each tier are reelected every three years.

CHAPTER 8

Prefectural Politics: Party and Electoral Stagnation

Robert J. Weiner

PREFECTURAL-LEVEL POLITICS' IMPORTANCE WITHIN JAPANESE democracy has been on the rise. Decentralization measures are advancing, national policy innovations like *kaigo hoken* (long-term care insurance) rely heavily on local governments for implementation, local-level innovations like *joho kokai* (freedom-of-information statutes) influence national policy, and local governments are increasingly players in such international issue areas as immigration and siting of military bases (Krauss 2000; Horiuchi et al. 2001).

Prefectural politics also has considerable potential to help shape party realignment, not the least by developing the politicians who serve as the lieutenants of Diet campaigns and who often aspire to the Diet themselves (Scheiner 2005). Since the fleeting fall from government of the dominant Liberal Democratic Party (LDP) in 1993, some have pointed to the prefectures as a source of renewed competitiveness in the Japanese party system (see, e.g., Jain 1999; Bouissou 2000; "Asu no hanashi o shiyo (5): chihosen" 2001). Opposition forces appear more willing and better able to join electoral combat there than any since the "progressive local government boom" of the late 1960s and 1970s.

But these views are off the mark. First, and most plain, is that the LDP remains even more entrenched at the prefectural level than it does in the Diet. Though independent and opposition party gubernatorial candidates have enjoyed attention-getting victories, these are little more than occasional exceptions to the continued success of LDP-backed candidates—not only in governors' elections (Weiner 2004), but also in prefectural assembly elections, the focus of this chapter.

Second, I argue that we have theoretical reasons to expect uncompetitive elections as a default outcome—not only because of political challengers' structural handicaps, but also because of their strategic choices. Scholars have long and rightly pointed to a variety of incumbency advantages that hamstring challengers, many of which involve electoral institutions and policy regimes that encourage pork and personalism over issue-based and other broad-based linkages with voters. These hurt the Democratic Party of Japan (DPJ), the current and longest-lived leader of the postrealignment opposition (Scheiner 2005), just as they did the DPJ's prerealignment opposition party counterparts—and as they do challengers in general, including independent candidates and mavericks within the LDP. But challengers don't languish simply because their efforts are thwarted. Often, they choose not to exert effort in the first place.

General Duvergerian principles should remind us that weaker parties and candidates tend to act "strategically" and ultimately abandon lost-cause districts (Duverger 1954). This gives us strong reason to expect uncompetitive elections in general, and especially at the prefectural level in Japan. Indeed, as shown below, simple simulations rooted in an assumption that candidates will strategically exit unpromising districts appear to go a long way toward explaining prefectural-level patterns of uncompetitiveness. The LDP, and incumbents more generally, have yet to relinquish their hold on most voters, and opposition party organizations remain piecemeal at best. The small populations and small seat magnitudes of prefectural assembly districts—single-member districts and two-member districts account for three-quarters of all prefectural assembly districts and nearly half of all seats—make it easy for weaker parties and candidates to perceive their poor chances of winning. The result is a host of lopsided romps over token challengers, and sometimes no opposition at all.

Prior to 1993, these dynamics had already made uncompetitiveness the norm in prefectural assembly races. Since 1993, we have had no reason to expect this to change, notwithstanding other significant changes in Japanese electoral politics.

Defining Competitiveness

I measure the competitiveness of any given prefectural assembly district in two straightforward and related ways. The first measure is based on an individual-level "closeness ratio": the ratio of a losing candidate's vote to the vote of the district winner (or, in multimember districts with M winners, the lowest winner, or Mth finisher). In general, the higher a loser's closeness ratio, the more confident we can be (post hoc) that he or she was indeed "competitive" or "viable"—that he or she posed a significant threat to the eventual winner and enjoyed some reasonable chance of winning. As a simpler benchmark, we can also follow Richard G. Niemi and John Fuh-sheng

Hsieh's "70 percent rule" (2002, 81) and establish a black-and-white measure of competitiveness: any candidate is considered competitive or viable whose individual closeness ratio is at least 0.70. A competitive district, in turn, is one in which at least one loser is viable (we might establish a separate, "hypercompetitive" category for races with two or more viable losers, but these seem infrequent enough to lump together with single-viable-loser outcomes).[1] Uncompetitive districts are ones in which no loser is viable, or in which no loser runs in the first place.[2]

Seventy percent is an arbitrary threshold, of course. But it is reasonable and conventional, and perhaps even a bit generous. In a two-entrant single-member district, for example, a runner-up who draws 70 percent of the winner's vote has only fought the winner to a 41–59 percent split of the overall vote. This is nearly as lopsided as a "competitive" district can be by US standards (Niemi and Hsieh 2002, 81). This liberal definition creates a bias in favor of observing competitive candidates, and so it makes any findings of *non*competitiveness all the more robust.

The second measure, "district closeness," simply uses the strongest runner-up's closeness ratio as a proxy for overall district competitiveness. This reduces a district's overall competitiveness pattern to the gap between its strongest runner-up and its lowest winner. Higher closeness ratios indicate more competitive races. A race in which two or more candidates finish in an exact tie for the lowest seat—which does happen occasionally in small districts—would have a closeness ratio of 1, the highest possible. Uncontested races—ones with no runner-up at all—have a closeness ratio value of 0, the smallest possible.

A more comprehensive measure would account for other candidates too: all else equal, we might like to see whether a district's strongest runner-up was its *only* one that strong, or whether higher winners as well as the lowest might have felt threatened by a viable runner-up. But where competitiveness is concerned, the two candidates immediately straddling the win-loss line are the most important, and no measure incorporating both these two and other candidates' votes has yet been developed (see Reed and Shimizu 2007 for groundbreaking work to this end).

Persistent Uncompetitiveness in Prefectural Assembly Elections

I examine the results of all Japanese prefectural assembly elections from 1985 through 2007.[3] Since 1947, forty-four of Japan's forty-seven prefectures have held their prefectural assembly elections on a single unified local election date every four years. For these prefectures, this chapter covers six election years: 1987, 1991, 1995, 1999, 2003, and 2007. In order to incorporate results from the other three prefectures, I group elections into four-year "cycles" below. Each cycle includes not only those elections from the unified election year by which it is labeled, but also Ibaraki elections held one year before, Okinawa elections held one year after, and Tokyo elections held two years after.[4] Thus, the 1987 and 1991 cycles fall entirely within the prerealignment, 1955 System period—that is, they fall before mid-1993—while later cycles fall entirely within the postrealignment period.

Prefectural assembly elections are held in single nontransferable vote (SNTV) districts, the same type used until 1993 in Japanese Lower House elections. But unlike Lower House SNTV districts, most of which returned between three and five Lower House members, most prefectural assembly districts have fewer seats and some have many more seats.[5] In the 2007 election cycle, single-member districts accounted for 42 percent of all districts and 18 percent of all seats, and two-member districts for 30 percent of all districts and 25 percent of all seats. But districts of six or more seats accounted for 6 percent of all districts and 24 percent of all seats, and the largest district held nineteen seats.[6]

Figure 8.1 shows closeness ratios for prefectural assembly races by

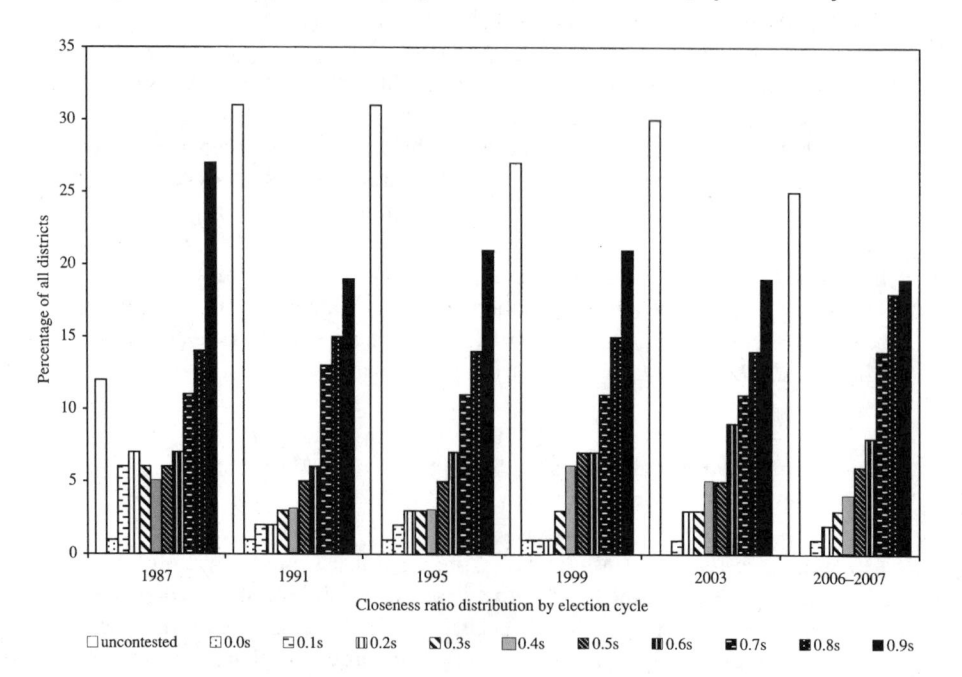

Figure 8.1 Prefectural Assembly Election Closeness Ratios, by Election Cycle

Note: Closeness ratio is the ratio of the first runner-up's vote to the lowest winner's vote.

election cycle. Table 8.1 lists percentages of uncompetitive districts (those with no viable losers, as defined by the 70 percent standard), and competitive districts with one, two, or more viable losers. Together, they paint a bleak picture of the state of competitiveness. Uncompetitive races are quite common. About half of all districts lack even one viable challenger to the eventual winners. About half of these uncompetitive districts, or one-quarter overall, simply go uncontested: no challenger even runs against the eventual winners, let alone mounts a viable challenge.

Outcomes in postrealignment elections hardly differ from their prerealignment counterparts. Uncontested and uncompetitive elections have increased on average since 1993, but this largely reflects the unusual competitiveness of the 1987 election cycle. The 1987 unified local elections were the first to be held amid the wave of voter unrest that ultimately cost

Table 8.1 Percentage of Uncompetitive and Competitive Districts, by Number of Viable Losers

	Uncompetitive (and Uncontested) Districts	Competitive Districts			Total Number
	0	1	2	3+	
All districts	52 (26)	39	7	2	7,355
1987 cycle	48 (12)	42	8	2	1,233
1991 cycle	53 (31)	38	6	2	1,237
1995 cycle	55 (31)	38	6	1	1,246
1999 cycle	53 (27)	37	8	2	1,246
2003 cycle	56 (30)	37	6	1	1,253
2007 cycle (2006–2007)	49 (25)	43	6	2	1,100
1-seat districts	68 (40)	30	2	0	3,086
2-seat districts	51 (22)	43	6	0	2,179
3-seat districts	38 (11)	50	10	1	1,010
4-seat districts	32 (6)	52	14	2	434
5-seat districts	29 (5)	51	16	5	219
6-seat+ districts	11 (2)	42	28	20	427
Gun (county)	64 (38)	33	3	0	2,263
Shi (city)	48 (22)	41	8	3	3,229
Ku (large-city ward)	41 (6)	45	13	1	763

Source: From the Japanese Local Democracy Project, a nationwide prefectural assembly election dataset (1985–2005) constructed with Yusaku Horiuchi, Ryouta Natori, Jun Saito, and Ethan Scheiner.

the LDP its Upper House majority in 1989. More important, after 1987, the Japan Communist Party (JCP) also drastically reduced its number of candidacies, leaving uncontested a number of districts where the JCP had provided the only challenge to the eventual winners. By the 1991 cycle, even before realignment had begun, competitiveness levels had already dropped. Realignment has hardly changed this. Competitiveness patterns through the 2003 cycle were no different than those of 1991. The proportion of competitive districts has increased during the 2007 cycle, but only slightly, and barely beyond the overall average.

In Prefectural Assembly Elections, the DPJ Is a Minor Party
One cause of prefectural assembly elections' low competitiveness—and perhaps, in turn, a consequence as well—is the almost complete absence of the "major" opposition. As of 2007, the DPJ had failed to establish itself as a viable local alternative to the LDP, either in name or in number. The party appears to behave "strategically," avoiding unpromising races and limiting its candidacies to districts where it expects to win. That is, it approaches prefectural elections much as Komeito approaches elections at all levels. In both the 2003 and 2007 election cycles, approximately 90 percent of the DPJ's candidates proved viable and approximately 75 percent won (contrast this with the JCP, less than one-third of whose candidates won seats). But the party is also weak. While most of its candidates run strong races, there are very few of them.

In the 1999 election cycle, the DPJ's first as Japan's main opposition party, 295 candidates ran under its banner. This represented only 7 percent of all candidates, and only one candidate for every ten seats up for election. The LDP, in contrast, accounted for 36 percent of all candidates—more than one candidate for every two seats up for election—and LDP-affiliated independents accounted for many of the rest. The DPJ did face a number of obstacles to candidate recruitment in its early years. Chief among these was the reluctance of local conservatives, whose survival in a clientelist political environment often depends on their ability to direct pork to constituents, to affiliate with an opposition party whose chances of gaining national-level power in the near future were quite uncertain (Scheiner 2005). Though the DPJ's national-level strength has waxed and waned since, its ability to take control of the more powerful Lower House at all, let alone for an extended period of time, remains suspect.

Even so, one might imagine that an additional eight years in which to pursue prefectural party building might have allowed the DPJ to expand its candidate base, especially with its understandably steep early "learning curve" now in the past. By the 2007 cycle, the DPJ had nearly doubled the size of its candidate slate—but this still left the party running only 13 percent of all candidates, or 1 for every 5.4 seats. The DPJ is, at best, a large minor party. Compare the DPJ's 13 percent of candidacies to the LDP's 39 percent, and then to the JCP's 8 percent, Komeito's 5 percent, and the Social Democratic Party of Japan's (SDPJ's) 2 percent.

The same imbalance of power holds when we turn to the DPJ's share of winners. In the 1999 election cycle, the DPJ won 7 percent of all seats; the LDP won 48 percent, Komeito 6 percent, the JCP 6 percent, and the SDPJ 3 percent. By the 2007 cycle, the DPJ had improved, but only by its own anemic standards. The party won 15 percent of all seats to the LDP's 48 percent, Komeito's 7 percent, the JCP's 4 percent, and the SDPJ's 2 percent. When we account for party-affiliated independents, the DPJ's percentage of seats increases to about 19 percent, but the LDP's similarly increases to about 57 percent.[7]

The DPJ's weakness in prefectural elections necessarily yields weak DPJ contingents in prefectural assemblies. The party frequently fails even to exist as such, its legislators often registering as a *kaiha* (intraparliamentary group) under a different name and joining forces with members of other parties. Prefectural assemblies remain dominated by the LDP and prepared to stand in the way of the few DPJ or independent governors who do manage to take office.

Table 8.2 ranks prefectures in descending order by the proportion of seats won by the DPJ and its affiliated independents in the April 2007 elections (columns 1 and 2). For comparison's sake, as described in Note 7, I report results based on both the "author's data" and "*Yomiuri* data" estimates of independents' partisan affiliations; prefectures are ranked according to the former (column 1), but the two measures are largely similar. Table 8.2 also reports a maximally generous measure of possible DPJ legislative strength: "max % DPJ camp" (columns 3 and 4). This category includes not only DPJ and de facto DPJ legislators, but also legislators affiliated with all other parties except the LDP, Komeito, and JCP, as well as any independent legislator whose party affiliation is unclear. That is, it represents each prefecture's upper bound of anti-LDP, non-Communist strength, or the largest percentage of legislators we might expect to side with the DPJ (even if few of them belong to the DPJ itself). Columns 5 through 8 report corresponding percentages for the LDP; "LDP camp" combines the LDP with the Komeito, an LDP ally.

Even by such liberal measures, the DPJ appears rather feeble, and the LDP still clearly dominant. The DPJ does not hold an outright majority in any prefecture, and the addition of other non-Communist, anti-LDP legislators only allows it to construct a majority in one prefecture, Iwate. The LDP, in contrast, would enjoy an outright legislative majority even without Komeito support in at least thirty-four of forty-seven prefectures, according to both the author's and the *Yomiuri* data (in five prefectures, only one of

Table 8.2 DPJ and LDP Shares of Prefectural Assemblies After the April 2007 Elections

Prefecture	(1) % DPJ (author)	(2) % DPJ (*Yomiuri*)	(3) Max % DPJ Camp (author)	(4) Max % DPJ Camp (*Yomiuri*)	(5) % LDP (author)	(6) % LDP (*Yomiuri*)	(7) % LDP Camp (author)	(8) % LDP Camp (*Yomiuri*)
Iwate	46	46	60	58	27	29	29	31
Hokkaidou	40	39	42	42	49	49	56	56
Aichi	37	37	37	37	57	57	63	63
Kanagawa	36	36	45	47	42	40	53	51
Shiga	30	34	49	45	40	45	45	49
Tokyo[a]	28	28	34	34	39	39	56	56
Fukushima	28	21	38	36	52	53	57	59
Shizuoka	27	32	36	36	54	54	62	62
Mie	25	35	47	47	45	45	49	49
Kyoto	24	23	27	26	42	44	52	53
Hyougo	23	22	34	29	47	51	61	65
Nagasaki	22	24	37	39	54	52	61	59
Chiba	22	22	31	27	58	61	65	68
Saitama	22	22	29	28	55	56	68	69
Osaka	21	23	27	25	44	46	64	66
Nara	20	20	30	27	52	55	59	61
Miyagi	20	16	28	34	62	56	69	62
Tottori	16	18	26	26	63	63	68	68
Shimane	16	16	27	27	68	68	70	70
Okayama	16	16	20	18	66	68	75	77
Fukuoka	15	15	27	32	51	50	68	67
Niigata	15	15	25	23	66	68	68	70
Gifu	15	15	24	17	70	76	74	80
Nagano	14	19	48	47	31	31	38	40
Tochigi	14	16	18	22	76	72	80	76
Kumamoto	14	10	31	22	63	71	69	78
Aomori	13	17	31	29	58	63	65	67
Yamanashi	13	16	24	26	71	68	74	71
Fukui	13	15	25	18	70	80	73	83
Wakayama	13	9	17	22	65	61	74	70
Tokushima	12	17	17	27	71	61	76	66
Yamaguchi	12	12	27	18	59	67	67	76
Hiroshima	11	14	29	27	61	62	70	71
Ehime	11	11	30	19	64	72	68	79
Yamagata	11	11	23	23	70	70	73	73
Akita	11	7	49	40	44	53	47	56
Saga	10	10	20	20	76	76	78	78
Ibaraki[a]	9	9	9	9	82	82	88	88
Toyama	8	5	23	23	73	73	75	75
Ishikawa	7	11	24	20	57	61	61	65
Ooita	7	9	36	45	55	43	61	52
Miyazaki	7	7	27	22	64	69	71	76
Kagawa	7	7	22	20	69	69	73	73
Gunma	6	10	28	22	66	72	70	76
Kagoshima	4	2	19	20	74	72	80	78
Kouchi	3	5	36	26	38	54	49	62
Okinawa[a]	0	0	40	40	42	42	54	54

Source: Based on "44 doufukengikai no shinseiryoku bunya" (2007).
Note: a. Not April 2007 election results, but *kaiha* membership as of May 2007.

the two datasets shows an LDP majority). In forty-one prefectures, the combined seats of the LDP and Komeito constitute a majority (in two more, only one of the two datasets shows a combined LDP-Komeito majority). In most prefectures then, even if a DPJ candidate (or any other candidate not backed by the LDP) were to win the governorship, the LDP's legislative veto power would remain formidable.

Uncompetitiveness Should Be No Surprise

The uncompetitiveness that we observe at the prefectural level betrays electoral system reformers' hopes. But reformers—and political scientists—should know better than to expect robust two-party competition in an environment marked by pragmatic parties, lopsided balances of party support, and a preponderance of single-member districts.

Elections are widely thought to be governed by Duverger's law, which holds that, in single-member districts with simple plurality voting, we should normally expect to see two candidates fight for the one seat at stake. Steven R. Reed (1990) and Gary W. Cox (1997), with Japan's former Lower House multimember districts in mind, reformulated Duverger's law into the more general "$M+1$ rule": in SNTV districts of M seats, we should normally expect to see $M + 1$ candidates fight for the M seats at stake (M stands for seat *m*agnitude, with $M = 1$ for single-member districts). Clearly weaker prospective candidates—ones who plainly expect to finish lower than $M+1$th place—expect to be strategically abandoned by supporters who want to avoid wasting their votes, and will ultimately choose not to run.[8] If more than $M + 1$ candidates are thought to have a reasonable chance of finishing in $M+1$th place or higher, however, then all of them have reason to run (though for all but $M + 1$ of them, these expectations will ultimately prove wrong, of course). Either way, at least $M + 1$ candidates enter the race. This is commonly interpreted to mean that at least $M + 1$ *viable* candidates will enter the race (i.e., that the $M+1$th candidate will be a viable one, not simply a token challenger), and thus make the election competitive.

This conventional wisdom suggests that Japanese prefectural-level elections have somehow strayed from the normal democratic path. But I argue that the conventional wisdom is wrong. First, it wrongly assumes that as many as $M + 1$ prospective viable candidates always exist in the district. Second, and more important, it wrongly assumes that a prospective candidate who clearly expects to finish in $M+1$th place will nonetheless choose to run—unlike all other candidates who clearly expect to lose. What actually governs elections is an "M rule." Strategic prospective candidates and parties who expect to finish in Mth place or above—that is, ones who expect to win—will run. Those who expect to lose, to the extent that they can clearly forecast this, will tend to drop out of the race. Japanese prefectural assembly elections offer textbook examples of how strategic decisionmaking drains competition from elections.

Not All Districts Contain M + 1 Viable Candidates

A competitive election initially requires that at least $M + 1$ viable candidates exist in a district in the first place, but we have no particular reason to expect this. The likelihood that any particular district will house at least two viable candidates remains an open theoretical question. Districts are heterogeneous, and some will prove uncompetitive simply because they contain no one strong enough to viably challenge the eventual winner.

This line of argument assumes that potential candidates can always assess their electoral strength with some degree of accuracy before they run.[9] This is an oversimplification, of course, but a common assumption. Most important, it already lies at the foundation of the Duvergerian approach, in which parties and candidates are assumed able to gauge each other's strengths before they decide whether to run, seek alliances or mergers, or stand down.[10] It emphasizes that not all potential candidates are created equal: some have preexisting and durable advantages rooted in incumbency, party affiliation, prior policy stances, or personal traits.

We can gain a better sense of how district heterogeneity might constrain competitiveness through a simple (and necessarily oversimplified) simulation. Imagine a set of election districts in which prospective candidates are able to predict—fully accurately—how well they would fare if they were to contest the race. Each district houses some number, varying between 0 and n, of "underdogs" (i.e., prospective candidates who, if they choose to run, expect to finish no better than runner-up), as opposed to prospective candidates who expect to win if they run as in the case of many incumbents, and as opposed to the vast majority of district residents who never even consider running and thus are not prospective candidates at all. By definition, an underdog expects his or her closeness ratio to fall somewhere between 0 and 1.[11] Prospective candidates with an expected closeness ratio of 0.7 or greater will be viable (by the definition above) should they choose to run.

Now imagine that the number of underdogs in each district falls between 0 and n, but varies from district to district, with each possible number between 0 and n equally likely. For example, if we judge that n should be 2, then an equal share of the simulated districts will have 0, 1, and 2 underdogs, respectively. In other words, each district's number of underdogs can be said to reflect a random draw from a uniform distribution of the integers between 0 and n (as opposed to, say, a bell-curved normal distribution in which extreme values like 0 and n are less likely than intermediate

PREFECTURAL POLITICS 161

values). Similarly, imagine that the electoral strength of underdogs—that is, each underdog's expected closeness ratio—varies from individual to individual, with every possible value between 0 and 1 equally likely (recall that a district's underdogs are its prospective candidates, including those who ultimately choose not to run).

How many such districts have the potential for a competitive race? That is, how many are home to at least 1 viable underdog? The answer depends on how large n is: the more underdogs there are, the more likely it is that at least 1 of them will be strong enough to run a viable campaign. To be exact, the proportion of districts containing at least 1 underdog with an expected closeness ratio above any particular value v will be $\Sigma^n_{i=0} (1 - v^i)/(n + 1)$. It follows that $\Sigma^n_{i=0} (1 - 0.7^i)/(n + 1)$ is the simulated proportion of districts containing at least 1 viable underdog. As shown in Figure 8.2, the simulation suggests that, for example, if districts may have as many as 2 underdogs, then 27 percent of districts will have at least 1 viable underdog and thus be competitive; and if districts may have at least 10 underdogs, then 70 percent of districts will have at least 1 viable underdog and thus be competitive.[12] Figure 8.3 shows the proportion of districts whose strongest underdog, under these conditions, would have a closeness ratio above 0.9 (or "in the 0.9s"), above 0.8 but below 0.9, above 0.7 but below 0.8, and so on.

Figure 8.2 Simulation: More Underdogs in a District Yield More Viable Candidates

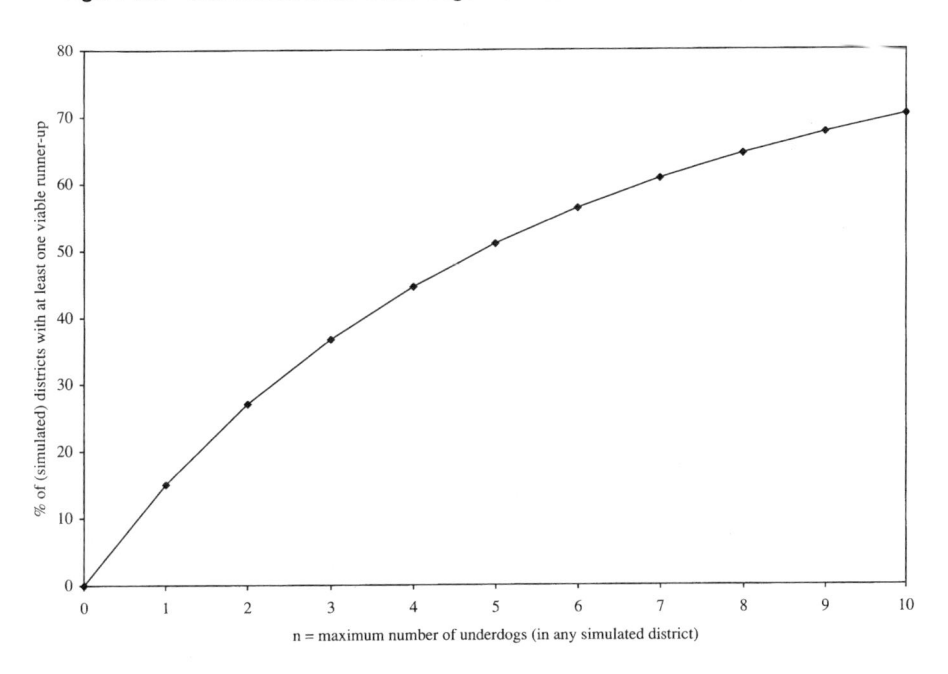

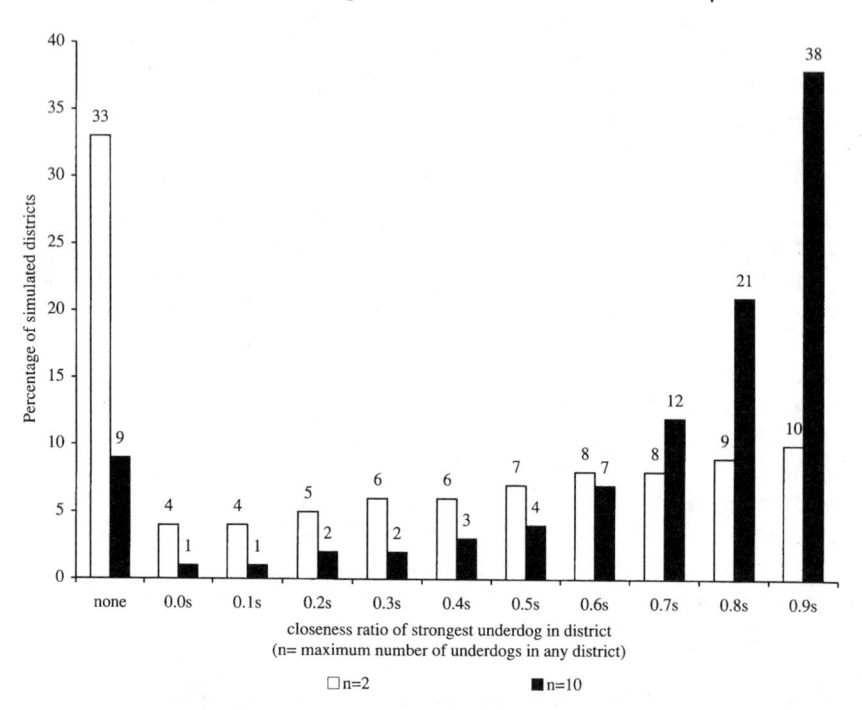

Figure 8.3 Strongest Underdogs Given Random Distributions of Expected Votes

closeness ratio of strongest underdog in district
(n= maximum number of underdogs in any district)

☐ n=2   ■ n=10

Three patterns are worth noting. First, some districts—$1/(n + 1)$ of them—simply have no underdogs waiting in the wings. Elections would always go uncontested in these districts. Similarly, some districts ($[1/(n + 1)]$ $\Sigma^{n}_{x=0}\, 0.7^{x}$ of them) have not a single viable underdog. Elections might be contested but can never be competitive, by the 70 percent standard, in these districts. Second, as shown in Figure 8.3, the more underdogs a district contains, the more likely it is that at least 1 has a closeness ratio of at least v. Third, so long as n is greater than 1, districts whose strongest underdogs have expected closeness ratios between 0.9 and 1 should be more common than districts whose strongest underdogs have expected votes between 0.8 and 0.9, and so on.

Not All Viable Challengers Run

But underdogs are only prospective runners-up. How many of them will run? If they are strategic, those who clearly expect to lose will choose not to run. Of course, citizens and political scientists might prefer to see them enter the race and instigate genuine competition. But from these viable-but-trailing candidates' own point of view, keeping the front-runners honest isn't reason enough to launch a campaign. Running is only worthwhile when one's odds of winning—not just coming close—are good enough to justify the effort.

Strategic entry theory tells us that potential candidates choose whether or not to run according to decision theory's familiar "$pb - c$" calculus: entering the race promises a payoff of $pb - c$, where b represents the benefits available to the winner, p the probability of winning, and c the inevitable costs of mounting a campaign. Staying out of the race, meanwhile, promises a payoff of 0. Entering, then, is only worthwhile when $pb - c > 0$ (or $pb > c$, or $p > c/b$). For a viable-but-trailing candidate, this requires at least one of three conditions: (1) candidates' relative strengths are uncertain enough—which makes the probability p great enough—to offset costs c, (2) costs c are low enough (relative to benefits b) to offset poor odds of beating the front-runner, or (3) the candidate abandons such strategic calculations altogether.

Why does uncertainty about candidate strengths encourage trailing-but-viable candidates to run? Two factors contribute to a candidate's perceived probability of winning: expected electoral strength relative to the front-runner (as expressible through a closeness ratio) and the degree of uncertainty underlying this expectation. Of course, greater strength implies a greater (or equal) probability of winning.[13] But probability of winning also reflects uncertainty, which establishes a margin of error around expected strength. Under (hypothetical) conditions of complete certainty, with no margin of error, candidates' expectations are perfectly accurate. This ruthlessly transforms any expected strength lower than the front-runner's—that is, any closeness ratio below 1—into 0 probability of winning, and drains away any incentive to run so long as running is at all costly. With greater uncertainty, though, the margin of error grows wider. At some point, this yields a value of p great enough to justify the cost of running. Ultimately, under (hypothetical) conditions of absolute uncertainty, the race becomes a perfectly random toss-up: all entrants are equally likely to win. In general, greater certainty tends to discourage entry by prospective runners-up; greater uncertainty tends to encourage it.

We can continue with the simulation above for a rough illustration. For simplicity's sake, imagine that a single level of uncertainty and a single benefit-cost ratio apply to all districts and all candidates. Under complete certainty and completely strategic behavior, all elections should simply go uncontested: all eventual losers know they will lose, so none run. When uncertainty and the benefit-cost ratio combine to make entry attractive for any candidate with an expected vote of at least v, however, any district housing at least 1 such candidate will be contested. When the effective entry threshold is 70 percent of the Mth finisher's vote, for example, districts should be contested either by viable eventual runners-up or not at all. Figure

8.4 illustrates the effect of a 70 percent threshold when applied to the results of Figure 8.3.

Not All Candidates Are Strategic

We have assumed so far that candidates—or the parties sponsoring them—approach entry decisions "strategically": they weigh expected benefits against expected costs, considering only the immediate district election at hand, and coolly choose not to run if the costs are greater. Many individual candidates do operate this way, and so do some parties. Komeito is the prototypical strategic party: it ruthlessly assesses its prospects in each race and runs candidates only when confident of winning. The party rarely overestimates its strength, and its candidates rarely lose. But other candidates and parties appear entirely *non*strategic, or "sincere," in their approach to elections. The JCP is the prototypical sincere party: it runs candidates in as many elections as possible, even when it fully expects to lose. Entering the election seems less a choice than a responsibility or an expressive act, and serves as an end in itself.[14] Of course, most candidates and parties fall in

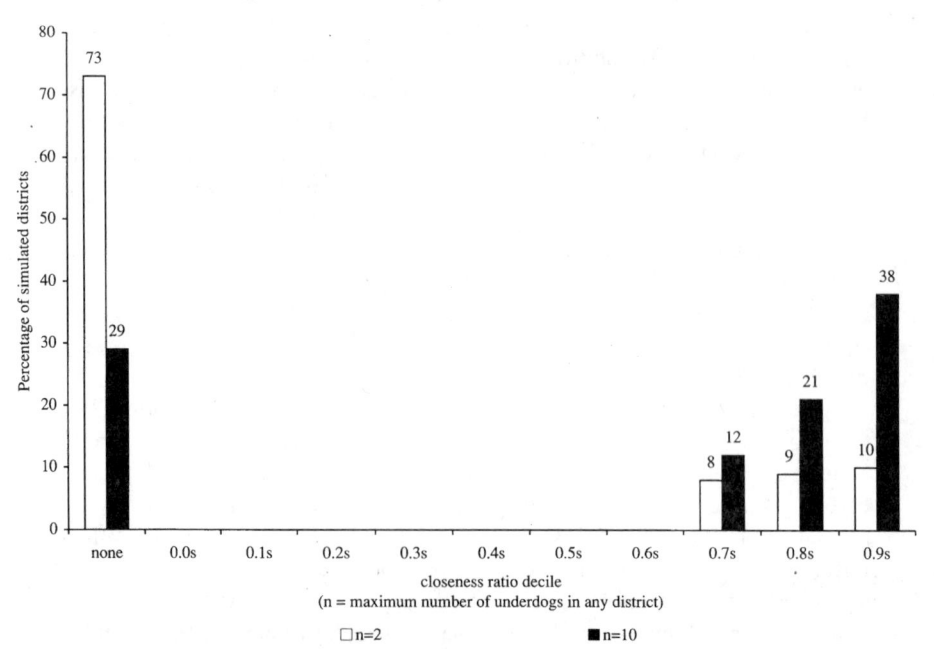

Figure 8.4 Simulated District Closeness Ratios

Note: Closeness ratios given an entry threshold at 70 percent of Mth finisher's vote and random distribution of expected vote.

between these extremes of strategy and sincerity. Whatever the particular balance, however, greater strategicness generally tends to discourage entry, all else equal.

We can continue with the simple simulation to illustrate the effect of sincere entry on competitiveness. Assume that, in every district, a fixed number f of sincere eventual runners-up, $f \geq 0$, exist alongside the n strategic prospective runners-up. The sincere runners-up always enter the race (and, hence, are "eventual" rather than "potential" runners-up). Also assume, as with strategic prospective candidates, that sincere candidates' closeness ratios are distributed randomly. Then, the proportion of districts with at least 1 potential or eventual runner-up with an expected vote of at least v equals $1 - v^f (1/(n + 1)) \Sigma^n_{x=0} v^x$.

Figure 8.5 illustrates how a single sincere entrant changes the simulated competition patterns of Figure 8.4. Sincere candidates turn uncontested races into contested ones. They also increase competitiveness levels in contested districts—if they happen to be stronger than any strategic entrants. In districts whose strongest sincere candidate is still rather weak, the result is a

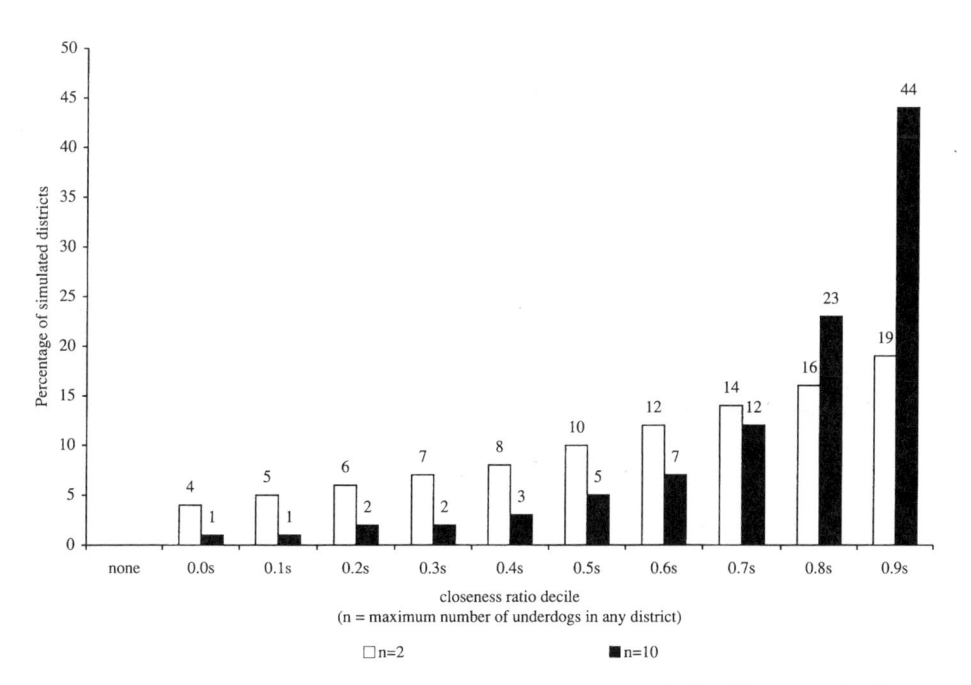

Figure 8.5 Simulated District Closeness Ratios Given One Sincere Entrant

Note: Closeness ratios given one sincere entrant, an entry threshold at 70 percent of Mth finisher's vote, and random distribution of expected votes.

lopsided, low-competition race that would never have arisen through strategic entry alone. Finally, as with strategic underdogs, the more there are in a district (e.g., when n is 10 rather than 2), the better the odds that at least 1 of them will be strong enough to produce a competitive race, and this increases competitiveness levels overall.

Prefectural Assembly Uncompetitiveness Follows Theoretical Predictions

In sum, entry by viable-but-trailing candidates will only be propped up by sufficiently low costs, uncertain outcomes, or disregard for myopically strategic cost-benefit calculations. To the extent that the opposite conditions hold (i.e., to the extent that elections are costly, outcomes can be predicted with certainty, and candidates and parties are strategic), we should expect such candidates to stand down despite their ability to provoke a competitive race.

At the prefectural level in Japan, we have particularly good reason to expect noncompetitive conditions. Prefectural assembly districts' small populations and often-small seat magnitudes make for smaller potential candidate pools and greater certainty. Smaller electorates have the same effect in prefectural assembly districts. Prefectural-level races are more candidate centered and less party centered than national ones, and this should favor the short-term, narrowly instrumental strategic decisionmaking that Duvergerian causal mechanisms assume: party sponsorship often gives life to weak candidacies that the potential candidates themselves might pass up if acting alone. Though office benefits and campaigning costs should both be lower than in national elections, the ratio of benefits to costs might be lower at more local levels.

Results in prefectural assembly elections appear to bear this out. Both before and after 1993, prefectural assembly closeness ratio distributions (Figure 8.1) closely match those of the randomized simulation, resembling a cross between the hypothetical patterns shown in Figures 8.4 and 8.5. One might infer that prefectural assembly elections are marked by conditions conducive enough to strategic decisionmaking that weaker strategic actors choose not to run, and that some—but not all—districts contain a sincere entrant as well. As noted above, prefectural elections do seem comparatively amenable to strategic decisionmaking. And most—but not all—districts house a single, consistent nonstrategic presence: the JCP.

That prefectural assembly closeness ratio distributions are consistent with the M rule and the randomized simulation of (mostly) strategic entry does not necessarily confirm that strategic entry produced them. After all, as Figure 8.3 illustrates, they could also represent a random distribution of numbers and strengths of sincere candidates, the strongest of which in each district enters without fail. We can dispel some of these doubts by grouping districts by their likely levels of uncertainty, and then comparing results across groups. We expect higher certainty districts to have greater proportions of uncontested and closely contested elections. If we do observe such a pattern in practice, then we can be more confident that strategic entry is actually at work: this pattern could only reflect nonstrategic entry if higher certainty districts were more likely to house either strong sincere candidates or none at all, and we have no reason to suspect this. Elsewhere I use multiple regression to establish the links between uncertainty and conformity to M rule predictions (Weiner 2003).[15] Here, I isolate two particular determinants of uncertainty—district magnitude and urbanness.[16]

Several studies have identified higher district magnitudes as a key instigator of competition. Higher magnitudes tend to lower the vote share needed to win a seat, putting victory in apparent reach for more candidates, and generally increase uncertainty (see, e.g., Reed 1990; Cox 1997, 105–106). If the population of eligible voters per seat is held constant, higher magnitude districts also require fewer viable candidates to produce competitive races—that is, the effective candidate pool is increased. Compare, for example, one five-seat district of 1,000 voters and five one-seat districts of 200 voters each. Competitiveness in the five-seat district only calls for one viable loser per 1,000 voters. The five one-seat districts together require five viable losers per 1,000 voters—and a distribution that places at least one in each individual district.[17]

Previous empirical research on multimember SNTV districts has indeed found lower magnitudes to be associated with less competition (Reed 1990; Cox 1997; Hsieh and Niemi 1999; Niemi and Hsieh 2002). Previous empirical research on uncontested elections has focused on single-member districts, and particularly US single-member districts (see, e.g., Squire 1989, 2000), in part because of the high rate of uncontestedness in those smallest of districts—ironically, precisely the district type that originally inspired Duverger's law. As Aaron Wildavsky noted in one of the earliest critiques of Duverger, "the two-party systems in America and Great Britain are, for the most part, alliances of predominantly one-party areas" (1959, 309).

Prefectural assembly results, whose M values here range from 1 to 19, illustrate this relationship sharply (they also foreshadow the effect of the Lower House's recent switch from multimember to single-member districts). Figure 8.6 and Table 8.1 present closeness ratio distributions and numbers of viable losers for six magnitude categories. More than 40 percent of single-member districts are uncontested, and fully 70 percent are uncompetitive by the 70 percent standard. As seat magnitudes grow larger, the proportions of uncontested and uncompetitive races steadily fall. Among districts with six or more seats, only 2 percent are uncontested, and only 11 percent are uncompetitive. That larger-magnitude districts are associated

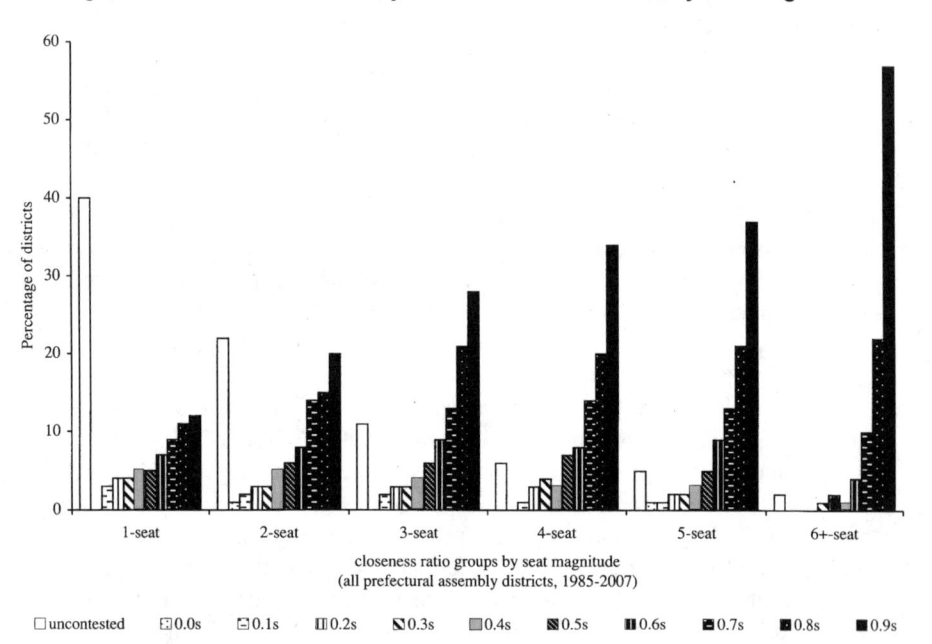

Figure 8.6 Prefectural Assembly Election Closeness Ratios, by Seat Magnitude

closeness ratio groups by seat magnitude
(all prefectural assembly districts, 1985-2007)

□ uncontested   ▣ 0.0s   ▤ 0.1s   ▥ 0.2s   ▨ 0.3s   ▢ 0.4s   ▩ 0.5s   ▦ 0.6s   ▧ 0.7s   ▬ 0.8s   ■ 0.9s

not only with more contested elections, but also a greater proportion of highly competitive races among contested elections, reflects the likely larger size of these districts' candidate pools. Seat magnitude is correlated with, though not a strict function of, electoral district population, and candidate pools should be roughly correlated with district population.[18]

Similarly, more urban districts should also be more likely to impose greater uncertainty. Although urban districts in Japan are the stronghold of the two Japanese parties whose vote support is most predictable, the JCP and Komeito, urban voters are generally more mobile and maintain weaker party and candidate loyalties, and this is likely to yield more uncertainty overall. We might also expect urban districts to house greater numbers of nonstrategic candidates, at least in Japan: the JCP's support base is heavily urban, and unaligned "cranks" of all stripes seem to surface more often in urban elections.

I use a crude, but reasonable, scale of urbanness. Nearly all prefectural assembly districts comprise a single large-city *ku* (ward), *shi* (city), or *gun* (county of towns and villages) in its entirety, and I simply categorize districts by these locality types.[19] Here, I omit elections falling after 2005, at which point large-scale amalgamation of municipalities began to convert dozens of rural areas into nominal cities, rendering tenuous the link between official city status and actual urbanness. Figure 8.7 and Table 8.1 present closeness ratio distributions and numbers of viable losers for the three urbanness categories. The difference in distributions between more rural and more urban districts again matches expectations, though differences across urbanness types are not as stark as those across magnitude categories. In rural counties, 38 percent of prefectural assembly elections are simply uncontested, and 26 percent more are contested without viable runners-up, for an overall uncompetitiveness rate of 64 percent. With increasing urbanness and uncertainty, uncontested and uncompetitiveness rates fall. In large-city wards, only 6 percent of elections go uncontested, and "only" 41 percent are uncompetitive. Note that while large-city wards have far fewer outright uncontested elections than cities do, a fair proportion of the corresponding increase in contested elections comes in districts with moderate closeness ratios—that is, districts that are contested but uncompetitive. The proportion of the most highly competitive elections, those in the 0.9s group, actually decreases slightly from cities to large-city wards. This suggests that while large-city ward elections feature greater uncertainty and lower strategic entry thresholds, or perhaps contain greater numbers of weak sincere entrants, their overall candidate pools are not appreciably larger than those of cities. This seems consistent with the fact that large-city

Figure 8.7 Prefectural Election Closeness Ratios, by District Urbanness

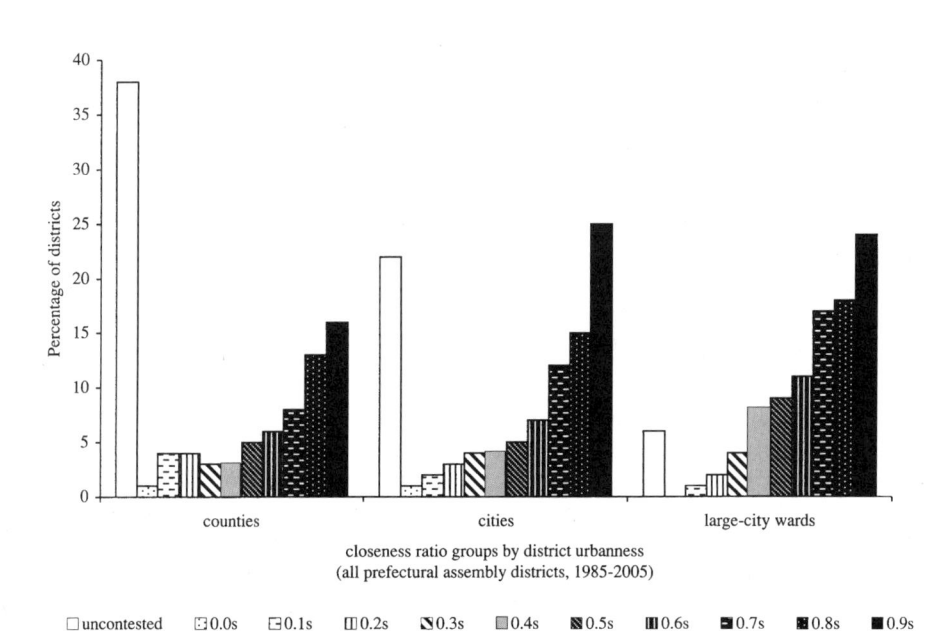

closeness ratio groups by district urbanness
(all prefectural assembly districts, 1985-2005)

□ uncontested ▩ 0.0s ▩ 0.1s ▥ 0.2s ▧ 0.3s ▪ 0.4s ▨ 0.5s ▦ 0.6s ▬ 0.7s ▩ 0.8s ■ 0.9s

wards' range of population roughly parallels the higher end of the population range of cities.

Conclusion

Even in the mid-1990s, when party realignment and electoral reform had only just been set in motion, expectations that genuine competition would become the norm had no basis either in Japan's electoral history or strategic entry theory. In theory, we have no particular reason to expect any district of M seats to house more than M viable potential candidates—and even viable potential candidates, if they expect to lose, have incentives not to run. Conditions in prefectural assembly elections seem to match this theory's assumptions quite well. And indeed, in practice, most prefectural assembly elections had been uncompetitive before 1993. Post-1993 Japanese electoral experience thus far should give optimists pause. Since 1993, prefectural assembly elections have been at least as uncompetitive as before.

The considerable and durable unevenness of vote support among individual candidates and political parties is important here. But just as important as the cards that candidates and parties are dealt is how they choose to play them. In recent years, the DPJ, in particular, has made an especially large contribution to prefectural-level electoral stagnation. In Lower House elections the DPJ may often fail to beat the LDP, but in prefectural-level elections, it doesn't even try. This may be in the party's short-term interests, saving it resources that would otherwise be spent on losing campaigns. But the party might also be undercutting its strength in the longer term by failing to invest resources in candidates who help publicize the party, serve as a vessel for any unanticipated wave of anti-LDP sentiment, and develop a pool of potential candidates for the Lower House. As the electoral entry theory detailed above argues, such a myopic strategy in prefectural elections should not surprise us, but neither should it reassure us if competitiveness is a concern.

The overwhelming prevalence of noncompetition in Japan, even with its new Lower House electoral system and new opposition parties, is not only significant in itself, but also might be profitably kept in mind in broader studies of Japanese local and electoral politics. Recent research has tended to give disproportionate attention to political underdogs and newcomers (e.g., progressive mayors and governors, independent upset winners, and citizen's group miniparties). This is all to the good—and, to some extent, simply necessary—and little different from research on other countries. But we should not lose sight of the fact that participation by such actors, let alone success, is exceptional. In particular, the idea of a vibrant local-level arena of democratic experimentation seems almost absurd where electoral politics is concerned, apt as it could be for policymaking. Established actors' continued anticompetitive stranglehold on electoral power might not be exciting, but it is certainly significant.

Notes

1. Of the 3,510 prefectural assembly races between 1985 and 2007 with at least one viable loser, only 490, or 14 percent, had two viable losers and only 128, or 4 percent, had more than two.

2. Closeness ratios and viability-based counts are conscious departures from measures based on "effective" numbers of candidates (Laakso and Taagepera 1979; Molinar 1991). Effective numbers are less appropriate for counting numbers of candidates within a district (Niemi and Hsieh 2002), and this is particularly so when measuring competitiveness. Because effective numbers are weighted counts of all entrants, they cannot distinguish between large numbers of weak losers and small numbers of strong losers. For example, a three-candidate race in which the winner draws 65 percent of the vote and two other candidates draw 25 percent and 10 percent, respectively, is said to have two effective candidates. So is a race in which two actual candidates each draw about 50 percent of the vote—something quite different by any intuitive standard of competitiveness.

3. Raw data on prefectural assembly election results are drawn from the Japanese Local Democracy Project dataset constructed from official government election reports and newspaper reports by Yusaku Horiuchi, Ryouta Natori, Jun Saito, Ethan Scheiner, and the author, with support from the Tokyo Foundation.

4. Because Tokyo's 1985 elections thus belong to the 1983 cycle, for whose other years data are unavailable, they are not included below when data are grouped by cycle. I include them in the overall analysis simply because the Japanese Local Democracy Project makes them available. Data for the 2007 cycle, meanwhile, exclude Okinawa's 2008 elections and Tokyo's 2009 elections, which had not yet occurred at the time of this writing. This may inflate the LDP's strength in the 2007 cycle relative to previous ones, since the LDP is weak in both Okinawa and Tokyo. It may also underestimate the DPJ's strength in the 2007 cycle, but only slightly, since the DPJ is strong in Tokyo but weak in Okinawa.

5. In most cases, district boundaries match the boundaries of a *gun* (rural county), *shi* (city), or *ku* (large-city ward).

6. These figures are nearly unchanged from the 2003 election cycle, despite the widespread *daigappei* (municipal amalgamation) that occurred in the interim.

7. Nominally independent candidates' true partisan affiliations are unofficial and not easily measured. Many prefectural legislators officially run as independents and, if they win, remain independents throughout their terms in office or join assembly-specific, non-national-party *kaiha* with names like "Green Forum" or "Citizen's Network." Some of these legislators are genuine independents, but others are de facto affiliates of major parties. To discern 2007 candidates' partisan affiliations (or lack thereof), I rely on two separate and slightly varying measures. First, I use the *Yomiuri Shimbun*'s report of partisan affiliations aggregated by prefecture ("44 doufukengikai no shinseiryoku bunya" 2007; hereafter, *Yomiuri* data). Second, I compare the *Yomiuri* data against separate, candidate-level data collected from a variety of sources, including parties' official "recommendation" lists, newspaper reports, and the Web pages of prefectural legislatures and individual legislators (hereafter,

author's data; specific sources are available on request). For the Ibaraki elections of 2006, both the *Yomiuri* data and author's data add data from the same third source (Ibaraki Prefecture 2007). The two data sources prove similar in the aggregate nationwide. The former finds that DPJ-affiliated candidates won 20 percent and LDP-affiliated candidates 58 percent of all seats in the 2007 cycle; the latter puts these percentages at 19 percent and 57 percent, respectively, as reported above. The two data sources vary more for individual prefectures.

8. Strictly speaking, the theory underpinning the $M+1$ rule holds that we should expect no more than $M + 1$ candidates to fight for the M seats at stake under these conditions (Cox 1997). Strategic voters abandon all but the strongest $M + 1$ prospective candidates, but additional prospective candidates (in particular, the $M+1$th strongest) could drop out of the race as well, for reasons beyond the scope of the theory. Cox's discussion implies, however, that this would be unusual, as does that of most other researchers.

9. Below, we also assume that the vote total a candidate actually receives is the vote total a candidate is expected to receive. That is, we assume complete information. Inferring candidates' preelection strength expectations through post hoc election results is not ideal, but measuring candidates' actual expectations is impractical when dealing with more than a few election districts.

10. Downsian approaches assume the opposite: candidates' strengths are determined only once they select policy positions (see, e.g., Osborne 1993; Besley and Coate 1997).

11. That is, between 0 and 1, exclusive. An expected closeness ratio of exactly 0 implies that the candidate expects 0 votes, which is impossible if we assume the candidate plans to vote for himself or herself. An expected ratio of 1 implies that the candidate expects to tie for a seat, which means the candidate is not an underdog.

12. The expression $\Sigma^n_{i=0} (1 - v^i)/(n + 1)$ is derived as follows: Since the closeness ratio of any individual underdog reflects a random draw from a uniform distribution of all possible values between 0 and 1 exclusive, the probability that the ratio falls below v simply equals v. Thus, in a district with i underdogs, the probability that all of them have closeness ratios below v equals v^i, and $1 - v^i$ equals the probability that not all of them have closeness ratios below v—in other words, the probability that at least 1 has a closeness ratio above v. But the number of underdogs i varies randomly from 0 to n across districts, with each possible number equally likely. This means that each possible number of underdogs will be found in $1/(n + 1)$ of all districts (there are $n + 1$ possible numbers of underdogs, not n, because the numbers range from 0 to n, not 1 to n). Thus, $1/(n + 1)$ of the districts have 0 underdogs, and these districts' probability of having at least 1 underdog with a closeness ratio above v is $1 - v^0$ (that is, 0); $1/(n + 1)$ of the districts have 1 underdog, and a probability $1 - v^1$ of having 1 underdog with a closeness ratio above v; $1/(n + 1)$ of the districts have 2 underdogs, and a probability $1 - v^2$ of having 1 underdog with a closeness ratio above v; and so on, up to and including the $1/(n + 1)$ share of districts with n underdogs, whose probability of having at least 1 underdog with a closeness ratio above v is $1 - v^n$. Thus, across all districts with all possible numbers of underdogs, the probability that any single district will house at least 1 underdog with an expected closeness ratio above v is the sum of the probabilities associated with each possible number of underdogs i, with each probability weighted by the share of districts in which it is found, or $1/(n + 1)$: $\Sigma^n_{i=0} (1 - v^i)/(n + 1)$.

13. Beyond this first-order relationship, precisely how p should be linked to closeness ratios is an open question. See Rui de Figueiredo (2002) and Robert James Weiner (2003) for two possibilities.

14. Sincerity recalls the "d term," for "duty," sometimes appended to the standard "$pb - c$" expression in attempts to explain why citizens ever turn out to vote despite the tiny probability their vote will prove decisive (Aldrich 1997).

15. Note again that, even when we do observe the closeness ratio patterns that the M rule produces, this constitutes nothing more than weak support for the rule. True tests of the rule itself must account for all runners-up, not only the strongest.

16. Note that the hypothesized link between higher magnitudes and urbanness, on the one hand, and greater uncertainty and deviation from strategic behavior, on the other, is different from the idea that strategic considerations lead parties to make different strategic decisions in districts of different magnitudes or urbanness. For example, if smaller parties with more urban bases of support act strategically in all districts, they should choose to field candidates more often in larger-magnitude (Kohno 1997) and more urban districts (Scheiner 1999).

17. Of course, this reflects a measure of competitiveness that ignores vote gaps among winners. See Steven R. Reed and Kay Shimizu (2007) for a measure that accounts for these.

18. Within most prefectures, voter-per-seat ratios are fairly consistent across districts. But there are cross-prefecture disparities, as larger prefectures' assemblies contain more voters per seat. A medium-magnitude district in a small prefecture may have as many voters as a small-magnitude district in a large prefecture.

19. A small number of districts combine a city and all or part of a county. Because the city portion generally dominates, I include these districts in the "city" category. A few other districts combine localities of the same category.

CHAPTER 9

The Potential and Limits of Antiparty Electoral Movements in Local Politics

Robin M. LeBlanc

IN THE POSTREFORM ERA, JAPANESE PARTY POLITICS HAVE changed in some ways at the national level. In particular, the dominant Liberal Democratic Party (LDP) has a much more centralized internal structure, as Ellis S. Krauss and Robert Pekkanen explain in Chapter 2 of this volume. Redistricting and the introduction of some proportional representation seats in the Diet's House of Representatives have helped to shift the organizational incentives for candidates and parties. Nonetheless, some argue that change in the national-level party system is coming very slowly (Reed 2003). Getting elected remains largely a personal affair in which candidates with strong organizations, rather than sound partisan credentials, win (see Dyron Dabney in Chapter 3). Experiments in new kinds of electoral cooperation between old and newly formed political groups have not borne fruit consistently enough to challenge LDP control (Otake 1998; Christensen 2000a; Park 1998a). Moreover, the patronage politics on which the LDP has long grounded its electoral success is still a powerful element in the Japanese system (Scheiner 2006).

If we turn our attention to the electorate or to local-level elites, we might find it more tempting to conclude that, in fact, Japanese politics *is* changing. First, growth in the sector of the electorate unaligned with any party as well as a steady decline in voter turnout suggest the environment in which elites seek votes has been altered substantially, even though elites have been at a loss for how to turn this change into political power (Campbell and Cox 2000; Tanaka and Martin 2003; Christensen 1998, 2000a, 185–189). Second, the scattered development of new forms of citizens' movements at the local level have led many to point to the growth of a political consciousness and an organizational style which are neither that of the LDP nor any variant of the national-level opposition parties. In a number of cases, these new movements have led to the election of nonconservative, nonsocialist independents in local assembly and executive positions, and the enactment of citizens' referenda as well as other forms of grassroots challenges to the postwar political establishment (Jain 2000; Smith 2000; Watanabe 1997; Shimizu 1999; Takayose 1999; Igarashi 2003; Lam 2005; Numata 2006; Imai 1997).

Students of nonelites do see more change in Japanese democracy than those who focus on control of government at the national level. Nonetheless, even scholars who point to the increasing number of successful challenges to traditional electoral machines at the local level are uncertain about the impact these new political ventures will have. Robert J. Weiner (Chapter 8 of this volume) and Ethan Scheiner (2006) point to the persistence of strong barriers to the electoral success of candidates at the local level who are not affiliated with the LDP or its former members. Single-issue electoral or referendum movements do present temporary obstacles to the long-term governing alliance between the LDP and bureaucrats, and sometimes, as in the case of public works decisionmaking or nuclear power plant construction, this new sort of activism has changed the set of choices available to national elites (Lam 2005; Numata 2006). Still, these local movements will require great transformation before they can provide the vision for a sustained challenge to the stalwart remnants of the LDP-dominant system (Takayose 1999; Bouissou 2000). The institutional weakness of the most penetrable structures, local assemblies, reduces the scope of action of even the most coherently organized among the alternative politics movements (Eguchi 1999; Sato 1999). Moreover, when ambitious independents take the helm at the prefectural and city level, conservative-dominated local assemblies can become unruly. The result is often deadlock and, in several cases, assembly votes of no confidence against governors or mayors (Lam 2005; Smith 2000).

Are changes in the Japanese electorate and in the types of politics practiced at the local level enough to change Japanese democracy at the national level? The answer is important not only to Japanologists, but also to students of other advanced industrial democracies where a similar divorce between citizens and their elected officials seems pending. This phenomenon is sometimes described as the rise of "critical citizens," an increase in the portion of citizens who value democracy generally but greatly distrust their particular leaders and institutions and are often less likely than in the past to affiliate with political parties or turn out to vote (Dalton 1999, 2000). Japan certainly has many of these critical citizens: ranks of disaffected, unaligned Japanese voters that include a substantial number who seem to be consciously waiting for an alternative better than those offered by the current system (Takabatake and Yasuda 1997; Tanaka and Martin 2003).

In this chapter, I use two case studies to investigate whether new electoral movements at the local level have the potential to be a force for political competition at the national level, thus offering an alternative to an electorate hungry for better choices. The two groups I describe here have successfully challenged LDP hegemony at the local level, and their leaders have articulated a robust notion of self-government, something quite different from the patron-client relationships that have been so powerful in postwar Japanese democracy. In pioneering new organizational tactics, changing the demographics of electoral movements, and motivating their followers with an assertive, individualist rhetoric of self-determination, these local groups are radically altering their participants' experience of Japanese democracy. Nonetheless, when it comes to reshaping national-level politics, these antiestablishment efforts also face challenges, including some limits that come, paradoxically, through their assertive democratic rhetoric.

The Two Cases: Handmade Elections Take on a Kingdom of Money-Power Politics

The groups in my case studies are especially interesting because they have been successful in making substantial changes to the demographics and behavior of elected officials, despite the fact that both of these groups are located in a rural prefecture where some of the practices that won the LDP its reputation as a corrupt, money-power electoral machine got their start and where politicians well known for their leadership in machine politics have historically been well supported.[1] I call this prefecture Nashiyama, and I have named the towns in which I followed these movements Take Town and Shima City.[2] My studies of antiestablishment electoral movements in the town of Take and the city of Shima are based on a combination of participant observation and interviewing done in short bursts of a few months each and then set against a decade's worth of observation and interviewing among other participants in Nashiyama's politics, from the governor's level down. My first work in Nashiyama began in the early 1990s, when the governor was forced to step down because of his connection to a construction scandal that eventually had widespread effects on the national leadership of the LDP. During that scandal, a local newspaper looking for a fresh perspective commissioned me to conduct interviews and write two articles about the by-election following the governor's resignation.

In the early 1990s, the leaders in all of the major parties, as well as many of the journalists with whom I spoke, argued that the progressive-conservative standoff that had structured political conflicts since the formation of the LDP in 1955 was on its way out. This was also the end of the "organization" era in electoral politics, they told me. In that early 1990s election, the "end of organization" meant the winning candidate was a man handpicked by a group known to politicians and journalists as the *wakai keizaijin* (young economy types), a collection of forty- and fifty-something businessmen who were powerful in Nashiyama's capital, Shima City, but not democratically accountable to anyone. In fact, all negotiations about the candidate were held behind the scenes, and because only the Communist Party chose to contest the election, Nashiyama voters were actually given no practical choice of governor. The new governor served for three terms, facing only nominal opposition each time. Throughout this period, voter turnout in governors' elections declined.

The governor's three elections demonstrated one potential outcome of the gap between Japan's elites and its critical citizens: unaccountable elites chose leaders while the electorate became less and less involved in the process of self-government. But this was not the only trend observable during Nashiyama's past decade. Grassroots alternatives to the old parties and the young economy types were also making headway. The citizens' movement that unfolded across several elections in Take Town in the latter half of the 1990s and the election of a nonparty mayor in the prefecture's capital, Shima City, are two good examples of alternative responses to the postorganization era in Nashiyama politics. Antiparty activists in these elections worked according to distinct but related visions of a more vigorous, transparent democracy.

The small town, Take (population 30,000), became suddenly and intensely conflictual in the 1990s, surrounding a grassroots demand that the siting of a nuclear power plant be put to a citizen vote in a referendum. In this town, the long-dominant conservatives lost much of their electoral support, and antiparty organizations claimed a new centrality for citizens in the governing process. In fact, Take held one of the first ever citizens' referendums on a major project of this sort, helping form a long string of similar attempts in localities throughout Japan. Following the first citizens' initiative referendum executed in 1996, citizens' movements for referendums increased drastically. For example, between 1991 and 1995, there were an average of four attempts at local referendums a year in Japan. In 1996, there were seven attempts; in 1998, there were sixteen; in 1999, fifteen—although only seven of these movements were successful in getting local legislatures to pass referendum ordinances (Numata 2006, 23). The success of the Take referendum movement rippled through Japanese local politics elsewhere. However, after they successfully stopped the nuclear power plant project, some of the new organizations in Take disbanded; it is unclear if the claims of citizen centrality produced in the conflict over the nuclear power plant will transform Take politics over the long run. Certainly, Take activists have made little effort to network with referendum enthusiasts in other towns.

In my second case, an independent mayor, Akio Ito, was elected in Shima City, in 2002. Surprisingly, he won his bid for office against a traditional candidate backed by nearly every established political organization in the city. Ito's campaign was one example of a new sort of antiparty politics that has been successful around the country. Ito, like the independent governors of two prefectures as well as a long string of nearly 100 assembly members at other levels of government, including a member of the House of Councilors, received support from an unusual political consulting endeavor, the Citizen's Party. Importantly, although this consulting group is called "Citizen's *Party*," it is not actually a political party in any major sense. It did help to recruit candidates and to run campaigns, much as well-organized interest groups from labor unions to religious groups might in the United States. But the Citizen's Party lacked even the sort of organizational apparatus for doing policy work that a well-funded US interest group would have and, significantly, it did not seek to be recognized by the electorate as a party. In fact, many workers in the Ito campaign did not even know that a group called Citizen's Party was providing consulting services. Toward the end of this chapter, I examine the vision of this consulting enterprise, focusing especially on the idea of a new politics espoused by its leader, Hiroshi Kakuda. In part because of Kakuda's role in shaping it, the citizens' politics discourse of Ito's campaign can be more easily stretched to a national scope than that practiced in Take. Moreover, Ito's citizens' politics is backed by an organizational structure with much greater resources and much stronger supralocal connections than that which backed the citizens' movement in Take. Nonetheless, this new vision also faces undeniable limits.

Case 1: Take and the Right to Say No
Shortly after I moved to Take in March 1999, I joined Akihito Baba, a small-shop owner and one of the founders of the Referendum Association, for a meeting with a journalist from the *Asahi Shimbun* to talk about the strategy that the Referendum Association, a collection of allied groups and individual local assembly members, planned to use in a fight to win the majority of seats in the Take town assembly. In that interview, Baba, the unofficial spokesperson for the Referendum Association, articulated a justification for the movement that I will call the "autonomy principle." According to Baba's view, local governments should have robust rights to assert the needs of their communities against the central state and, as a corollary, local political processes should, as much as possible, protect citizen sovereignty by granting citizens ample opportunity for making their voices heard in an open, nonhierarchical atmosphere.

This autonomy principle set of ideas Baba articulated to the *Asahi Shimbun* journalist, and in many other contexts, framed and justified major changes in political practices in Take. First, autonomy principle thinking justified citizens' demands for an unprecedented citizens' initiative referendum that lacked clear support in Japanese law. The autonomy principle also provided an ideological structure along which groups that were otherwise ideologically incompatible could be mobilized for common action. The autonomy principle encouraged and justified newcomers' vigorous incursion into political activities from soliciting votes to running for office, greatly altering the demographics of those either holding elected office or playing prominent organizational and informal roles in Take politics. And the autonomy principle helped to shape an organizational ethic for members of the Referendum Association who opposed the development of organizational hierarchy, exclusiveness, and secrecy, especially within the Referendum Association. I illustrate all of these claims in the description of the case study below. But I am also forced to admit that Baba's autonomy principle has limits, as becomes clear toward the end of my discussion of the Take case study. While those who adhered to the views Baba expressed were both encouraged and enabled to play a new and important role in Take politics, they were simultaneously led to be suspicious of movements and organizations with a scope of action greater than a single locality and of political action strategies that smacked of professionalism. The autonomy principle mobilized new groups of citizens and helped them to manage a new politics, but it was strictly self-limiting.

When Baba's interview with the *Asahi Shimbun* reporter was conducted in the spring of 1999, the Referendum Association leaders were seeking more seats in the town assembly in order to strengthen support for Mayor Jiro Akeboshi, who belonged to the Referendum Association and had been elected with its help. The mayor needed support in the local assembly in his continuing bid to hold off the building of a nuclear power plant within the Take boundaries.[3] Mayor Akeboshi and the Referendum Association justified their resistance to the plant project on the basis of a town referendum held in 1996, in which more than 60 percent of the voters (in a greater than 80 percent turnout) voted against the plant in a straight yes-or-no ballot. The Japanese Local Autonomy Law offers no provisions binding a mayor to the results of a citizens' referendum like that held in Take, but the Take town ordinance on which the referendum was based urged the mayor to "respect" the citizens' choice. Mayor Akeboshi wanted more public support for his fight against national bureaucrats; plus, the power company planned to build the plant regardless of the referendum. Baba was a key leader in the alliance that was fighting to build the support that Akeboshi needed.

The *Asahi Shimbun* reporter suggested that the Referendum Association's unusual resistance to Japan's national energy policy was merely another case of not in my backyard (NIMBY) politics and asked why the Referendum Association did not offer alternatives to the power plant they resisted. Baba's response was simple: "Localities have the 'right to say no.'" In actuality, Referendum Association representatives had worked in the local assembly to get solar panels installed on public facilities; many had installed them on their own homes. But in response to the reporter, Baba did not point to any of these initiatives. Instead he repeated his conviction that localities have the right to say no to facilities they don't want. "If every locality turns down a national policy, then the national bureaucrats will have to reconsider the policy," Baba explained. "The national bureaucracies have lots of experts," Baba pointed out. "They ought to be able to come up with workable alternatives."

Baba's insistence that towns have the right to say no might seem a bit quirky, but it was precisely this sort of rhetoric of local veto—an autonomy principle—that pulled together a range of disparate constituencies into a force for political change.[4] The local battle between opponents of the power plant and national authorities and one of Japan's largest power companies had raged for more than thirty years by the time the reporter and I heard Baba's justification of a locality's right to say no. But for more than the first twenty of those years, organized opposition to the plant was concentrated in a handful of small groups with clear connections to members of the local Social Democratic Party of Japan (SDPJ) and Japan Communist Party (JCP). The plant did not get built in the decades between its announcement and the project's cancellation in 2003 because two conservative factions attached to the two LDP politicians who represented the district in the Diet competed with each other to control the mayor's office and the local assembly. Cynics say the conservative factions each wanted to control key offices when it came time to parcel out the lucrative public works contracts and other pork sure to come with the plant's construction. The two LDP factions traded the mayor's office back and forth over the years. New candidates won by claiming to be "cautious" about the plant project, but eventually each would be sniffed out as pro-plant and replaced by another cautious conservative. Money from power plant supporters greased the wheels. Bribery was rampant and ethically questionable tactics, such as the removal of pro-plant town assembly members to hotels in nearby Shima City prior to pro-plant ordinance votes, became standard fare.

In 1994, when the change in the House of Representatives electoral system leading to only a single seat for the Take District coincided with a détente between competing conservative factions in local politics, conservatives united to speed building of the plant. But Baba and a group of several other men (most of whom, like him, had not previously vocalized their opposition to the plant) demanded a citizens' referendum on the issue. Eventually, after electing members of their group to the local assembly, using recall petitions to get the conservative mayor to step down, and electing one of their own as mayor, the Referendum Association succeeded in getting the town to hold the official referendum.

Take had been widely known for its *nomase kuwase* (let them drink; let them eat) elections—a euphemism for bribing voters, often done with sake and sushi. Money from pro-plant sources flowed so freely that documentaries about the process of winning and enacting the referendum ordinance actually caught plant supporters on tape wining and dining potential voters.[5] Because there are no laws governing referendum campaigns, much of the activity filmed was not technically illegal, but merely unethical. Yet every Take voter with whom I talked during my time there attested to the fact that this sort of behavior was typical during elections in which it *was* officially illegal.

In this atmosphere, a group of politically inexperienced individuals that pulled together a starting fund of less than $100,000 (the contributions of about 1.5 million yen each from seven small businessmen who helped found the Referendum Association) built a headquarters with a prefabricated building kit, ran its own unofficial referendum (even hiring an impartial accounting service to supervise the voting), and elected enough of its members and allies to office to be able to bring about an official referendum. The power company finally canceled its plans to build the plant after the mayor, arguing it was his duty to *soncho* ("respect") the results of the nonbinding referendum, sold a small piece of municipal land within the town site to a consortium of plant opponents.

When I interviewed them, local leaders on either side of the nuclear plant issue agreed that the linchpin of the referendum movement's success was the formation of the Referendum Association by Baba and his friends. Political scientists might be reluctant to accept the notion that one grassroots organization with creative leaders can bring important changes to the structure of a local political system. For example, we might ask if the rise of the Referendum Association could not instead be attributable to changes in local political opportunity structures (e.g., chances for new mobilization provided by new laws). But, in fact, little support for such an argument exists. As many scholars have noted, the Japanese Local Autonomy Law has never provided clear legal justification for citizens' initiative referendums; citizen's groups that want to bring about a referendum are forced to use assembly petitioning and threats of elected representative recall that have been little used, but nonetheless available, tools in the Local Autonomy Law since the 1940s (Numata 2006, 22; see also Imai 1999). Changes in law that might seem to lend some legitimacy to grassroots movements such as the Nonprofit Organization Law came after the movement in Take. Nor were referendums yet an interest of either the Japanese media or political scientists specializing on Japan.

The real question then is, Why were tools that had long been ignored by local activists suddenly used so effectively? The answer at hand is that the Referendum Association and the strategies it chose for constituency mobilization provided a basis for changing the demographics of those who sought a voice in local policymaking at the same time that the autonomy principle provided a justification for using all legal means to make elected representatives responsive. As Lee Ann Banaszak's (1996) study of the differences in the success of the women's suffrage movements in Switzerland and the United States demonstrates, the existence of political opportunity alone cannot explain movement success. The strategies that a group chooses in response to existing opportunity structures are an important part of the success equation, but strategies are often as much a product of a group's collective belief structures as any rational assessment of the group's chances (Banaszak 1996).

Baba's simple claim was that the Referendum Association would give ordinary people a voice they had not been allowed under the LDP-dominated system of old. Baba emphasized the fact that ordinary people were not enriched by the real estate speculation surrounding the plant siting nor benefited in any crucial way by money flowing through the town's electoral machines. "Sure, they drank the sake and ate the sushi provided by the pro-plant conservatives," he said, "but when they did not have real political choices, when they knew their voices would not be heard, who could blame them for taking the small compensations available?"

Baba and his followers' notion of true democracy—what I have labeled the autonomy principle—is one in which the commonsense responses of hardworking, ordinary people are not subordinated to claims in the national interest. According to Baba's account, large organizations cannot be trusted, and major political parties are always willing to sacrifice the little guy in order to assuage their leaders' hunger for money or power. As Baba explained it, particular economic interests will never serve the majority of individuals who serve them; in fact, the contemporary national fixation on boosting economic growth is misguided. He argued that macroeconomic numbers reveal little about the quality of life for regular people who just "work *isshokenmei* (with all their effort) to maintain their *seikatsu o tateru* (standard of living)." The dignity of self-determination is the democratic citizen's only real friend. Baba and the other leaders of the Referendum Association believed that the set of notions about voice contained in the autonomy principle applied in even relatively small organizations like the Referendum Association. Candidates were judged acceptable on the basis of their willingness to respect the voice of the townspeople as displayed in the referendum. Congruence in other ways was not necessary. When candidates asked what they should write in their campaign flyers, Baba insisted that each candidate make an independent decision, emphasizing whatever personal qualities or policy preferences (beyond the pro-referendum stance) he or she chose.

The autonomy principle had some real organizational benefits. In a town where electoral mobilization had been intense and Red-baiting as well as competition among conservatives had sharpened the divides among different camps, Baba's insistence on the individual's autonomy from organizational pressure made it possible for him to build a movement where one man who bragged about his longtime loyalty to a powerful LDP Diet member who had done him a favor to aid the international portion of his business could work happily alongside another man who had left the Communist Party because the party seemed insufficiently true to its ideals. Tobacco farmers and restaurateurs, engineers and milk truck drivers could claim a common ground in the right to speak one's mind. Similarly, the area's long-term landholders and the residents of new suburban developments could forge a new identity as *chomin* (townspeople) who exercise the right to say no.[6]

Baba's autonomy principle had two downsides. First, his "live and let live" approach to managing multiple candidates was not the most effective strategy for getting all of the Referendum Association's people in office. It simply defied the logic of Japanese multimember districts in which similar candidates must compete against each other. In the election I observed, the Referendum Association had enough votes to have won seats for all five of its candidates but, because the votes were distributed unevenly among candidates with overlapping territory and differing degrees of attractiveness, only three candidates won office. Better strategy with less concern about independence of voice might well have changed the outcome.

Second, Baba's right to say no logic prevented the group from becoming more ambitious. Despite the fact that Baba and many other group members actually did see their local policy problems as connected to, even determined by, politics on other levels of government, the Referendum Association firmly resisted any attempt to build connections with related movements elsewhere. When the association's success drew grassroots activists from around the country seeking to learn the lessons that Take could teach for defeating the conservative hegemony in their own towns, the top leaders of the Referendum Association were generally uninterested in meeting them. More than once, Baba complained about these citizens' movement networkers. "Every town is different," he said. "They should go back to their own town and find out what the people there want to do." But of course, Baba's insistence on only homegrown politics meant that his movement would never have the resources or reach to challenge the foundations of the power structures that thrust nuclear power plant projects on small towns like Take.

The Referendum Association's activism vastly increased the political participation of its members, most of whom had never been directly involved in standing for office or canvassing for candidates before. This was especially true for women. By the end of April 1999, three women from the Referendum Association and two from allied groups had been elected to a local assembly that had had only one woman member prior to 1995. As women sought office, they drew their friends directly into the Referendum Association's activities and altered in a very obvious way the demographics of election mobilization. In fact, pro-plant leaders blamed their loss of the referendum on the activism of "young mothers" who let their emotions cloud their judgment about nuclear safety. Thus, in their own way, even conservatives acknowledged that the gender basis of the town's politics had shifted. But after court challenges to the mayor's land sale failed in 2003, the Referendum Association totally disbanded. Even before that date, the association sold its land and took down its prefab headquarters building. In 1999, I talked with many association members who claimed their activism had changed them in surprising and good ways as well as expanding their network of friends. Yet many of these same activists spoke wistfully of the day when the power company would give up on the plant and they could return to their less hectic, preassociation lives. Of course, one of these was a woman assembly member who ran in 2004, unsuccessfully, as the first woman candidate for mayor. Had she won, she would have taken her activism to a new level.

Will the new type of assembly members bred by the Referendum Association's activities continue to hold office in Take? Will the new spirit of activism justified by the autonomy principle thrive now that the most obvious threat to local autonomy— the money-power politics surrounding the nuclear plant—has been put to bed? I do not know the answer to these questions. In his study of Japanese environmental movements, Jeffrey Broadbent finds that respected local leaders like Baba who "had the internal moral fiber to resist enticements and threats" could effectively stop conservative political machines from pressing their priorities on a community (2003, 223). However, Broadbent claims that these movements do not entail a reworking of vertical relationships in the town. Instead, loyal followers continue to pursue the "boss" to whom they have been attached by other traditional community structures. The boss's "activist leader morality" is what makes for a different political outcome (Broadbent 2003, 223). I agree with Broadbent that moral fiber in leaders like Baba is an undeniably important part of the success of movements like Take's referendum movement. However, in Take, the breakdown of at least some of the traditional, vertical relationships that structured the community prior to the rise of the Referendum Association (e.g., the breakdown of gender barriers to political participation) was essential to the movement's success. But whether this sort of success improves the long-term connection of citizens and their political leaders remains an open question.

Case 2: Making Friends Instead of Cronies in Shima City
In many ways, the case of Akio Ito's election to Shima City's mayoralty is far less dramatic than the Referendum Association's nearly ten-year battle to stop a nuclear power plant. What is striking about the Ito case is the claim that the kind of antiparty, "ordinary citizens" organizing Ito did is not local in scope. Members of Ito's campaign, especially the members of the Citizen's Party, which provided much of the organizational expertise and some of the material goods necessary to pull the campaign together, saw Ito's campaign as one piece of a long-term strategy to change the structure of the entire Japanese political system. This meant that the campaign straddled a curious tension between its grounding in localist claims not unlike Baba's and its bigger agenda as part of a nationwide battle to replace the prevalent model of partisan mobilization.

As a candidate, Ito was a nontraditional, but not shocking, choice. Unlike the previous three mayors and his opponent, Ito had not worked his way up through the Shima City civil service, a trend that had held steady since 1975. Moreover, as a journalist he had eschewed ties with any partisan or economic interest groups. This meant he had not been able to use his career to build connections with potential supporters in the way that his predecessor and opponent had. But he was the son of a local inn owner and, as a journalist who had frequently covered prefectural and city politics over the years, he knew a great deal about political processes. Moreover, in the later years of his journalism career, he had become more and more interested in citizens' movements like the one in Take (which he and his colleagues had followed with great interest). Citizen's groups often invited him to be a speaker or panel moderator at their events. Ito was not quite the political novice that the Take Referendum Association members had been.

Two things motivated Ito's decision to run for office. First, no viable opponent was willing to announce a race against the deputy mayor Koji Washida. (Of course, the Communist Party fielded a candidate.) Ito and his friends were especially frustrated by Washida's candidacy because they thought that he had used his control over city finances to reward and build connections with key constituencies of the then incumbent mayor, Tanaka. People in Ito's office believed that, once he had won over the loyalties of a large number of Tanaka supporters, Washida essentially forced out the popular mayor Tanaka who surprised the city by announcing he would not run for another term. Washida presented himself as a candidate with the support of every established party except the Communists and with the support of major labor and business groups as well. Ito and his campaign staff were careful not to make direct claims that Washida had run a corrupt city office. But the tone of their discussion hinted at as much. Indeed, in 2004, Japan's Fair Trade Committee found that the Shima City civil servants had long managed collusive arrangements for the bidding of public contracts in areas like sewer and public housing construction—evidence that all was not well under Washida's watch. The other motivating factor behind Ito's candidacy was the sudden death of his brother earlier in the year, a fact that seems to have increased Ito's desire to do something significant with his life like taking the risk of standing for election when he felt citizens' interests were not being well served.

Ito had two local organizational resources. The first was a fairly wide personal network of relationships with successful entrepreneurs and professionals, mostly men and women who, like himself, were in their mid-fifties. They could afford to contribute money to his campaign effort and had networks of their own on which to draw. A key segment of this group was active in the *machizukuri* (city planning) field. In fact, the campaign office manager described his career as "*machizukuri* production," which, when I pressed him for details, seemed to boil down to a kind of master planning consultancy. For example, he had worked with a variety of public and private constituencies in an Okinawan municipality on a city revitalization plan. Ito's second basic resource was a large group of volunteers who came to the office to stamp envelopes, staff phones, and the like. Perhaps the most important job that these volunteers did was run a postcard campaign to expand the list of potential supporters by soliciting names and addresses from those already on the campaign *meibo* (supporters' list). When I asked Ito's wife how many potential supporters had provided the volunteers with names and addresses of other potential supporters, she replied that she did not know, but pointed to a stack of papers listing their names and addresses that was 4 or 5 inches high. Even "citizen's" campaigns like Ito's are cagey about their *meibo*, but I was told that the goal was to build a *koenkai* (constituent organization) member list of about 10,000. The Shima City electorate is around 100,000; the city population about 530,000.

The volunteers were mobilized and assigned duties under the direction of campaign consultants who came from Ito's chief, nonlocal resource, the Citizen's Party. Ito's friends in journalism, city planning, and other fields lacked campaign experience but, when I first visited his office in early October, a little more than a month before the election, as many as four or five "volunteer" campaign staffers from the Citizen's Party had come from outside Shima. They were knowledgeable about politics, and spoke of other campaigns in which they had been involved. They seemed to be devoted full time to Ito's election effort, sometimes even sleeping in the office. They computerized the supporters' database (something still fairly new in local-level elections in Japan), maintained a Web page, provided and drove the sound truck, and directed much of the work of area volunteers who would come by the office to work for an hour or two at a time.

The Citizen's Party professionals had a remarkably unified message. They were moving among various *shiminha* (citizens')—as opposed to established party—elections, providing technical assistance. They told me proudly about their previous involvements in elections of independent governors, mayors, and members of assemblies. As they explained, the typical campaign is costly because of money spent to pay temporary personnel who hang posters, address postcards, make phone calls, and keep the growing *meibo*. In my experience, most staffers in an LDP campaign office in an electorate the size of Shima would receive financial compensation for their services in some way, whether this consisted of generous reimbursement for travel costs, actual wages, or pay from a third party ostensibly employing and lending the staffers. But Citizen's Party members were able to volunteer full time without pay from the Ito campaign because either they were elected officials from other towns who had flexible schedules or, as was true with one staffer I spoke to at length, they had financial resources of their own. That staffer drew income from real estate and did not have to work full time. Ito's affiliation with the Citizen's Party also meant that he could have the public support of popular independent politicians at the gubernatorial or Diet level.

The Citizen's Party leader, Hiroshi Kakuda, explained that he and others who had worked with him on the Nashiyama House of Councilors election in July 2002 had assumed there would be a citizen's challenger to Shima's *ainori* mayoral candidate Washida. (An *ainori* election is one in which every established party except the Communist Party backs the same candidate.) Ito had heard about Kakuda and the services provided by the Citizen's Party and somehow they fell together; it was a sort of gut-level connection, they said. According to Kakuda, the Citizen's Party was not a formal organization. It had no official membership list, no rules, and no officers other than Kakuda who acted as *daihyo* (representative, or chair). Of course, it did have people who behaved as members, and a quick Web search showed that local assembly members in the Kanto area who ran for office with the assistance of the Citizen's Party shared platform planks including support for greater freedom of information and opposition to the consumption tax. Nonetheless, as I explain above, in a very important way the Citizen's Party clearly was *not* a party, not even a proto-party. The Citizen's Party did not seek to be recognized as an organizational force by either the bulk of campaign workers in Ito's office or the electorate of Shima City.

Kakuda described his work and the work of candidates like Ito as building a new politics for the twenty-first century, something that would replace what he characterized as the *rieki dantai* ("interest group") politics of the *kisei seito* (establishment parties). The key problem according to Kakuda was to structure something that would bring citizens into politics as *honto no kojin* ("real" individuals) and pull them together without squashing their diversity. "Voters are ready for this," he said, insisting that low voter turnout was the result of voter dislike for establishment parties. In order to receive Citizen's Party support, candidates had to be truly independent and willing to run clean, volunteer elections. The one point of commonality among the nearly 100 candidates with whom Kakuda claimed to have worked was, as he said it, "a conviction that the way politics has been is unacceptable." The main job of the Citizen's Party was to provide technology and advice to political newcomers. The Citizen's Party also used its connections to previously elected officials and their supporters to call for contributions that could be used as starter funds in newcomers' campaigns, and it maintained some resources (like the sound truck Ito used) that could be shared among campaigns in an effort to reduce the costs to any one campaign. Kakuda's discussion of the "networked" style by which citizens would be brought into the new politics of a postorganization Japan sounds almost like a scholarly piece on new social movements or postmaterialist values. Kakuda explains that, as he sees it, the era of the class conflict in rich societies is over. New concerns such as the threat to the global environment are uniting voters, but politicians in the prevailing system have served particularist interest groups, business interests, or labor unions and do not respond to new concerns in the electorate.

Except for the fact that his rhetoric is replete with the vocabulary of a formal student of politics, Kakuda's vision of politics accomplished by collaborations of diverse "real individuals" is not terribly different from Baba's autonomy principle. But Kakuda's ambitious networking of politicians and supporters around the country is very different from Baba's tactics, and his understanding that the future of this citizens' politics would rest on technical know-how accentuates that difference. The skills employed by the traveling "volunteers" of the Citizen's Party were out of the reach of nearly the entire membership of Take's Referendum Association, as well as most of the Shima City residents who manned phones or addressed postcards in Ito's office. The vision of what any given campaign is about is also correspondingly different. This was brought home to me when I returned to Ito's office in November. One of the *machizukuri* group staffers in his office, a campaign novice, told me that he had learned a great deal about elections in the past month. "Elections," this staffer said, "are all about *nakama zukuri* (making friends). The more friends you make, the more likely you are to win." "The *seiji kanbu* (political managers) don't always understand that," he grumbled. I took his vague reference to managers to include some of the professionalized people in his own office. "The *seiji kanbu* think politics is all about *tatakai* (fighting)," he said woefully. "But, they are wrong. It's about making friends," he repeated. By coincidence, I have a close friend who was active in a governor's campaign in which Kakuda and his Citizen's Party volunteers consulted; her response to the Citizen's Party's professionalized services was as negative as that of the campaign novice in Ito's office. She had been involved in a number of nonparty, grassroots elections at the local and prefectural assembly election level, but she felt that Kakuda's influence diminished the citizens' spirit of the campaign. Kakuda's Citizen's Party has vision, skills, and resources to knit disparate antiparty activities around the country into a larger electoral movement, but it is unclear whether that movement will have the same sort of democratic vigor that drove groups like Take's Referendum Association.

Conclusion

Kakuda's Citizen's Party provides technical resources that have made possible, in many different districts, the entry of a new sort of politician. These new politics elections, so heavily dependent on volunteer labor as a means of cutting costs and so hostile to traditional party organizations (both conservative and progressive) have necessarily brought other new participants into the electoral process. Who these participants are depends a bit on the nature of the individual candidate involved, but women and youth seem to be important. Ito's campaign, for example, mobilized a small but noticeable contingent of twenty-something men. The LDP campaign offices often have such young men working in their campaigns, but they are usually paid for their time. The young men I talked with in Ito's campaign office stressed the value of participating for participation's sake.

If the Citizen's Party or other consultancies like it can convince a broader pool of citizens to assert themselves in the political arena, then democracy ostensibly will be deepened, and perhaps a new and original means of drawing potential critical citizens (such as the twenty-something men in Ito's office) into the political process will be born. Yet tensions of the sort experienced between the local area volunteers and the Citizen's Party pros in Ito's campaign remain troubling. Kakuda insisted that politicians like Ito remain viable by building their own contribution-based constituency organizations. And the independence of real individuals will be protected because this new sort of politician's roots are based on his or her personally crafted following. Hearing this, I wonder how greatly Kakuda's vision differs from the electoral practices of the LDP (see Otake 1998). Kakuda's personal support organization is difficult to distinguish from an LDP *koenkai* (see Dyron Dabney in Chapter 3 and Naoko Taniguchi in Chapter 4 of this volume). But I can think of two differences. First, the candidates of the Citizen's Party have generally been grouped in a nonsocialist but progressive terrain on the Japanese policy preference landscape, a terrain that the established parties have had trouble representing. Second, the fund-raising practices of the Citizen's Party have been much more reliant on the contributions of private individuals with middle-class resources than on the wherewithal of business interests. These are not differences to be sneezed at, but do they really make for an entirely new politics? After all, the very antiparty rhetoric that makes the Citizen's Party shun formal organization means the technical professionals of the Citizen's Party are no more democratically transparent or accountable than are the young economy types who selected Nashiyama's governor in the early 1990s. Who will keep the Citizen's Party honest over the years?

In Take Town, Baba's autonomy principle shaped a movement identity that, like the Citizen's Party, was nonconservative but also distinct from existing SDPJ and JCP alternatives to LDP dominance. The autonomy principle encouraged a variety of political newcomers—housewives, salarymen, and progressive farmers, among others—to work with people who had long supported the local conservative establishment to stop that establishment and the nuclear power plant project it supported. These political newcomers made the mayor's office and the local assembly more accessible and transparent, and eventually they prevented the building of the nuclear plant. However, their attachment to the autonomy principle also led them to make some choices about electoral politics that were not strategic, limited their willingness to expand political activities beyond the local level by networking with similar movements elsewhere, and contributed to the literal and figurative deconstruction of their movement's edifice once its original goals were satisfied. While we might judge the movement a success in many ways, it is not the source of an alternative to the LDP dominance that continues to shape the larger environment in which towns like Take struggle for economic and policy independence.

Investigating the rhetorical and organizational challenges presented in these two cases of antiparty politics allows us to see the profound tensions inherent in any mass democracy. Of course, some balance must be struck between the organization that allows us to manage large-scale political transformation as well as see "who" is to be credited or blamed, and the disorganization that allows individuals to practice the self-determination that gives the public sphere true democratic vigor. Striking this balance is no mere matter of building the correct institutions (although, of course, institutions are important). Political philosophy matters, too. Baba's autonomy principle helped him to lead former enemies together into battle against both local corruption and a policy that the majority of the townspeople did not want. The promise that "this time, real individuals will really count" helped Kakuda's professionals organize a volunteer base that keeps itself going by seeing electoral work as the building of friendships.

To the extent that electoral movements openly challenging the longstanding web of patron-client relationships on which the electoral basis of LDP power has rested can be successful in Nashiyama Prefecture, I think we can safely say that in some ways Japanese democracy is changing. Unfortunately, because these new groups are often mobilized behind a rhetoric that promises to eschew these patronage connections, the new groups are in some ways self-limiting. They find it hard to justify the kind of organization building that would expand the scope of possible change. The challenges present in the vigorous democratic rhetoric of critical citizen activists in Take and Shima are instructive for students of the critical citizen dilemma not only in Japan, but more generally in the advanced industrial democracies. Creative responses to disillusionment with the current political establishment may have disconcerting, paradoxical effects on electorates—teaching critical citizens an even stronger attachment to democratic values, but simultaneously further reinforcing their cynicism about their institutions and leaders.

Notes

The research conducted for this chapter was supported by funding from the Japan Society for the Promotion of Science, the Fulbright program, and two grants from Washington and Lee University. Over the years, fellow political scientists Tokuko Ogai and Akio Igarashi have shared insights, connections, and sometimes even field notes from their own research among some of the same groups I treat here. Many other individuals whom I cannot name here have also given generously of time and mind. Without them, I could not have done this work.

1. Michitoshi Takabatake described this traditional patronage politics in several localities in *Chiho no okoku* (1997).

2. I have decided to use pseudonyms here and throughout the chapter. While everyone who met with me in the field was informed that I was there to conduct research, I cannot be certain that each person with whom I spoke was constantly aware that his or her words might appear in print. Moreover, some of the research reported here is part of a larger project that probes more deeply into individual consciousness and experience.

3. Some of the details of this story have been altered to protect privacy.

4. Baba's response was unusual in its vigor, but his claim that local NIMBYism can force more honest and creative thinking about policy is reinforced by Shuji Shimizu's study of several such conflicts (1999).

5. I am aware that I should cite this documentary, but to do so would be to declare the identities of the very informants I am trying to protect both in this project and in others based on more sensitive work in the same field.

6. I have tranlsated the word *chomin* as "townspeople," a very literal translation, rather than as "citizen," the word that might sound more natural in English. The reason is two-fold. First, no direct translation for "citizen" in the English sense exists in Japanese. All the words available in Japanese are quite specific to the entity to which a person belongs. For example, *kokumin* are "people of the nation," *shimin* are "people of a city" (*shi*), and *chomin* are "people of a town" (*cho*). Second, I might choose to obscure these distinctions in English, but I believe members of the Referendum Association, Baba especially, used the word *chomin* in a very specific way to distinguish themselves from the nation or locality, able to speak for themselves in ways other, more generalized bodies, could not.

CHAPTER 10

Civil Society and Democracy: Reforming Nonprofit Organization Law

Yuko Kawato and Robert Pekkanen

MANY CHAPTERS IN THIS VOLUME HAVE EXAMINED INSTITUtional changes and the resultant impact on democracy in Japan. This chapter likewise traces institutional changes in the arena of civil society, and studies the consequences for Japanese democracy. By the middle of the 1990s, a movement was under way to initiate legislation aimed at unfettering civil society. Spurred by popular dissatisfaction with government efforts, activists and ordinary citizens alike sought to transform the nature of state-society relations and even the quality of democracy. How successful has this attempt been? Specifically, what has the Special Nonprofit Organization Law (NPO Law) of 1998 accomplished?[1]

The NPO Law aimed to promote the development of independent NPOs by liberalizing conditions under which groups could form and operate. The law significantly expanded the scope of groups that qualify for legal status, and curtailed bureaucratic supervision. Many hoped that the law would transform Japanese society by spurring the growth of NPOs, and increase citizens' access to policymaking and implementation. It is therefore important to ask, Has the NPO Law improved the quality of Japanese democracy by altering the channels of interest articulation that connect masses to political elites?

There is some evidence that the legislation has had a positive impact on democracy. The NPO Law has led to a steady increase in the number of organizations that are more independent from bureaucratic supervision. New channels of communication have also opened up between NPOs and state officials. In addition, the law has given legitimacy to the NPO sector. These changes represent increasing political opportunities for Japan's civil society organizations, which are eroding the political insulation of the bureaucracy that has played a central role in policymaking and implementation.

However, the NPO Law has not led to a fundamental change in the Japanese civil society or the state–civil society relationship. There are several factors that have limited the transforming effect of the NPO Law. First, for many lawmakers, the main purpose of the law was to increase the number of NPOs that would support the state's provision of services at the local level, instead of increasing professional advocacy groups that operate nationally. Therefore, many small local groups and few large professional advocacy groups continue to make up the civil society, and NPOs' impact on policymaking and implementation remains more at the local level than at the national level. This suggests that it is important to explore the various ways in which NPOs relate to democracy and the NPO Law's impact on each. We argue that NPOs connect to democracy in four ways: (1) NPOs can support state provision of social services and contribute to democracy by participating in governance, (2) NPOs can create social capital and increase the performance of democracy, (3) NPOs can increase citizens' access to politics through their relationship to political parties, and (4) NPOs can influence policymaking and implementation through advocacy and monitoring. Although the NPO Law had a positive impact on all four areas, NPOs providing social services remain the largest segment of NPOs and professional advocacy groups remain few. Also, NPOs' activities remain more at the local level than the national level. Therefore, the legislation did not fundamentally change Japanese civil society.

The second factor that has limited the transformative effect of the NPO Law is the inadequate financial support for NPOs. Although the NPO Law allows groups with legal status to receive tax breaks and grants, many NPOs remain short of funds. The Cabinet Office's research in 2004 shows that on average 34.6 percent of NPOs' funding comes from different levels of government (although 58.0 percent of NPOs receive no funding from government), 33.2 percent comes from membership fees, and 6.8 percent comes from donations (Cabinet Office 2004b, 2007). Eighty-five percent of NPOs hope to obtain funding from the government in the future, but not all will be funded (Cabinet Office 2007). Securing funding from membership fees is not easy because Japanese NPOs are generally small: 35.4 percent of NPOs in 2006 had no members besides the officers that ran the groups, 29.7 percent had between 1 and 19 members, 13.5 percent had between 20 and 49 members, 8.9 percent had between 50 and 99 members, and 12.6 percent had more than 100 members (Cabinet Office 2007). Depending on donations is also difficult. The Cabinet Office's research in 2000 shows that 60.0 percent of those polled from the general public had the will to donate to NPOs, but only 6.1 percent of them would donate voluntarily without any request from NPOs. Forty-three percent said they would donate if NPOs ask, and 13.2 percent said they would donate if others around them did (Cabinet Office 2001a). For these reasons, NPOs often suffer from a shortage of funds, and the NPO Law did not fundamentally change this situation. Scarcity of resources constrains both NPOs' activities and their contribution to democracy.

Third, although the NPO Law made group formation and operation easier in many ways, some disincentives to obtaining legal status remain and many organizations continue to operate as voluntary groups. Many organizations do not apply for legal status because they consider the accounting and finance reporting requirements too onerous, and they fear that bureaucrats might still control the objectives or activities of the NPOs (Pekkanen 2004b, 227; Noumi 1997).

For these reasons, the effect of the NPO Law on the quality of Japanese democracy has not been as dramatic as many proponents hoped. However, the increasing number of NPOs and new channels of interest articulation clearly show that the NPO Law has had some positive effects on the development of the Japanese democracy and civil society. NPOs' provision of social services, enhancement of social capital, access to political parties, and advocacy and monitoring roles also relate to core concepts of democracy such as participation, representation, and accountability. The NPO Law improved participation, representation, and accountability, even though the improvement was not dramatic enough to change the existing state–civil society relationship in a fundamental way.

Emergence of the NPO Law

Several key factors enabled the establishment of the NPO Law.[2] First, civil society organizations, including an organization established specifically to push for an NPO law, participated actively in the lawmaking process in the early 1990s. These organizations wanted a law that would allow them to obtain legal status more easily because legal status offered multiple benefits that would help them develop. To begin with, organizations with legal status receive tax breaks and gain access to public funds in the form of grants. Organizations without legal status are deprived of these financial benefits. In addition, organizations without legal status cannot sign contracts. This means that they "cannot open bank accounts, hire staff, own property, sign lease agreements for office space, undertake joint projects with domestic government bodies, or even, on a mundane level, lease a photocopy machine" (Pekkanen 2000, 113). In organizations without legal status, individuals must sign contracts on behalf of their organization. This makes the individuals incur large costs, and creates various other problems. For example, when an individual dies with an organization's funds in his or her bank account, the organization cannot regain the funds without the family's consent (Keizai Kikaku Chou 2000, pt. 1, chap. 5, sec. 3). Such inconvenience tends to constrain the growth of organizations. For these reasons, a lobbying effort by organizations for legislation to attain legal status led to the founding of study groups on NPOs in several political parties.

Second, the Hanshin earthquake in 1995 accelerated the lawmaking process. In the aftermath of the earthquake, jurisdictional disputes among ministries paralyzed government relief efforts. In contrast, volunteer groups mobilized quickly to deliver relief. When the media publicized the differences between the government and volunteer responses, and the fact that volunteer groups without legal status lacked any kind of work insurance, public pressure for the government to provide legislative assistance to these volunteer groups increased.

Also important were the electoral changes of 1994, which increased political parties' interest in NPOs as a vote coordination mechanism. The electoral reform replaced the previous multimember district system with a single nontransferable vote (SNTV) with a hybrid system of 300 single-member districts and 180 (initially 200) regional party list or proportional representation seats. Small parties like Sakigake and the Social Democratic Party of Japan (SDPJ), which had been disadvantaged in the single-member districts, would do better with proportional representation seats. They considered NPOs a mechanism for coordinating votes, and therefore supported the NPO Law.[3] The change in electoral institutions also encouraged the Liberal Democratic Party (LDP) to support the law. Under the old SNTV system, the LDP had to have multiple candidates win in many districts to secure a majority in the Diet, and this promoted the development of groups that supported each legislator, but not the LDP as a whole. In the new electoral system, the LDP believed the NPOs could deliver voting blocs in the single-member districts where a few thousand votes could make a difference (Pekkanen 2000, 139–140). In closely contested districts—especially urban districts—the LDP wished to tap into floating voters traditionally aloof from the LDP, especially the educated and young voters who were more likely to be partial to or affiliated with NPOs. The LDP was also familiar with using the group-oriented voter mobilization tactics. In addition, the LDP wanted to avoid conceding this voting bloc entirely to the Democratic Party of Japan (DPJ), which was a strong supporter of the NPO Law.

Furthermore, the pressures of coalition politics on the LDP created a favorable environment for the establishment of the NPO Law. In 1994, the LDP formed a coalition government with Sakigake and the SDPJ. Sakigake and the SDPJ had been enthusiastic about legislation to support civil society groups, and the LDP leadership thought to use the NPO Law as a glue that would hold together the coalition (Sato 2006, 114; Yomiuri Shinbun Seijibu

2003, 34). In the process of drafting the NPO Law, the LDP made a compromise with Sakigake and the SDPJ on the law's content. In addition, the existence of a credible opposition party, the New Frontier Party (although now defunct) pushed the LDP to accept the NPO Law (Pekkanen 2000, 140). The DPJ also emerged as a major challenger to the LDP. The DPJ, a strong supporter of the NPO Law, sought to expand the civil society groups at the expense of the bureaucracy and as a means to erode LDP power. An increasing number of DPJ Diet members and staffers had also come from NPOs (Pekkanen 2004a, 380–381).

While bureaucrats write most legislation in Japan, the NPO Law emerged as a series of laws written by Diet members (*Giin rippou*). This exclusion of bureaucrats made sense, given the new electoral incentives that politicians were responding to as well as the purpose of the law—to promote the development of independent NPOs by reducing bureaucratic guidance. Indeed, the NPO Law emerged as a part of the administrative reform in the 1990s. In 1996, the Official and Private Sector Activity Allotment Subcommittee of the Administrative Reform Committee concluded that administrative activities should be minimized if the private sector can perform the same task. The NPO Law was born partly as a result of the government's effort to encourage division of labor between the public and private sectors, deregulation, and decentralization (Ota 1999, 126). The law was established in March 1998, and went into effect in December 1998.

How the NPO Law Has Encouraged Formation and Development of Organizations

The NPO Law has encouraged the formation and development of organizations in three ways. First, the law reduced bureaucratic supervision and regulation of NPOs by allowing groups to obtain legal status without bureaucratic screening. Previously, the bureaucracy could contain civil society groups' formation by deciding which groups could obtain legal status. More specifically, the state categorized NPOs with legal status as public-interest legal persons (PILP), and a competent bureaucratic authority granted the legal status to groups based on its definition of "public interest." Therefore, groups that the bureaucracy did not recognize as serving the public interest had no legal basis to form. The bureaucracy could define public interest in a narrow or arbitrary manner, and it did not need to justify its decisions about withholding legal status from groups. The NPO Law replaced this bureaucratic screening with an application either to the governor of the prefecture where a group's office exists (if the office is in one prefecture), or to the Cabinet Office (if the group has offices in multiple prefectures) (Japan NPO Center n.d.).[4] The law also states that reasons for rejection of applications will be explicitly stated. Additionally, the NPO Law also aims to reduce bureaucratic administrative guidance over NPO activities.

Further evidence of the bureaucracy's diminished power is the decentralized implementation process of the NPO Law. The NPO Law came about as a Diet member's bill, and therefore the prefectures had to draft their own provisions for the NPOs without a model from the Ministry of Home Affairs. Furthermore, the NPO Law requires NPOs to publicly disclose information about their activities and budgets every year. This is a change from before the NPO Law, when groups reported to bureaucrats and the information was not publicly disclosed. This change also reflects the weakened power of the bureaucracy.

Second, the NPO Law has encouraged the formation and development of organizations by eliminating a financial requirement for obtaining legal status. Previously, citing the Civil Code, bureaucrats often required the applicant groups to have capital of approximately 300 million yen, or about $3 million (Pekkanen 2000, 118). Many civil society groups could not raise this much money, and therefore the financial hurdle hindered groups from obtaining legal status. Under the NPO Law, in contrast, there is no requirement for starting capital, and this has expanded the scope of groups that qualify for legal status.

Last but not least, by helping more groups obtain legal status, the NPO Law has given legitimacy to the NPO sector as having a socially valued purpose. In a 1999 survey of NPOs, 81 percent said they acquired legal status because they thought it would increase public trust in their work, and 62 percent said they wanted the public to understand that they were nonprofit organizations (Keizai Kikaku Chou 2000, pt. 1, chap. 5, sec. 3). Indeed, the NPO Law has significantly increased public recognition of the sector. According to Cabinet Office research in 2000, 47.3 percent of those surveyed answered that they had never heard the term "NPO," 31.6 percent said they had heard the term, 19.4 percent said they knew what "NPO" was to some extent, and 1.7 percent said they knew very well what "NPO" was. In 2003, in contrast, those who said they had never heard the term "NPO" decreased to 10.5 percent, those who had heard the term increased to 39.2 percent, those who knew what "NPO" was dramatically increased to 44.3 percent, and 5.9 percent said they knew very well what "NPO" was (Cabinet Office 2004c; Sato 2006, 117). The legitimating function of the NPO Law and the public recognition may have increased the public interest in NPOs and their activities.

These provisions of the NPO Law have led to the steady increase in the number of NPOs with legal status, from 1,176 NPOs in December 1999 to 31,581 in May 2007 (Figure 10.1).[5] Does this increase in number of groups mean that the NPO Law has improved the quality of Japanese democracy? In order to answer this question, it is necessary to examine the four ways in

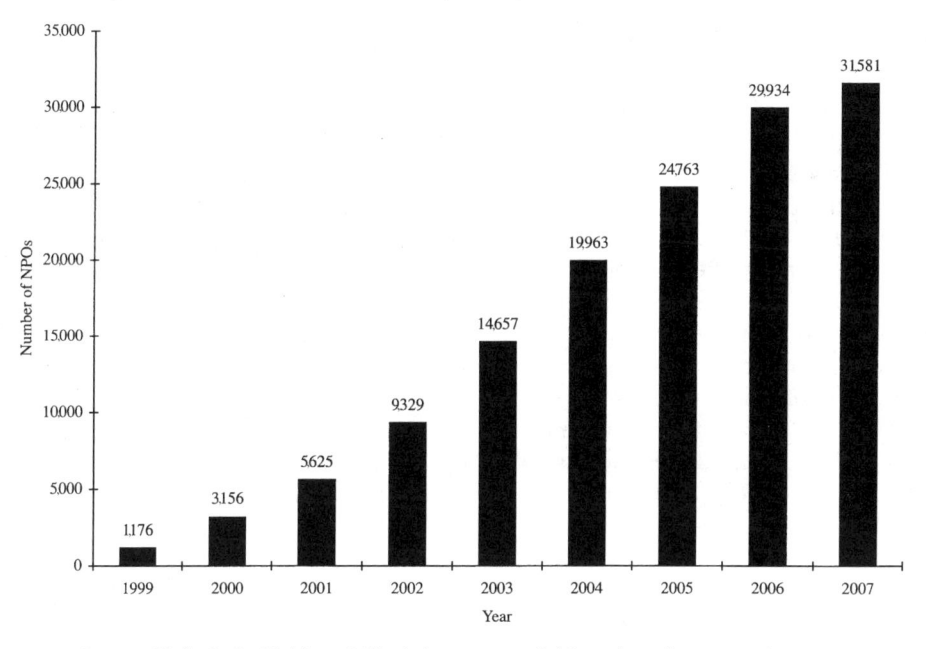

Figure 10.1   The Number of Nonprofit Organizations After the NPO Law

Year	Number of NPOs
1999	1,176
2000	3,156
2001	5,625
2002	9,329
2003	14,657
2004	19,963
2005	24,763
2006	29,934
2007	31,581

Source: Naikakufu (Cabinet Office) data set, available at http://www.npo-homepage.go.jp/data/pref history.txt.
Note: The figure for 2007 is from the end of May (retrieved June 29, 2007).

which NPOs relate to democracy, and what impact the NPO Law has had on each.

The Effects of the NPO Law

There are four ways in which NPOs relate to democracy. First, NPOs can support state provision of social services and contribute to democracy by participating in governance. Second, NPOs can create social capital and increase the performance of democracy. Third, NPOs can increase citizens' access to politics through their relationship to political parties. Fourth, NPOs can influence policymaking and implementation through advocacy and monitoring.

Provision of Social Services
Again, the first way in which NPOs relate to democracy is that NPOs can support state provision of social services and contribute to democracy through participation in governance. For many in the LDP, increasing the

number of NPOs that support the state's provision of social services (health, medical, and welfare services) was the main purpose of the NPO Law. Akiko Domoto, a former Sakigake member who was involved in the legislative process for the NPO Law, writes that the LDP hoped to have more NPOs in "fields like nursing" (Domoto 2000, 166–167; Sato 2006, 115).[6] Iwao Sato also says that the government has encouraged the NPO sector's growth so that it will take on more tasks while the government implements administrative reforms to become more streamlined and efficient (2006, 109–110, 112). Akihiro Ogawa also argues that volunteer activities organized under NPOs not only augment, but also replace, the government's provision of social services. He attributes this NPO policy to cost cutting in public administration (Ogawa 2004, 73).[7]

How can NPOs help the government cut costs and improve the provision of social services? Hiroko Ota (1999) argues that NPOs can compensate for market and government failures in providing social services. First, government failures such as "bureaucratic bloat and corruption, inefficiency, and inflexible decision making" can happen. NPOs can supplement government services to reduce such failures. Second, government provides uniform services that may not meet everyone's needs. NPOs can improve the provision of services by offering different services. Third, NPOs can utilize donations and subsidies to provide services more adequately and cheaply than businesses. Finally, in case of information asymmetry, NPOs that do not distribute profits can gain trust more easily than for-profit businesses (Ota 1999, 128–129).

Ota also points out that NPOs' provision of social services allows them to participate in governance and improve the quality of democracy in several ways. First, NPOs' provision of services that did not exist before—guided by demand—"constitute expressions of opinion regarding governance" (1999, 140). Second, Ota expects that consumers of social services will assess the services offered by suppliers (the government, NPOs, and businesses), and this will lead to supply-side accountability. Third, Ota foresees that "the top-down decision making, with the public sector above the private sector and the central government above local governments, will give way to horizontal, citizen-participatory decision making" (1999, 140). It may take a while for this expectation to be fulfilled, but there has been increasing cooperation between NPOs and local governments in provision of services.[8]

As the government hoped, the number of NPOs in the field of health, medical, and social welfare services has steadily increased since the NPO Law, and a substantial number of NPOs support, augment, and replace the state's provision of social services.[9] In fact, the number of NPOs that provide social services is the largest of all NPO fields (Figure 10.2).[10] The NPO Law facilitated the increase in number of NPOs in this field, and thus

Figure 10.2 The Number of Nonprofit Organizations, by Category

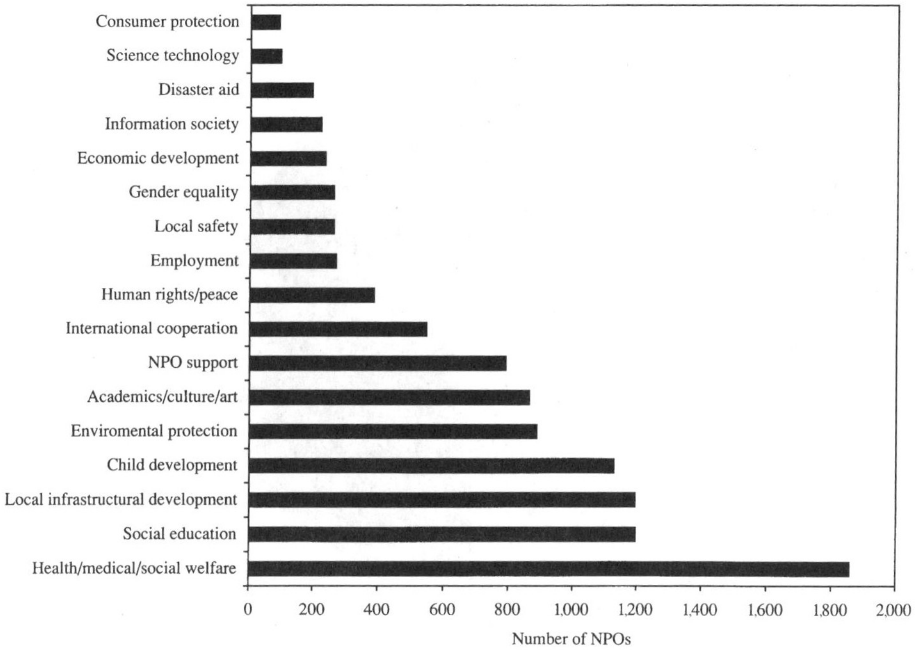

Category	Number of NPOs
Consumer protection	~100
Science technology	~100
Disaster aid	~200
Information society	~220
Economic development	~240
Gender equality	~270
Local safety	~270
Employment	~280
Human rights/peace	~400
International cooperation	~550
NPO support	~800
Academics/culture/art	~850
Enviromental protection	~900
Child development	~1,150
Local infrastructural development	~1,200
Social education	~1,200
Health/medical/social welfare	~1,850

Source: Cabinet Office (2004a).

contributed to democracy through NPOs' increased participation in governance.

Creation of Social Capital

The second way in which NPOs relate to democracy is through NPOs' creation of social capital. When compared to other countries' civil societies, Japan has many small, local groups and few large, national, professionalized groups (Pekkanen 2004a, 2004b, 2006). Most NPO activities remain at the local level (Figure 10.3). According to the Tokyo Metropolitan Government's (2001) survey, NPOs see their relationship with the ward, city, town, and village administrations as most important, and their relationship with the metropolitan government as second in importance. NPOs ranked their relationship with the national government as third in importance (Tokyo Metropolitan Government 2001). It is likely that NPOs create social capital most effectively at the local level.

The Cabinet Office sponsored a study by leading Japanese civil society scholars in 2002, which concludes that NPOs and other volunteer and civil society organizations can increase social capital (Cabinet Office 2002).

Figure 10.3 Breakdown of Activities of Civil Society
Organizations in Ibaraki Prefecture, 1997

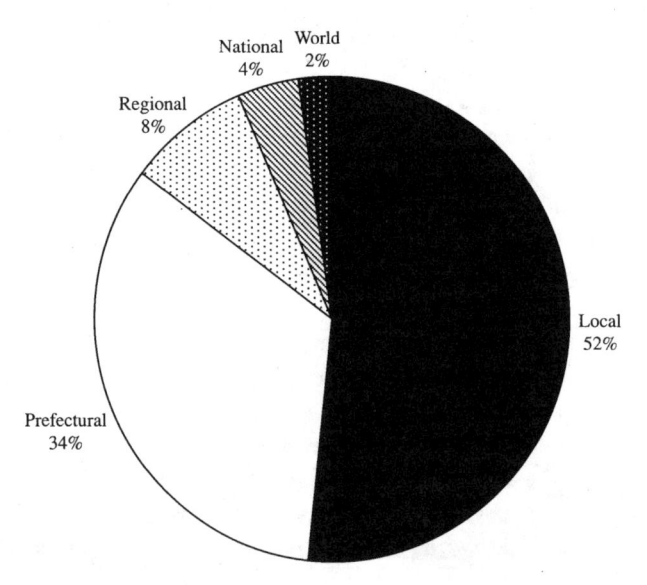

[Pie chart showing: Local 52%, Prefectural 34%, Regional 8%, National 4%, World 2%]

Source: Mori and Tsujinaka (2002), chart 105.
Note: n = 191.

According to the study, NPOs both create new social capital and influence preexisting social capital in the following manner. When, for example, NPO organizers realize that their region lacks a service that it needs, they look for people in the region who can help them achieve their goal. NPOs can seek cooperation from preexisting social capital groups like neighborhood associations and PTAs and, as they work together, a new network for communication and cooperation emerges. This process creates new social capital and also transforms the preexisting social capital from being "bonding" (or internal to the preexisting groups) to being "bridging" (or bringing together various groups). The increase in social capital in turn positively influences future NPO activities.

The NPO Law has steadily increased the number of NPOs over the years and thus has provided new opportunities for citizens to participate in various projects that they think are important, to build social networks and support, and to increase trust among residents in their neighborhoods. These components of social capital are important for democracy. Although there is no direct evidence to show increased social capital since 1998, it is likely that the NPO Law has contributed to democracy by increasing the number of NPOs and social capital.

Access to Political Parties

Third, NPOs can contribute to democracy through their relationship to political parties. In the NPOs' effort to have the NPO Law passed and even after the law's passage, new channels of communication between the public and politicians emerged, and preexisting channels became stronger. For example, political parties have established NPO committees and this has institutionalized NPO access to politicians. In February 2005, the LDP held a meeting with representatives from nineteen NPOs, about ten party representatives, and officials from the Cabinet Office and the National Tax Agency (Jiyuu Minshutou 2004). In October 2005, the LDP's special committee on the NPOs held a meeting with twelve NPOs and twelve Diet members, where the NPOs handed a written request to the party (C's 2005, 7). There have been similar meetings between NPOs and other political parties, in both committees and study groups (C's 2005, 8).[11] Furthermore, the LDP's website on NPOs has links to some NPO support groups such as C's, the Japan NPO Center, and the NPO Support Center, suggesting a close working relationship between the party and the NPOs.

In addition, many of the major political parties have made election promises to further promote NPO activities.[12] For example, the DPJ issued a manifesto containing a section on NPOs in the run-up to the November 2003 Lower House elections. The manifesto proposed to vastly expand tax benefits to NPOs, increase the number of NPOs providing after-school care to 20,000, and use NPOs to lower unemployment (Pekkanen 2004a, 380). Many parties also promised further tax reform for NPOs in the 2005 Lower House election (C's 2005, 4).

Political parties have also expected that NPOs serve as a vote collection mechanism. However, there are limits to NPOs' effectiveness to gather votes. First, the NPO Law states that NPOs cannot be established for "political activities." For example, NPOs cannot be created to support or oppose a political party or an individual candidate (Pekkanen 2000, 136).[13] This has belied the political parties' hope that NPOs would serve as vote collection vehicles. Second, NPOs' ability as a vote collection mechanism depends on NPO support for parties. Few NPOs support the LDP, for example, and therefore they may not be very useful for the LDP. Finally, NPOs have yet to demonstrate the ability to deliver votes like Soka Gakkai or labor unions. Shoji Takahira of the Kodomo Gekijo National Center (an organization promoting the performing arts among children, with 400,000 members nationwide) ran in the 2001 Upper House election as a national proportional representation candidate for the DPJ, but earned only 11,175 votes (Pekkanen 2004a, 380). Without serving as a vote-gathering mechanism, NPOs may not get much attention from some politicians and NPO impact on policy may be reduced.

Last but not least, in the NPO-party relationship, frequent changes in party personnel responsible for NPO activities create headaches for NPOs. This forces the NPOs to make appointments with new representatives, explain the situation facing the NPOs, and convince the representatives about the importance of change, only to repeat this process (C's 2005, 7). This delays necessary changes, and limits NPOs' positive influence on democracy.

Advocacy and Monitoring

Fourth, NPOs relate to democracy by participating in policymaking and implementation through advocacy and monitoring. In addition to building new channels of communication with political parties, NPO efforts include organization of symposiums and publications (C's n.d. "Koremade no katsudou"). Also, many prefectural governments now have NPO activity promotion offices, and NPOs and prefectural governments cooperate in policymaking and implementation. According to the Tokyo Metropolitan Government's (2001) research, 27.0 percent of the NPOs polled said they submit petitions and requests to various levels of government, 21.8 percent submit specific policy proposals, and 21.1 percent send NPO officials to deliberative councils and study groups.

Yet another channel of communication for advocacy is the NPO Giin Renmei, which is a league of Diet members that gives further legislative support for NPO activities. The league was established in August 1999, eight months after the NPO Law came into force. There were 204 starting members from various parties (C's 1999). Using the various communication channels, NPOs have let the politicians know about the NPO Law's shortcomings and advocated change. As a result, revisions of the law have been enacted. For example, in 2001, in order to ameliorate the difficult funding situation for many groups, NPOs helped create a law that allowed individuals and corporations to obtain tax privileges for donating to NPOs with special certification from the National Tax Agency. These certified NPOs are a subcategory of NPO legal persons to which individuals or corporations can make a contribution that is deductible from their income tax (Pekkanen 2003, 124). However, the selection process for the certification has been stringent, limiting the number of certified NPOs (Japan NPO Center n.d.). With NPO monitoring and advocacy, the law was further revised in 2002, 2003, and 2005 (C's n.d. "Koremade no katsudou"). Yet in July 2005, there were still only thirty-four certified NPOs.[14] NPOs continue to ask the government and political parties to relax the certification requirements, simplify the certification process, and lower the minimum amount of donations that qualifies for tax exemption (C's 2005, 6). In addition, because the certification process involves public disclosure of names and addresses of donors who have donated more than 200,000 yen in the past two years as well as salaries of NPO employees, NPOs wish to increase protection of personal information in the application process (Cabinet Office 2004a, 52).

Another example of NPO impact on policymaking is the NPO Law's revision in December 2002.[15] The new law increased the categories of NPO activities from twelve to seventeen (adding, e.g., consumer protection, development of scientific technology, and promotion of employment). The law also simplified the application process and strengthened the measures to prevent gangs from obtaining legal status as NPOs.

Despite the growing number and influence of NPOs, according to the Johns Hopkins Global Civil Society Index which measured the robustness of civil societies around the world based on their capacity, sustainability, and impact, Japan ranks nineteenth out of thirty-four countries. This is the second lowest rank of all developed nations (Yamauchi 2005, 58; Salamon and Sokolowski 2004). It suggests that Japanese NPOs' role in advocacy and monitoring is limited, compared to other countries' civil society organizations. One of the most important reasons for this is that the Japanese civil society organizations are underprofessionalized. While Japan has many small local groups, it has few large professional groups that operate nationally (Pekkanen 2004a, 2004b, 2006; Mori and Tsujinaka 2002, 105). Professional organizations with full-time employees can develop expertise, institutionalize movements, and influence policies better than small, local groups (Pekkanen 2004b, 240). For example, Robert Pekkanen's data analysis in 2004 shows that there is a strong correlation between group size (in terms of number of permanent employees) and the media coverage a group can attract (2004a, 371–372). In Japan, the small number of employees in professional advocacy groups cannot produce much research for the media to cover. This constrains their ability to influence public discourse over policies, especially at the national level (Pekkanen 2004a, 372). Indeed, our new research data show that the government was the most frequent contributor of policy-related research to *Nihon Keizai Shinbun* between 2002 and 2004, and contributions from civil society organizations were significantly less (Figure 10.4).[16] This comes in stark contrast to the United States where there are more professional advocacy groups, and newspapers use civil society groups' research more than any other sources (Pekkanen 2004b, 243; Berry 1998, 379). The Japanese civil society's ability to contribute research findings to public debates has not improved since Pekkanen compiled his data for 2001–2002 (Pekkanen 2004a, 370–371).

There are some other reasons for the limited advocacy and monitoring roles of NPOs in Japan. First, many NPOs are short of funds, and this constrains their growth and activities. According to the Tokyo Metropolitan Government's (2005) research on NPOs, 68 percent of the groups wished to receive subsidies from the government. This is only a slight decrease from 2001, when 71 percent of the NPOs wanted subsidies (Tokyo Metropolitan

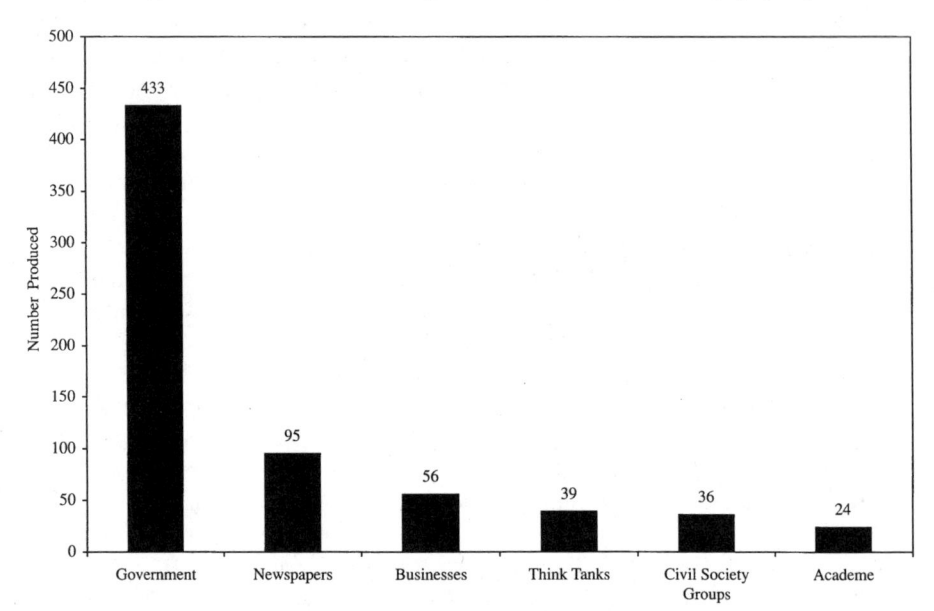

Figure 10.4   Amount of Policy-related Research Produced, by Group

Group	Number Produced
Government	433
Newspapers	95
Businesses	56
Think Tanks	39
Civil Society Groups	36
Academe	24

Source: Compiled from fifty randomly selected dates per year from *Nihon Keizai Shimbun* between 2002 and 2004.

Note: The civil society category includes both NPO legal persons and groups without legal status.

Government 2001). Nationally, 85 percent of the NPOs in 2006 wished to receive government funding (Cabinet Office 2007). The weak financial foundation also makes many NPOs overly dependent on *itaku jigyou* (tasks entrusted from the government), and this undermines the independent position of NPOs (C's n.d. "NPO to jichitai: paatonaashippu"). In addition, about 20 percent of NPOs funded by government in 2006 reported that restrictions on the usage of funding constrained the organizations' activities (Cabinet Office 2007, 10). With dependence on the government, monitoring and advocacy could become more challenging.

Second, the NPO Law is designed to allow groups to obtain legal status without bureaucratic screening, but in reality bureaucrats have asked many groups to change their application. This is a violation of the spirit of the law, and has led to many organizations choosing not to seek state recognition of their legal status (Pekkanen 2000, 138–139, nn. 86, 87). In addition, the state continues to engage in administrative guidance of organizations, and requires organizations to submit accounting and finance reports. Organizations must also submit reports on annual activities, lists of assets, accounts of changes in membership, and financial statements for the past year as well as planned activity reports and budget estimates for the coming year. A nationwide Economic Planning Agency survey of NPOs shows that the most common reason for not applying for legal status was that accounting and finance reporting requirements were too onerous (61 percent of the responding groups), and the third most common reason was the fear that bureaucrats might control the objective or activities of the NPO (45 percent) (Pekkanen 2004b, 227; Noumi 1997). Many organizations do not apply for legal status in order to remain independent from state control (Pekkanen 2003, 124). The monitoring and advocacy function of NPOs becomes weakened when many groups withhold application for legal status, because working without legal status constrains their growth.

Conclusion

NPOs and the government must continue to work together to encourage further NPO development. Many NPOs have weak foundations, and more tax reforms are necessary. Conducting research about the needs of the public and engaging in other activities require resources that are in short supply. However, considering the fact that many of the NPOs are new, and there is a positive correlation between a group's age and budget size, the budget of NPOs that survive will probably continue to grow.[17]

Many NPOs also lack expertise, or information on how to run their organizations and expand their activities. Nobuko Kawashima (2005) points out that the NPO Law leaves the structure of governance in NPOs unclear. Governance, separate from management, is about leading and controlling the NPOs, and it helps increase accountability and makes sure that NPOs remain socially responsible. Because the NPO Law does not guarantee governance, Kawashima argues that each NPO would have to strengthen governance and policymakers should consider legal requirements for governance (2005). NPOs can also rely on NPO support organizations' seminars and publications to further their development (C's n.d. "Koremade no katsudou").

Many politicians and the public acknowledge that NPOs have an important role in the society because they engage in various political, economic, and social issues. It is likely that NPOs will continue to be a significant part of the further development of the Japanese democracy and civil society. The NPO Law has contributed to the development of NPOs by liberalizing conditions under which groups can form and operate. As a result the number of NPOs has steadily increased, and the law has enhanced NPOs' contribution to democracy. Through more provision of social services, enhancement of social capital, greater access to political parties, and improved opportunity for advocacy and monitoring, NPOs have increased citizen participation, representation, and accountability. For example, as the national government has asked local governments and NPOs to provide more social services, NPO involvement has enhanced participation by allowing local residents to decide which services should be provided and how. As residents have engaged in more NPO activities and events, participation has increased and social capital has further enhanced democratic governance. Improved NPO access to political parties has also increased representation and accountability, as demonstrated in the political parties' election manifestos on NPO development. In addition, the improved access to political parties and enhanced advocacy role of NPOs has led to increased participation in policymaking processes, as in the many revisions of the NPO Law. The NPO Law has improved participation, representation, and accountability, and therefore the quality of democracy in Japan.

However, the structure of the civil society in Japan and the way in which state and civil society relate to each other have not changed fundamentally after the NPO Law. There are still many small, local grassroots organizations and few large, national professional advocacy organizations. This structure continues to limit NPO advocacy and monitoring through national campaigns. Yet this in itself does not necessarily hinder democracy because local grassroots organizations often enhance participation. Their organizational, financial, and other limits may not allow their policy preferences to be represented at the national level, however. In other words, there may be trade-offs between participation and representation. If more nationwide professional advocacy groups are born, they may give their members' voice greater representation, but potentially at the cost of the members' participation. That is, members of national groups often only write checks for their organizations and do not participate in the organizations' operations and events as much as grassroots organization members. In any case, more local grassroots organizations than national and professional advocacy organizations continue to make up the Japanese civil society after the NPO Law. Furthermore, many NPO leaders believe that the relationship between NPOs and government has not changed much. In a Cabinet Office questionnaire in 2006, for example, many NPO leaders said that government offices still take the leadership role when they work together, and their relationship is not equal (Cabinet Office 2007).

In sum, the NPO Law has improved the quality of democracy by increasing citizens' grassroots participation as well as representation and accountability in the policymaking and implementation processes. Such changes, however, have not led to a fundamental change in the structure of civil society and the state–civil society relations. NPOs are continuing to work for more revision of the NPO Law to improve their operations and the sector as a whole. If such efforts are successful, Japanese democracy and civil society will continue to develop further.

Notes

This research was assisted by a grant to Robert Pekkanen from the Abe Fellowship Program administered by the Social Science Research Council and the American Council of Learned Society in cooperation with and with funds provided by the Japan Foundation Center for Global Partnership.

1. Before answering this question, it is important to define both civil society and nonprofit organizations (NPOs). "Civil society" is the organized, nonstate, nonmarket sector. It does not include government bureaucracies, businesses, or other profit-oriented groups. This definition of civil society is contested. For example, Japan's leading scholar of civil society, Yutaka Tsujinaka, includes business organizations in his analyses (2002, 2003), although otherwise his approach is consistent with this definition. In any event, this chapter focuses on the empirically observable organizational dimension, not on a public sphere. Here, civil society encompasses nonprofit organizations (NPOs), nongovernmental organizations (NGOs), and other voluntary associations. In Japan, "NPOs" usually refer to domestically active groups, while "NGOs" are groups that engage in international activities, although NPOs increasingly include groups that are involved in global issues. Many Japanese people tend to view NPOs as the most vital, citizen-oriented part of the civil society.

2. For a more detailed discussion of the law's emergence, see Pekkanen 2000.

3. Their hopes were not realized, however. Even large and powerful groups have not delivered proportional representation bloc votes consistently, with the important exception of Soka Gakkai.

4. As a result of this system, we can vividly capture the variation in the number of NPOs by prefecture. We find unsurprisingly that Tokyo has by far the most NPOs per 100,000 population (35.18), with Kyoto next at 21.61 and Nagano just behind with 20.85, while Saitama (9.48) and Ibaraki (9.13) bring up the rear (Hirashita 2006, 74). Unfortunately, we do not have the space here to investigate the cause of this regional variation.

5. The total for 1999 is from the LDP website "LDP shimin katsudo NET." The total for 2006 is from the Naikakufu NPO home page, "Tokutei hieiri katsudou sokushin hou ni motozuku shinsei jyurisuu oyobi ninshousuu, funinshousuu tou."

6. According to Iwao Sato (2006), Akiko Domoto writes that the political parties in coalition had different aims for encouraging NPO activities. The LDP hoped to have more NPOs in fields like nursing. The SDPJ wished to answer the demands of the peace and environmental movement organizations, and Sakigake saw NPOs as essential in reforming the society from the one characterized by bureaucratic dominance to one characterized by citizen leadership.

7. In an interview in 2000, DPJ's Yukio Hatoyama also linked NPO activities with cost reduction (see "Chiisana seifuni NPO no chikara wo" 2000).

8. C's, an organization that supports NPOs in Japan, has a list of prefectural offices that promote NPO activities under NPOWEB daigaku. See C's website for stories about partnership between local governments and NPOs, http://www.npoweb.jb/modules/feature/index.php?cat_id=5 (retrieved January 24, 2008).

9. NPOs in this category can be divided into two types, according to a 1996 survey by Kansai Inter-Discipline Studies Inc. Some are the "government-backup type" that local governments helped set up and provide support, while others operate independent of the government (see Ota 1999, 141).

10. This does not mean, however, that the number of NPOs in this field has increased more rapidly than other fields. The Cabinet Office's research on NPOs

from 2004 shows that the percentage of NPOs in the field of social welfare between 1996 and 2004 remained steady at 37 percent (see Cabinet Office 2004b).

11. The newsletter discusses meetings with Komeito and the Democratic Party of Japan.

12. For a comparison of party election promises, see C's (2005, 4).

13. See also Japan NPO Center (n.d.). For more on the argument of this paragraph, see Pekkanen (2004a).

14. C's (2005, 6), citing a request from the Cabinet Office; Ministry of Foreign Affairs; Ministry of Health, Labor and Welfare; Ministry of Economy, Trade and Industry; and Ministry of the Environment to the Ministry of Finance.

15. The revised law came into effect in May 2003.

16. These data support earlier analyses (see Pekkanen 2004a, 370–371, 2006).

17. Pekkanen (2004b, 231) shows this correlation between age and budget size.

PART 3

Conclusion

CHAPTER 11

Contemporary Japanese Democracy

Sherry L. Martin and Gill Steel

JAPAN HAS REVOLUTIONIZED ITS PROCESSES OF GOVERnance and administration. The research presented in this volume describes patterns of political change that extend over two decades of reform. Reforms have profoundly transformed the bureaucracy, the electoral system, nonprofit organizations (NPOs), transparency in government, and freedom of information, to name but some of the changes. As a whole, they have produced change along multiple dimensions by which we analyze how well democracy works.

Legislation, however, can only go some of the way toward effectively reinvigorating democracy. The reforms have set the stage for a deepening of democracy to occur, but whether the actors embrace change is another matter. Political elites and everyday voters alike may fail to make full use of the potential that the reforms offer due to inertia, the high costs of change, or because the ability to take advantage of new opportunities and resources is a learned process that takes time. Well into the second decade of reform processes, Japanese politics has not stabilized at a new equilibrium. Yet developments over this period of time reveal patterns of change on which we can predict the future path of reform and the deepening of Japanese democracy.

We conclude this volume with an overview of salient findings, note areas of concurrence and conflict, and discuss the implications for democracy. We organize our concluding thoughts under four broad themes that emerge across all chapters: (1) a concern with whether institutional change can produce new political norms, (2) how the bifurcation of Japanese politics effects patterns of change, (3) the role of leadership in determining future directions in Japanese politics, and (4) the pace of democratic change.

Structure vs. Culture

Echoing the hopes of some of the Japanese architects of political, administrative, and economic reforms, the work in this volume is premised on the assumption that political outcomes are influenced by the surrounding institutional framework, rather than by the particularities of the cultural context. Each of the reforms was ambitious in seeking to accomplish multiple tasks in the service of improving the quality of Japanese democracy. Electoral reform and campaign financing regulations, for example, were seen as crucial to generating a competitive two-party–dominant system with regular alteration in power, producing programmatic parties and issue-based politics, reducing patronage politics and corruption, and fostering deeper citizen engagement with politics.

Under the 1955 System, the Liberal Democratic Party (LDP) was able to maintain its dominant position in part by being responsive to a fairly wide range of demands. As citizens began to support new issues and vote for the opposition on the basis of these issues, conservative politicians at all levels of government co-opted the issues (although not always in a timely fashion). The political opposition was not completely marginalized; not only were their ideas co-opted, they also were able to force concessions through procedural delays, or threats thereof. This political flexibility or "creative conservatism," to use T. J. Pempel's (1982) resonant phrase, has averted an LDP government-versus-opposition policy cleavage that might have cost the LDP dearly, speeding its decline. It also undercut any policy agenda that the opposition might have developed, outside of criticism of political corruption. Some of these trends continue in the postreform era. Yet all of the chapters in the first half of this volume uncover some change, even though the LDP continues its dominance.

In contrast to the rapid splintering, dissolution, and reconstitution of opposition parties around the time of electoral reform, the Democratic Party of Japan (DPJ) has stabilized as the largest opposition party, but it has yet to unseat or provide a viable alternative to the LDP. The continuation of the DPJ struggle to craft a stable, substantive, and ideologically coherent policy profile evokes counter-responses from the LDP, and introduces electoral pressures that benefit voters. As findings from Ellis S. Krauss and Robert Pekkanen (Chapter 2) and Gill Steel (Chapter 5) show, the LDP and the DPJ are two centrist parties that are now more responsive to the median voter, and their manifestos symbolize a shift toward more programmatic campaigns. When Komeito entered into a governing coalition with the LDP, this long-term political outsider was propelled to the center of politics and used its new position to win a number of policy concessions from the LDP.

Ellis S. Krauss and Takeshi Ishida's summation of party politics preform remains an apt description of the dynamics we have observed to date in the aftermath of electoral reform: *"alternating power* is replaced by simultaneous, shared, but unequal influence" (1989, 335, emphasis in original). Many pundits argue that Japan is heading toward a two-party system but, as of the time of writing, the reforms have done little to change the asymmetry in electoral politics; though the DPJ may well be here to stay, one-party dominance continues to be the norm in Japan. Despite the fact that the DPJ managed to triumph in the 2007 election to the less powerful Upper House, it is unclear whether the party will be able to build on this victory. Robert J. Weiner (Chapter 8) finds that uncompetitiveness continues to hinder the DPJ's ability to establish itself as a grassroots party. Weiner's assessment is supported by Naoko Taniguchi (Chapter 4), who finds that incentives remain for voters to support second-generation politicians, locally and nationally, because their pre-existing networks and ties to central government actors ensure voters continued access to pork barrel projects.

Theorists do not usually think of one-party dominance as democratic, but is Japan any less democratic than other nations in which parties do alternate in power? Concerns that Krauss and Ishida raise about the sufficiency of institutional incentives in forcing the LDP to respond to change as experienced by a broad array of societal interests (1989, 334) remain pertinent in the postreform era. As Dyron Dabney indicates in Chapter 3, the continued importance of the *koenkai* and other traditional vote-gathering mechanisms prompt concerns about whether reforms have truly brought a wider array of interests into the political process. A further sign that reform has not achieved this increased incorporation of interests is the citizen disengagement from national-level politics in terms of decreasing voter turnout.

Even when the authors in this volume conclude that the reforms have not lived up to expectations, the continuation of practices developed under the 1955 System is attributed to the failure of new institutions to alter incentives, or a learning curve associated with the reforms. Authors in this volume are less likely to attribute continuity to the enduring strength of cultural norms, agreeing that most people are not yet fully conversant with, and able to take advantage of, the opportunities that the reforms afford. This is most clear when we are talking about change at the local level and in rural constituencies, bastions of conservatism where traditional clientelist politics are strongest, giving rise to an expectation of more continuity than change.

Bifurcation in the Political System

Finding continuity or change in the quality of Japanese democracy depends on where one is looking in this "bifurcated" political system. Researchers generally focus on electoral politics at the national level for evidence that reforms have produced substantive changes in democratic practices in Japan. The chapters in the second half of this volume examine the dynamics of local politics and civil society. Here, we find that incremental changes at the national level are counterbalanced by more dramatic change at the grassroots level where we see evidence of increased citizen participation and shifting attitudes about quality representation.

While Robert J. Weiner finds that subnational elections in the aggregate remain largely uncompetitive (Chapter 8), Robin M. LeBlanc's examination of local elections in Chapter 9 uncovers citizens' movements to put the authority and powers guaranteed under the Local Autonomy Law into practice; local politicians are challenging incumbents because they want to exercise the right to say no to incursions of the central government into local politics. This is a marked departure from politics under the 1955 System when rural voters supported conservative politicians locally and nationally, and benefited from the LDP's redistributive policies that favored rural development. While these policies have been a source of contention for urban voters and opposition party supporters, public works projects—one foundation of pork barrel politics—have seemingly reached a point of diminishing returns for citizens in LeBlanc's study who represent a perspective that might be on the rise among rural voters. Similarly, Sherry L. Martin addresses changes in women's patterns of subnational officeholding (Chapter 7) that suggest a broadening trend of women challenging seats in rural races we would foresee to be the most uncompetitive, with the highest barriers to entry by political outsiders. Whereas Weiner predicts stagnancy in subnational politics, LeBlanc and Martin suggest that fresh faces might have a long-term impact beyond their presently small numbers.

We also see scattered grassroots-level democracy, with ordinary citizens acting on matters of concern regardless of the institutional changes. LeBlanc describes groups that did not actively pursue or anticipate national-level efforts toward decentralization (Chapter 9). However, faced with new opportunities to exercise political influence that institutional changes provide, the future potential exists for a broader array of civil society actors to participate in the political process. Yuko Kawato and Robert Pekkanen show in Chapter 10 that the numbers of citizens participating in NPOs has increased steadily and NPOs' impact on policymaking, particularly at the local level, has also increased.

At the grassroots level, citizens are learning to take advantage of freedom-of-information laws and NPO legislation to more directly intervene in the political process by holding officials accountable for unethical and unfair political practices; registered NPOs and unregistered groups provide social services independently of and in collaboration with local and national government; and voters are monitoring local budgets in anticipation of the challenges that accompany municipal amalgamations. Participatory local politics and the vibrancy of civil society generate expectations of the pressures for change from the bottom up, resulting in a widening of access points in this traditionally top-down political system.

Importance of Leadership

Leadership is of increasing importance to this nation where political leaders, especially the prime minister, with few exceptions have been weak. Joseph A. Massey (1975) refers to Japan's leader as "missing" and, in his absence, the nation lacked an essential contributing component of the political socialization process. Former prime minister Junichiro Koizumi was one marked departure from this tradition. And the enthusiasm that the public showed for the Koizumi administration was a brief interlude in a long-term downward trend in voter turnout and engagement with politics, and it may prove unsustainable in the post-Koizumi era. Koizumi used the momentum and opportunities unleashed by early reforms, described within this volume, to introduce new norms and rules that would increase the decisionmaking potential of the *kantei* (prime minister's office). These reforms were produced in part by a shift in public expectations of the political process that made Koizumi, and other innovative policy-oriented leaders like him, a political possibility.

Whether future leaders will take full advantage of existing resources to centralize decisionmaking in the office of prime minister is doubtful. Although Shinzo Abe did not reverse economic reforms during his short tenure, he allowed the momentum that grew under Koizumi to dissipate. Abe essentially put Koizumi's structural reform ideas on hold, leading an *Asahi Shimbun* editorial to ask whether dependence on the bureaucracy was returning. Abe's various reforms were not a coherent structural reform program in any sense, prompting the *Asahi Shimbun* to suggest that the bureaucracy was regaining its former power—bringing an end to drastic change to Japanese economy and society (*Asahi Shimbun* editorial 2007).

Administrative reforms, as Eiji Kawabata discusses in Chapter 6, divert power from bureaucrats to elected political leaders. But the potential of these reforms to alter the relationship between elected officials and their constituents over the long term is contingent on the vision and initiatives of politicians who seek to alter the status quo, circumstances that are familiar and vital to their past electoral success. Substantive change in state-society relations, from the administration of Yasuhiro Nakasone onward, has proceeded in fits and starts depending on innovative skills of the prime minister and renegade junior politicians who formed the core of new parties.

At the local level, victories by independent candidates in gubernatorial races were seemingly indicative of a new style of leadership that had gained purchase among voters—young, reformist, political outsiders. In grassroots involvement, LeBlanc emphasizes in Chapter 9 the importance of the ethical stances adopted by activist leaders who seek to replace vertical relationships between constituent and representative with horizontal relationships. Conditions seem ripe for the entry of more politicians who embody inclusive leadership styles. Weiner, however, argues in Chapter 8 that a handful of successful candidates unaffiliated with any party barely constitutes an "independent wave," as some commentators imply. Such candidacies are the exception, and not the norm; strong opposition challengers are unlikely to emerge in local elections when making rational, strategic decisions. Weiner asserts that it is natural for competition to decrease over time. If Weiner's predictions hold true, voters' expectations that reforms will produce more electoral choices, and stronger leadership, will go unfulfilled with potential consequences for rebuilding positive affective orientations toward government.

The Pace of Change

A final common theme that emerges across all chapters is attention to the pace of change. Even the authors whose tone is pessimistic hold an air of anticipation with regard to what the future will hold. But it is clear when we talk about "deepening democracy" that we are talking about a variety of phenomena, and that these phenomena are not occurring simultaneously. There has been no unified linear progression toward a deepened democracy. Authors in the first half of this book all suggest that national-level change is on the horizon; we just have to wait. The latter chapters imply that long-term predictions about the future direction and pace of change rest on a more thorough understanding of change in local politics, the electoral base.

In addition to the institutional barriers to change identified in this project, more time is required for politicians, bureaucrats, and citizens to cast off standard operating procedures developed under the old system, and respond to the potential of the new. The most evident sign of continuity is that the LDP, in coalition with the small Komeito, remains the dominant party within the Japanese system. At the local level, potential challengers are acting strategically by not entering races with strong LDP candidates (see Weiner, Chapter 8).

Change exists more in attitudes about representation and participation, transparency and accountability, and in norms of fairness that the reforms advance among Japanese elites and voters. While the political culture tradition recognizes how important it is that voters internalize beliefs, values, and norms that support democracy, political scientists have not untangled endogenous patterns of causality. Does culture shift institutions, or do institutions shift culture? The authors here do not resolve this issue, but their discussion of the incentives behind reform, how elites and voters have responded, and observed changes in political outcomes to date all suggest that fundamental shifts in attitudes have been operative at every stage of the reform process. Krauss and Pekkanen propose in Chapter 2 that the pace of change depends on how secure voters feel in installing new political elites, or forcing the existing ones to abandon practices still associated with Japan's postwar achievements. The vibrancy observable in grassroots politics might be experimentation in "laboratories of democracy." Citizens' expectations of and orientation toward politics have shifted at the individual level with ripple effects that spill over into local communities where pressures mount to influence the course of national politics over the long term.

Japanese democracy is stable, and far from endangered. That said, we know more about the democratization process in the transitional and stabilization stages than in mature democracies. Japanese democracy offers us a rare opportunity to observe rapid changes in the functioning of democracy over a truncated period of time; in sixty years, state-society relations in Japan have undergone changes that have taken a century and a half in other advanced industrialized democracies. As such, Japan tells us something about the strength of continuity and the limits of institutional change. Though we wait with impatient anticipation for the changes that stem from administrative, fiscal, and political reforms, we forget that we are talking about a relatively short period of time. Even so, we find changes in democratic norms and practice occurring in predictable patterns. Citizens and elites are armed with more tools than ever to facilitate a two-way channel of influence and communication. How rapidly and how much farther changing norms of representation, accountability, pluralism, and competitiveness progress is contingent on how leaders use their resources to realize a political and economic agenda with broad appeal, and the lengths that voters are willing to go to hold them accountable.

Acronyms

ARC	Administrative Reform Council
ASSK	Akarui Senkyo Suishin Kyokai (Society for the Promotion of Clean Elections)
CP	Conservative Party
DMS	direct mobilization strategy
DPJ	Democratic Party of Japan
DSP	Democratic Socialist Party
FILP	Fiscal Investment and Loan Program
FSI	fiscal strength index
HC	House of Councilors (Upper House)
HR	House of Representatives (Lower House)
IMS	indirect mobilization strategy
JCP	Japan Communist Party
JES	Japan Election Study
JSP	Japan Socialist Party
LDP	Liberal Democratic Party
LP	Liberal Party
MITI	Ministry of International Trade and Industry
MPHPT	Ministry of Public Management, Home Affairs, Posts and Telecommunications
MPT	Ministry of Posts and Telecommunications
NCP	New Conservative Party
NFP	New Frontier Party
NGO	nongovernmental organization
NIMBY	not in my backyard
NLC	New Liberal Club
NPO	nonprofit organization
NPO Law	Nonprofit Organization Law
NTT	Nippon Telegraph and Telephone

ODC	ordinance-designated city
PARC	Policy Affairs Research Council
PILP	public-interest legal persons
RRP	ratio of recurring profit
SDPJ	Social Democratic Party of Japan
SNTV	single nontransferable vote

References

"44 doufukengikai no shinseiryoku bunya." (2007, April 9). *Yomiuri Shimbun*, evening edition.
"44 doufukengisen tousenshasuu." (2003, April 14). *Yomiuri Shimbun*, online edition.
Aberbach, Joel, and Bert Rockman. (2000). *In the Web of Politics: Three Decades of the U.S. Federal Executive*. Washington, DC: Brookings Institution Press.
"'Ainori haiboku' ni yureru Minshutou: Shiga chijisen shokku." (2006, July 12). *Asahi Shimbun*, online edition.
Aldrich, John. (1997). "When Is It Rational to Vote?" In D. Mueller (ed.), *Perspectives on Public Choice: A Handbook*, pp. 373–390. Cambridge: Cambridge University Press.
Almond, Gabriel, and Sidney Verba. (1963). *The Civic Culture: Political Attitudes and Behavior in Five Nations*. Princeton: Princeton University Press.
Alvarez, R. Michael, and Jonathan Nagler. (1995). "Economics, Issues, and the Perot Candidacy: Voter Choice in the 1992 Election." *American Journal of Political Science* 39: 714–744.
Anderson, Christopher J., and Christine A. Guillory. (1997). "Political Institutions and Satisfaction with Democracy: A Cross-national Analysis of Consensus and Majoritarian Systems." *American Political Science Review* 91, no. 1: 66–81.
Anderson, Christopher J., and Yuliya V. Tverdova. (2001). "Winners, Losers, and Attitudes Toward Government in Contemporary Democracies." *International Political Science Review* 22, no. 4: 321–338.
Asahi Shimbun editorial. (2007, June 10). "Honebuto no houshin kanryouizon ni modosukika." Retrieved January 24, 2008, from http://database.asahi.com/library2/main/start.php?loginSID=19670621eddfe23f1031ee303dd8e38e.
Asahi Shimbun Senkyo Honbu. (1980–1997). *Asahi Senkyo Taikan Books 1–7*. Tokyo: Asahi Shimbunsha.
Asano, Masahiko. (2003). "Senkyo Seido Kaikaku to Kohosha Konin." *Senkyo Kenkyu* 18: 174–189.
ASSK (Akarui Senkyo Suishin Kyokai Shugiin Giin Sosenkyo) (Society for the Promotion of Clean Elections, House of Representatives Election Studies), various years, made available through the Leviathan Data Bank, Tokyo.
"Asu no hanashi o shiyo (5): chihosen—kasoku suru seito banare; tsuyou shinai chinjogata seiji." (2001, January 7). *Yomiuri Shimbun*, Chuubu edition, p. 30.

Banaszak, Lee Ann. (1996). *Why Movements Succeed or Fail: Opportunity, Culture, and the Struggle for Woman Suffrage*. Princeton: Princeton University Press.

Berry, Jeffrey M. (1998). "The Rise of Citizens Groups." In Theda Skocpol and Morris P. Fiorina (eds.), *Civic Engagement in American Democracy*, pp. 367–394. Washington, DC: Brookings Institution.

Besley, Timothy, and Stephen Coate. (1997). "An Economic Model of Representative Democracy." *Quarterly Journal of Economics* 112, no. 1: 85–114.

Bochel, Catherine, and Hugh Bochel. (2005). "Exploring the Low Levels of Women's Representation in Japanese Local Government." *Japanese Journal of Political Science* 6, no. 3: 375–392.

Bochel, Catherine, Masashi Kasuga, and Hideko Takeyasu. (2003). "Against the System? Women in Elected Local Government in Japan." *Local Government Studies* 29, no. 2: 19–31.

Bouissou, Jean Marie. (2000). "Ambiguous Revival: A Study of Some 'New Civic Movements' in Japan." *Pacific Review* 13, no. 3: 335–366.

Broadbent, Jeffrey. (2003). "Movement in Context: Thick Networks and Japanese Environmental Protest." In Mario Diani and Doug MacAdam (eds.), *Social Movements and Networks: Relational Approaches to Collective Action*, pp. 204–229. New York: Oxford University Press.

C's. (1999). "NPO giin renmei hassoku." Retrieved March 29, 2006, from www.npoweb.jp/daigaku/shokatucho_info.php?article_id=1252.

———. (2005). News Letter no. 54, November 10.

———. (n.d.). "Koremade no katsudou." Retrieved March 29, 2006, from www.npoweb.jp/cs/cs_home_print.php?article_id=1963.

———. (n.d.). "NPO to jichitai: paatonaashippu." Retrieved May 28, 2006, from www.npoweb.jp/special/special_info.php?article_id=1818.

———. (n.d.). "Shokatsu chou ichiran jyouhou." Retrieved February 6, 2006, from www.npoweb.jp/daigaku/shokatucho_info.php?article_id=1252.

Cabinet Office. (2001a). "Shimin katsudou dantai no hyouka ni kansuru chosa." Research summary available online. Retrieved January 24, 2008, from http://www5.cao.go.jp/seikatsu/2001/0409shiminkatsudou/main.html.

———. (2001b). "Shimin katsudou dantaito kihon chosa." Retrieved May 27, 2006, from www5.cao.go.jp/seikatsu/2001/0409shiminkatsudou/main.html.

———. (2002). "Sousharu kyapitaru: yutaka na ningen kankei to shimin katsudou no kojynkan wo motomete." Retrieved May 28, 2006, from www.npo-homepage.go.jp/report/h14/sc/honbun.html.

———. (2004a). "NPO hojin no jittai oyobi nintei NPO hojin seido no riyo jyoukyou ni kansuru chosa." Retrieved May 12, 2006, from www.npo-homepage.go.jp/report/h16a-2.html.

———. (2004b). "Shimin katsudo dantai kihon chosa hokokusho." Retrieved May 28, 2006, from www.npo-homepage.go.jp/report/h16kihonchousa.html.

———. (2004c). "Kokumin seikatsu senkodo chosa." Research summary available online from http://www5.cao.go.jp/seikatsu/senkoudo/h15/senkoudo15_1.pdf.

———. (2006). "Tokutei hieiri katsudou sokushin hou ni motozuku shinsei jyurisu oyobi ninshousu, funinshousu to." Retrieved May 15, 2006, from www.npo-homepage.go.jp/data/pref.html.

———. (2007). "Shimin katsudou dantai kihon chosa hokusho." Research summary available online. Retrieved January 24, 2008, from http://www.npo-homepage.go.jp/data/report22.html.

Calder, Kent E. (1988). *Crisis and Compensation: Public Policy and Political Stability in Japan.* Princeton: Princeton University Press.

"Campaigning Begins for Hundreds of Mayoral, Assembly Races." (2007, April 16). *Japan Times.* Retrieved June 25, 2007, from http://search.japantimes.co.jp/cgi-bin/nn20070416a2.html.

Campbell, John. (1989). "Democracy and Bureaucracy in Japan." In Takeshi Ishida and Ellis Krauss (eds.), *Democracy in Japan*, pp. 113–138. Pittsburgh: University of Pittsburgh Press.

Campbell, John Creighton, and Karen E. Cox. (2000). "Age and Political Attitudes in Japan: With a Nod to the United States." Paper presented at the conference "Losing Faith in Politics," Quebec City, August.

Carlson, Matthew M. (2006). "Electoral Reform and the Costs of Personal Support in Japan." *Journal of East Asian Studies* 6, no. 2: 233–258.

Carmines, Edward G., and James A. Stimson. (1989). *Issue Evolution: Race and the Transformation of American Politics.* Princeton: Princeton University Press.

"Chiisana seifuni NPO no chikara wo." (2000, February 7). *Asahi Shimbun*, p. 13.

Childs, Sarah, and Mona Lena Krook. (2006). "Should Feminists Give Up on Critical Mass? A Contingent Yes." *Politics and Gender* 2, no. 4: 522–530.

Cho, Kangi. (1993). "Nihon no Rieki Haibun Seisaku to Jiminto no Shihai." *Senkyo Kenkyu* 8: 66–84.

Christensen, Ray. (1996). "The New Japanese Electoral System." *Pacific Affairs* 69, no. 1: 50–70.

———. (1998). "The Effects of Electoral Reforms on Campaign Practices in Japan: Putting New Wine into Old Bottles." *Asian Survey* 38: 986–1004.

———. (2000a). *Ending the LDP Hegemony: Party Cooperation in Japan.* Honolulu: University of Hawaii Press.

———. (2000b). "The Impact of Electoral Rules in Japan." In Rose J. Lee and Cal Clark (eds.), *Democracy and the Status of Women in East Asia*, pp. 25–46. Boulder: Lynne Rienner.

"Citizens and Elected Officials Can Work Together." (2003, April 28). *Asahi Shimbun.* Retrieved May 22, 2007, from www.newsbank.com.

Cox, Gary W. (1997). *Making Votes Count: Strategic Coordination in the World's Electoral Systems.* Cambridge: Cambridge University Press.

Crozier, Michael, Samuel. P. Huntington, Joji Watanuki, and Trilateral Commission. (1975). *The Crisis of Democracy: Report on the Governability of Democracies to the Trilateral Commission.* New York: New York University Press.

Curtis, Gerald L. (1971). *Election Campaigning, Japanese Style.* New York: Columbia University Press.

———. (1988). *The Japanese Way of Politics.* New York: Columbia University Press.

———. (1999). *The Logic of Japanese Politics.* New York: Columbia University Press.

Dahlerup, Drude. (2006). "The Story of Critical Mass." *Politics and Gender* 2, no. 4: 511–522.

Dahlerup, Drude, ed. (2006). "Introduction." In *Women, Quotas and Politics*, pp. 3–31. London: Routledge.

Dalton, Russell J. (1999). "Political Support in Advanced Industrial Democracies." In Pippa Norris (ed.), *Critical Citizens: Global Support for Democratic Governance*, pp. 57–77. New York: Oxford University Press.

———. (2000). "The Decline of Party Identifications." In Russell J. Dalton and Martin P. Wattenberg (eds.), *Parties Without Partisans: Political Change in*

Advanced Industrial Democracies, pp. 19–36. New York: Oxford University Press.
Darcy, R., Charles D. Hadley, and Jason R. Kirksey. (1993). "Election Systems and the Representation of Black Women in American State Legislatures." *Women and Politics* 13, no. 2: 73–89.
Darcy, R., and David L. Nixon. (1996). "Women in the 1946 and 1993 Japanese House of Representatives Elections: The Role of the Election System." *Journal of Northeast Asian Studies* 15, no. 1: 3–19.
de Figueiredo, Rui. (2002). "Electoral Competition, Political Uncertainty, and Policy Insulation." *American Political Science Review* 96, no. 2: 321–333.
Diamond, Larry, and Leonardo Morlino. (2004). "An Overview." *Journal of Democracy* 15, no. 4: 20–31.
Domoto, Akiko. (2000). "NPO hou no rippou katei." In Hiroyuki Torigoe (ed.), *Kankyou borantia: NPO no shakaigaku*, pp. 164–174. Tokyo: Shinyousha.
Downs, Anthony. (1957). *An Economic Theory of Democracy*. New York: Harper.
Duverger, Maurice. (1954). *Political Parties: Their Organization and Activity in the Modern State*. New York: Wiley.
Eguchi, Seizaburo. (1999). "Chiho gikai to shimin sanka." *Toshi Mondai* 90, no. 2: 25–36.
"Election 2005—Showdown Over Reform / Poll: LDP Support Growing Among Swing Voters." (2005, September 9). *Yomiuri Shimbun*, online edition.
Feddersen, Timothy. (1992). "A Voting Model Implying Duverger's Law and Positive Turnout." *American Journal of Political Science* 36, no. 4: 938–962.
Feddersen, Timothy, Itai Sened, and Stephan Wright. (1990). "Rational Voting and Candidate Entry Under Plurality Rule." *American Journal of Political Science* 34, no. 4: 1005–1016.
Flanagan, Scott C. (1980). "National and Local Voting Trends: Cross-level Linkages and Correlates of Change." In Kurt Steiner, Ellis Krauss, and Scott C. Flanagan (eds.), *Political Opposition and Local Politics in Japan*, pp. 131–184. Princeton: Princeton University Press.
———. (1991). "The Changing Japanese Voter and the 1989 and 1990 Elections." In Scott C. Flanagan et al. (eds.), *The Japanese Voter*, pp. 431–468. New Haven: Yale University Press.
Flanagan, Scott C., and Bradley M. Richardson. (1977). *Japanese Electoral Behavior: Social Cleavages, Social Networks, and Partisanship*. London: Sage Publications.
Flanagan, Scott C., Kurt Steiner, and Ellis S. Krauss. (1980). "The Partisan Politicization of Local Government: Causes and Consequences." In Kurt Steiner, Ellis Krauss, and Scott C. Flanagan (eds.), *Political Opposition and Local Politics in Japan*, pp. 427–469. Princeton: Princeton University Press.
Foljanty-Jost, Gesine, and Carmen Schmidt. (2006). "Local-level Political and Institutional Changes in Japan: An End to Political Alienation?" *Asia Europe Journal* 4: 381–397.
Foreign Press Center Japan. (2005a). "Prime Minister Koizumi Calls General Election After Upper House Rejects Postal Privatization Bills." *Japan Brief* No. 562, August 10. Retrieved June 2, 2006, from www.fpcj.jp/e/mres/japanbrief/jb_562.html.
———. (2005b). "Postal Reform Bills Narrowly Passed by the Lower House, but the Political Situation Might Get Unstable." *Japan Brief* No. 549, July 11. Retrieved June 2, 2006, from www.fpcj.jp/e/mres/japanbrief/jb_549.html.
———. (2007). "Women." In *Facts and Figures of Japan 2007*. Retrieved May 23, 2007, from http://fpcj.jp/old/e/mres/publication/ff/index_07.html.

Fuchs, Dieter, and Hans-Dieter Klingemann. (1995). "Citizens and the State: A Changing Relationship?" In H.-D. Klingemann and D. Fuchs (eds.), *Citizens and the State: Beliefs in Government,* vol. 1, pp. 1–24. Oxford: Oxford University Press.
Funabashi, Kuniko. (2004). "The History and Future of Women's Participation in Politics in Japan." *Voices from Japan* 13: 27–31. Retrieved June 24, 2007, from www.ajwrc.org/english/sub/voice/13-2-2.pdf.
Gender Equality Bureau, Cabinet Office, Government of Japan. (2007). *Gender Equality in Japan 2007.* Retrieved June 24, 2007, from www.gender.go.jp/.
Gotoda, Teruo. (1985). *The Local Politics of Kyoto.* Berkeley: Institute of East Asian Studies, University of California.
Grey, Sandra. (2006). "Numbers and Beyond: The Relevance of Critical Mass in Gender Research." *Politics and Gender* 2: 492–502.
Hasegawa, Yuki. (2000, September 18). "Souyotou kensei 'min' ga hanki: Nagano chijisen—Tanaka-shi nanori de konsen moyou: 'kenchou OB shihai' 40 nen, jimoto zaikai kara mo fuman." *Asahi Shimbun,* p. 3.
Hashimoto, Hiroko. (2001). "State of the Women in Urban Local Government in Japan." Retrieved April 15, 2006, from www.unescap.org/huset/women/reports/japan.pdf.
Hasunuma, Linda Choi. (2002). "Electoral Rules and the Gender Gap in Representation: Evidence from Japan." Paper presented at the annual meeting of the American Political Science Association, Boston, August.
Hayao, Kenji. (1993). *The Japanese Prime Minister and Public Policy.* Pittsburgh: Pittsburgh University Press.
Hickman, John C. (1997). "The Candidacy and Election of Women in Japanese SNTV Electoral Systems." *Women and Politics* 18, no. 2: 1–26.
Hirashita, Osamu. (2006). *Nihon Rettou Deetamappu.* Tokyo: Daiyamondosha.
Horiuchi, Yusaku. (2005). *Institutions, Incentives and Electoral Participation in Japan: Cross-level and Cross-national Perspectives.* London: Routledge Curzon.
Horiuchi, Yusaku, and Jun Saito. (2003a). "Reapportionment and Redistribution: Consequences of Electoral Reform in Japan." *American Journal of Political Science* 47: 669–682.
———. (2003b). "Senkyoseido Kaikaku ni Tomonau Giinteisuu haibun kakusa no Zesei to Hojyokin haibun kakusa no Zesei." *Leviathan* 32: 29–49.
Horiuchi, Yusaku, Jun Saito, Ethan Scheiner, and Robert J. Weiner. (2001). "Building an Infrastructure for Local Democracy Research: A Japanese Local Election Data Base." Unpublished manuscript.
Hrebenar, Ronald J. (2000). *Japan's New Party System.* Boulder: Westview Press.
Hsieh, John Fuh-sheng, and Richard G. Niemi. (1999). "Can Duverger's Law Be Extended to SNTV? The Case of Taiwan's Legislative Yuan Elections." *Electoral Studies* 18, no. 1: 101–116.
Ibaraki Prefecture. (2007). "Kengikai giin meibo (ichiran)." Retrieved May 2007, from www.pref.ibaraki.jp/gikai/.
Ichikawa, Taiichi. (1990). *"Seshu" Daigishi no Kenkyu.* Tokyo: Nihon Keizai Shimbun Sha.
Ichikawa Fusae Kinenkai. (2003). *Zen chiho gikai josei giin no genjo: josei sansei shiryoshu 2003-nen ban* (Local Assemblies, Handbook of Data on Japanese Women in Political Life, 2003). Tokyo: Ichikawa Fusae Kinenkai Shuppanbu.
Igarashi, Akio. (2003). "Chokusetsu minshushugi no atarashii nami—jī min tohyo:

maki machi no rei wo chushin ni." In Michitoshi Takabatake (ed.), *Gendai shimin seiji ron*, pp. 139–170. Yokohama: Seori shob.
Iio, Jun. (1993). *Min'eika no seijikatei: Rincho-gata kaikaku no seika to genkai*. Tokyo: Tokyo Daigaku Shuppankai.
Imai, Hajime. (1997). *Jumin tohyo: niju seikimatsu ni meueta nihon no shin ruru*. Osaka: Nikkei Osaka PR.
———. (1999). *Jumin tohyo Q & A*. Tokyo: Iwanami bukkuretto.
Inoguchi, Takashi, and Tomoaki Iwai. (1987). *Zoku giin no kenkyu*. Tokyo: Nihon Keizai Shimbunsha.
Inter-Parliamentary Union. (2007). "Women in National Parliaments." Retrieved May 22, 2007, from www.ipu.org/wmn-e/classif.htm.
Ishibashi, Michihiro, and Steven R. Reed. (1992). "Second-Generation Diet Members and Democracy in Japan: Hereditary Seats." *Asian Survey* 32: 366–379.
Iwai, Tomoaki. (1990). *Seiji Shikin no Kenkyu*. Tokyo: Nihon Keizai Shimbun Sha.
———. (2003, January 21). "Giin no Seshu, Jiminto de 4 wari ijo." *The Economist*.
Iwamoto, Misako. (2001). "The Madonna Boom: The Progress of Japanese Women into Politics in the 1980s." *PS: Political Science and Politics* 34, no. 2: 225–226.
Izumi, Hiroshi. (2005). "Koizumi Stakes All on Snap 'Postal Election.'" *Japan Echo* 32, no. 5 (October 10): 42–46.
Jain, Purnendra. (1999). "Japan's 1999 Unified Local Elections: Electing Tokyo's Governor." *Japanese Studies* 19, no. 2: 117–131.
———. (2000). "Jumin Tohyo and the Tokushima Anti-dam Movement in Japan." *Asian Survey* 40, no. 4: 551–570.
Jaquette, Jane S. (2001). "Women and Democracy: Regional Differences and Contrasting Views." *Journal of Democracy* 12, no. 3: 111–125.
Japan NPO Center. (n.d.). "NPO Q&A." Retrieved February 6, 2006, from www.jnpoc.ne.jp.
"Jiminto Asshou '296' yotou 3 bun no 2 chou . . . yuseihou anseiritsu." *Yomiuri Shimbun* (2005, September 12). Retrieved January 24, 2008 from http://www.yomiuri.co.jp/election2005/.
Jiyuu Minshutou. (2004). "LDP shimin katsudou NET." Retrieved March 28, 2006, from www.jimin.jp/jimin/npo/shiryo/naikaku.html.
Johnson, Chalmers. (1989a). *MITI and the Japanese Miracle: The Growth of Industrial Policy, 1925–1975*. Stanford: Stanford University Press.
———. (1989b). "MITI, MPT, and the Telecom Wars: How Japan Makes Policy for High Technology." In Chalmers Johnson, Laura D'Andrea Tyson, and John Zysman (eds.), *Politics and Productivity: How Japan's Development Strategy Works*, pp. 177–240. New York: Harper Business.
———. (1995). *Japan: Who Governs? The Rise of the Developmental State*. New York: W.W. Norton.
Kabashima, Ikuo. (1999). "An Ideological Survey of Japan's National Legislators." *Japan Echo* 26, no. 4: 9–16.
Kabashima, Ikuo, Jonathan Marshall, Takayoshi Vekami, and Dae-Song Hyun. (2000). "Causal Cynics, or Disillusioned Democrats? Political Alienation in Japan." *Political Psychology* 21, no. 4: 779–804.
Kabashima, Ikuo, and Yoshihiko Takenaka. (1996). *Gendai Nihonjin no Ideorogi*. Tokyo: Tokyo Daigaku Shuppankai.
Kabashima Ikuo Seminar. (2000a). *Gendai Nihon no Seijika Zo* (1990–1998). Vol. 1. Tokyo: Bokutaku Sha.

———. (2000b). *Gendai Nihon no Seijika Zo (1990–1998)*. Vol. 2. Tokyo: Bokutaku Sha.
Kanter, Rosabeth Moss. (1977). "Some Effects of Proportions on Group Life: Skewed Sex Ratios and Reponses to Token Women." *American Journal of Sociology* 82, no. 5: 965–990.
Katz, Richard S., and Peter Mair. (1995). "Changing Models of Party Organization and Party Democracy: The Emergence of the Cartel Party." *Party Politics* 1, no. 1: 5–28.
Kawabata, Eiji. (2001). "Sanction Power, Jurisdiction, and Economic Policy-making: Explaining Contemporary Telecommunications Policy in Japan." *Governance* 14, no. 4: 399–427.
———. (2004). "Dual Governance: The Contemporary Politics of Posts and Telecommunications in Japan." *Social Science Japan Journal* 7, no. 1: 21–39.
Kawashima, Nobuko. (2005). "The Governance of Not-for-Profit Organizations in Japan and the US: Nonprofit Corporation Laws and Issues for Reform." *The Nonprofit Review* 5, no. 1: 1–11.
Keizai Kikaku Chou. (2000). "Kokumin seikatsu hakusho—borantia ga fukameru kouen." Retrieved May 27, 2006, from www.cao.go.jp/j-j/wp-pl/wp-pl00/hakusho-00-1-51.html.
Kensei Shiryo Hensan Kai. (1978). *Rekidai Kakuryo to Kokkai Giin Meikan*. Tokyo: Life.
Klingemann, Hans-Dieter. (1999). "Mapping Political Support in the 1990s." In P. Norris (ed.), *Critical Citizens: Global Support for Democratic Government*. New York: Oxford University Press.
Kobayashi, Yoshiaki. (1985). *Keiryo Seijigaku*. Tokyo: Seibundo.
———. (1990). "Chiho Jichitai no Zaisei o Meguru Seijigaku." *Leviathan* 6: 69–92.
———. (1996). "The Electoral Process: How Does It Contribute to the Promotion of Local Autonomy in Japan?" *Policy Research* 9, no. 12. Tokyo: National Institute for Research Advancement.
———. (1997). *Gendai Nihon no Seiji Katei*. Tokyo: Tokyo University Press.
Kohei, Shinsaku, Ichiro Miyake, and Joji Watanuki. (1991). "Issues and Voting Behavior." In Scott C. Flanagan et al. (eds.), *The Japanese Voter*, pp. 267–296. New Haven: Yale University Press.
Kohno, Masaru. (1997). *Japan's Postwar Party Politics*. Princeton: Princeton University Press.
"Koizumi Gekijo ha owari minshu hantenkousei wo kyochou." (2005, September 5). *Yomiuri Shimbun*. Retrieved January 24, 2008, from www.yomiuri.co.jp/election2005/news/20050905ia02.htm.
Kokusai Mondai Chosakai. (1994). *Nihon no Naikaku*. Tokyo: Kokusei Mondai Chosakai.
Krauss, Ellis S. (1998). "Changing Television News and Politics in Japan." *Journal of Asian Studies* 57, no. 3: 663–692.
———. (2000). "Local Politics in Japan: Welcoming the Third Wave." In Sheila A. Smith (ed.), *Local Voices, National Issues: The Impact of Local Initiative in Japanese Policy-making*, pp. 1–8. Ann Arbor: Center for Japanese Studies, University of Michigan.
Krauss, Ellis S., and Takeshi Ishida. (1989). "Japanese Democracy in Perspective." In Takeshi Ishida and Ellis Krauss (eds.), *Democracy in Japan*, pp. 327–342. Pittsburgh: University of Pittsburgh Press.
Krauss, Ellis S., and Benjamin Nyblade. (2004). "'Presidentialization' in Japan? The Prime Minister, Media and Elections in Japan." *British Journal of Political Science* 34: 357–368.

Krauss, Ellis S., Benjamin Nyblade, and Robert Pekkanen. (2007). "The Logic of Ministerial Selection: Electoral Reform, Party Goals, and Choosing Cabinet Ministers in Japan." Unpublished manuscript.

Krauss, Ellis S., and Robert Pekkanen. (2004). "Explaining Party Adaptation to Electoral Reform: The Discreet Charm of the LDP?" *Journal of Japanese Studies* 30, no. 1: 1–34.

Kyodo Tsushinsha. (2007, April 23). "Chosongi, josei wa 8% somusho ga kaihyo kekkan happyo." Retrieved May 26, 2007, from http://topics.kyodo.co.jp/feature47/archives/2007/04/post_140.html.

Laakso, Marku, and Rein Taagepera. (1979). "Effective Number of Parties: A Measure with Application to West Europe." *Comparative Political Studies* 12, no. 1: 3–27.

Lam, Peng Er. (2005). "Local Governance: The Role of Referenda and the Rise of Independent Governors." In Glenn Hook (ed.), *Contested Governance in Japan: Sites and Issues*, pp. 71–89. New York: Routledge Curzon.

LeBlanc, Robin. 1999. *Bicycle Citizens: The Political World of the Japanese Housewife*. Berkeley: University of California Press.

Levi, Margaret. (1998). "A State of Trust." In Valerie Braithwaite and Margaret Levi (eds.), *Trust and Governance*, pp. 77–101. New York: Russell Sage Foundation.

Mabuchi, M. (2001). "Municipal Amalgamations." In M. Muramatsu, F. Iqbal, and I. Kume (eds.), *Local Government Development in Post-war Japan*, pp. 185–205. Oxford: Oxford University Press.

MacDougall, Terry. (2001). *Towards Political Inclusiveness: The Changing Role of Local Government in Japan*. Washington, DC: The World Bank. Retrieved June 24, 2007, from http://siteresources.worldbank.org/WBI/Resources/wbi37169.pdf.

Machidori, Satoshi. (2005). "The 1990s Reforms Have Transformed Japanese Politics." *Japan Echo* 32, no. 3 (June): 38–43.

Maclachlan, Patricia L. (2004). "Post Office Politics in Modern Japan: The Postmasters, Iron Triangles, and the Limits of Reform." *Journal of Japanese Studies* 30, no. 2: 303–313.

"Make Your Vote Count in Shaping Communities." (2003, April 24). *Asahi Shimbun*. Retrieved May 23, 2007, from www.newsbank.com.

Manin, Bernard. (1997). *The Principles of Representative Government*. New York: Cambridge University Press.

Manin, Bernard, Adam Przeworski, and Susan C. Stokes. (1999). "Introduction." In A. Przeworski, S. C. Stokes, and B. Manin (eds.), *Cambridge Studies in the Theory of Democracy*. New York: Cambridge University Press.

Massey, Joseph A. (1975). "The Missing Leader: Japanese Youths' View of Political Authority." *American Political Science Review* 69, no. 1: 31–48.

Matsuzaki, Tetsuhisa. (1991). *Nihongata Democracy no Gyakusetsu: Nisei Giin wa naze umareru no ka*. Tokyo: Toju Sha.

McKean, Margaret A., and Ethan Scheiner. (2000). "Japan's New Electoral System: La plus ça Change . . ." *Electoral Studies* 19: 447–477.

———. (2006). "Japan's Electoral System After Reform: Is It Indeed 'La plus ça change . . .'?" Paper presented at the annual meeting of the Association of Asian Studies, San Francisco, April.

Ministry of Internal Affairs and Communications. (2005a). "Members of Local Assemblies 1976, 1980–2005." Retrieved May 30, 2007, from http://winet.nwec.jp/cgi-bin/toukei/load/bin/tk_search.cgi.

———. (2005b). "Candidates and Persons Elected in Ordinary Elections for the

House of Councilors by Sex (1946–2003)." *Historical Statistics of Japan.* Retrieved May 30, 2007, from www.stat.go.jp/english/data/chouki/27.html.

———. (2005c). "Persons Elected and Votes Polled by Political Parties of Ordinary Elections for the House of Councilors by Sex (1958–2004)." *Historical Statistics of Japan.* Retrieved May 30, 2007, from www.stat.go.jp/english/data/chouki/27.html.

Minshuto Yusei Kaikaku Chosakai. (2005). *Yusei Kaikaku ni Kansuru Kangaekata.* Retrieved from www.eda-jp.com/dpj/2005/050329.

Mitsui, Mariko. (2003). "Advances in Politics by Women." *DAWN Newsletter of the DAWN CENTER.* Retrieved May 23, 2007, from www.dawncenter.or.jp/english/publication/edawn/0012/advances.html.

Miyake, Ichiro, Tomio Kinoshita, and Juichi Aiba. (1967). *Kotonaru reberu no senkyo ni okeru tohyo kodo no kenkyu.* Tokyo: Sobunsha.

Miyazaki, Jamie. (2003, November 12). "Japan: Two's a Party, Three's a Crowd." *Asia Times,* online edition.

Molinar, Juan. (1991). "Counting the Number of Parties: An Alternative Index." *American Political Science Review* 85, no. 4: 1383-1392.

Mori, Hiroki, and Yutaka Tsujinaka. (2002). "Katsudouchiikibetsuni mita dantai no zonritsu-koudou youshiki." In Yutaka Tsujinaka (ed.), *Gendai Nihon no Shiminshakai—Rieki Dantai.* Tokyo: Bokutakusha.

Mulgan, Aurelia George. (2000). "Japan's Political Leadership Deficit." *Australian Journal of Political Science* 35, no. 2: 183–202.

———. (2003). "Japan's 'Un-Westminster' System: Impediments to Reform in a Crisis Economy." *Government and Opposition* 38, no. 1: 73–91.

Müller, Wolfgang C., and Kaare Strøm. (eds.). (1990). *Policy, Office or Votes?* Cambridge: Cambridge University Press.

Murakami, Asako. (2001, April 17). "Women Stride Toward Parity in Shimamoto Assembly Poll." *Japan Times.* Retrieved May 23, 2007, from http://search.japantimes.co.jp/cgi-bin/nn20010417a3.html.

Muramatsu, Michio. (1987). "In Search of National Identity: The Politics and Policies of the Nakasone Administration." In Kenneth B. Pyle (ed.), *The Trade Crisis: How Will Japan Respond?* pp. 219–221. Seattle: Society for Japanese Studies.

Muramatsu, Michio, and Ellis S. Krauss. (1987). "The Conservative Policy Line and the Development of Patterned Pluralism." In K. Yamamura and Y. Yasuba (eds.), *The Political Economy of Japan. Volume 1: The Domestic Transformation,* pp. 536–554. Stanford: Stanford University Press.

Natori, Ryota. (2002). "Senkyo Seido Kaikaku to Rieki Yudo Seiji." *Senkyo Kenkyu* 17.

Nemoto, Kuniaki, Ellis Krauss, and Robert Pekkanen. (forthcoming). "Policy Defection and Party Discipline: The July 2005 Vote on Postal Privatization in Japan." *British Journal of Political Science.*

Newton, Kenneth, and Pippa Norris. (2000). "Confidence in Public Institutions: Faith, Culture, or Performance?" In S. J. Pharr and R. D. Putnam (eds.), *Disaffected Democracies: What's Troubling the Trilateral Countries?* Princeton: Princeton University Press.

Nichigai Associates. (1999). *Gendai Seijika Jinmei Jiten.* Tokyo: Nichigai Associates.

Niemi, Richard G., and John Fuh-sheng Hsieh. (2002). "Counting Candidates: An Alternative to the Effective N (With an Application to the $M+1$ Rule in Japan)." *Party Politics* 8, no. 1: 75–99.

Nihon Keizai Shimbun. (2002–2004). Various articles.
———. (2005, August 30). Pp. 1, 3–4.
Noble, Gregory W. (2005). "Stealth Populism: Administrative Reform in Japan." Paper presented at the conference "The Repositioning of Public Governance: Global Experience and Challenges," Taipei, November.
Nomoto, Yuji. (2006). "Municipal Mergers in Japan." Report presented at an OECD workshop titled "Performance Indicators and Local Government Collaboration," May 19, 2006. Retrieved May 24, 2007, from www.oecd.org/dataoecd/57/61/38270172.pdf.
Norris, Pippa. (2001). "Confidence in Australia's Democracy." In M. Sawer (ed.), *Elections: Full, Free and Fair*, pp. 202–215. Sydney: The Federation Press.
———. (2002). *Democratic Phoenix: Reinventing Political Activism.* New York: Cambridge University Press.
———. (ed.). (2004). *Australian Democracy in Comparative Context.* Melbourne: Allen & Unwin.
Norris, Pippa, and Ronald Inglehart. (2005). "Women as Political Leaders Worldwide: Cultural Barriers and Opportunities." In Sue Thomas and Clyde Wilcox (eds.), *Women and Elective Office: Past, Present, and Future.* New York: Oxford University Press.
North, Christopher T. (2005). "From Technocracy to Aristocracy: The Changing Career Paths of Japanese Politicians." *Journal of East Asian Studies* 5: 239–272.
Noumi, Yasushi. (1997). "Koekiteki dantai ni okeru koekisei to hierisei." *Juristo* 1105: 50–55.
Numata, Chieko. (2006). "Checking the Center: Popular Referenda in Japan." *Social Science Japan Journal* 9, no. 1: 19–31.
Ogai, Tokuko. (2001). "Japanese Women and Political Institutions: Why Are Women Politically Underrepresented?" *PS: Political Science and Politics* 34, no. 2: 207–210.
———. (2004). "Advancement of Japanese Women in Politics: The General Local Election of 2003." *PS: Political Science and Politics* 37, no. 2: 58–59.
Ogawa, Akihiro. (2004). "Invited by the State: Institutionalizing Volunteer Subjectivity in Contemporary Japan." *Asian Anthropology* 3: 71–96.
"Osaka-fu chiji ni Oota-shi saisen, Emoto-shi-ra yaburu: touhyouritsu kako saitei." (2004, February 2). *Asahi Shimbun*, online edition.
Osawa, Mari. (2000). "Government Approaches to Gender Equality in the Mid-1990s." *Social Science Japan Journal* 3, no. 1: 3–19.
Osborne, Martin. (1993). "Candidate Positioning and Entry in a Political Competition." *Games and Economic Behavior* 5, no. 1: 133–151.
Ota, Hiroko. (1999). "Sharing Governance: Changing Functions of Government, Business, and NPOs." In Tadashi Yamamoto (ed.), *Deciding the Public Good: Governance and Civil Society in Japan.* Tokyo: Japan Center for International Exchange.
Otake, Hideo. (1998). "How a Diet Member's Koenkai Adapts to Social and Political Changes." In Hideo Otake (ed.), *How Electoral Reform Boomeranged: Continuity in Japanese Campaigning Style.* Tokyo: Japan Center for International Exchange.
———. (2000). "Political Realignment and Policy Conflict." In Hideo Otake (ed.), *Power Shuffles and Policy Processes,* pp. 125–151. Japan: Japan Center for International Exchange.
Otake, Hideo, ed. *How Electoral Reform Boomeranged: Continuity in Japanese*

Campaigning Style. Tokyo and New York: Japan Center for International Exchange, 1998.

Otsuru, C. K. (2004). "Incorporating Gender Equality in Local Politics: The Case of Toyonaka." *PS: Political Science and Politics* 37, no. 1: 58.

Pacek, Alexander, and Benjamin Radcliff. (1995). "The Political Economy of Competitive Elections in the Developing World." *American Journal of Political Science* 39, no. 3: 745–759.

"Package of Redistricting Bills Approved by Lower House." (2002, 19 July). *Japan Times*, online edition. Retrieved January 24, 2008 from http://search.japantimes.co.jp/cgi-bin/nn20020719b2.html.

Park, Cheol Hee. (1998a). "The Enduring Campaign Networks of Tokyo's Shitamachi District." In Hideo Otake (ed.), *How Electoral Reform Boomeranged*, pp. 56–96. New York: Japan Center for International Exchange.

———. (1998b). "Electoral Strategies in Urban Japan: How Institutional Change Affects Strategic Choices." Ph.D. dissertation, Columbia University, 1998, UMI Dissertation Services.

Pekkanen, Robert. (2000). "Japan's New Politics: The Case of the NPO Law." *Journal of Japanese Studies* 26, no. 1: 111–148.

———. (2003). "Molding Japanese Civil Society: State-Structured Incentives and the Patterning of Civil Society." In Frank J. Schwartz and Susan J. Pharr (eds.), *The State of Civil Society in Japan*, pp. 116–134. New York: Cambridge University Press.

———. (2004a). "After the Developmental State: Civil Society in Japan." *Journal of East Asian Studies* 4: 363–388.

———. (2004b). "Japan: Social Capital Without Advocacy." In Muthiah Alagappa (ed.), *Civil Society and Political Change in Asia*, pp. 223–255. Stanford: Stanford University Press.

———. (2006). *Japan's Dual Civil Society: Members Without Advocates.* Stanford: Stanford University Press.

Pekkanen, Robert, Benjamin Nyblade, and Ellis S. Krauss. (2006). "Electoral Incentives in Mixed Member Systems: Party, Posts, and Zombie Politicians in Japan." *American Political Science Review* 100, no. 2: 183–193.

———. (2007). "Where Have All the Zoku Gone? Electoral Reform and MP Policy Specialization in Japan." Paper presented at the annual meeting of the Midwest Political Science Association, Chicago, April.

Pempel, T. J. (1982). *Policy and Politics in Japan: Creative Conservatism.* Philadelphia: Temple University Press.

Pharr, Susan. (1997). "Public Trust and Democracy in Japan." In Joseph S. Nye Jr., Philip D. Zelikow, and David C. King (eds.), *Why People Don't Trust Government,* pp. 237–252. Cambridge: Harvard University Press.

Pharr, Susan J., and Robert D. Putnam. (2000). *Disaffected Democracies: What's Troubling the Trilateral Countries?* Princeton: Princeton University Press.

Pierson, Paul. (2004). "Positive Feedback and Path Dependence." In Paul Pierson, *Politics in Time: History, Institutions, and Social Analysis*, pp. 17–53. Princeton: Princeton University Press.

Powell, G. Bingham Jr., and Guy D. Whitten. (1993). "A Cross-national Analysis of Economic Voting: Taking Account of the Political Context." *American Journal of Political Science* 37: 391–414.

Ramseyer, J. Mark, and Frances McCall Rosenbluth. (1993). *Japan's Political Marketplace.* Cambridge: Harvard University Press.

"Record High Proportion of Women Wins Seats in Local Assembly." (2001, April 23). *Japan Policy and Politics*. Retrieved May 23, 2007, from http://findarticles.com/p/articles/mi_m0XPQ/is_2001_April_23/ai_73597798

Reed, Steven R. (1990). "Structure and Behaviour: Extending Duverger's Law to the Japanese Case." *British Journal of Political Science* 20, no. 3: 335–356.

———. (ed.). (2003). *Japanese Electoral Politics: Creating a New Party System*. New York: Routledge Courzon.

Reed, Steven R., and Kay Shimizu. (2007). "Measuring Competitiveness in Multi-Member Districts." Paper presented at the Stanford Conference on Japanese Politics, Stanford, CA, June 11–12.

Reed, Steven R., and Michael F. Thies. (2001). "The Consequences of Electoral Reform in Japan." In Matthew Soberg Shugart and Martin P. Wattenberg (eds.), *Mixed-Member Electoral Systems: The Best of Both Worlds?* pp. 381–403. Oxford: Oxford University Press.

Richardson, Bradley M. (1991). "Japanese Voting Behavior in Comparative Perspective." In S. C. Flanagan et al. (eds.), *The Japanese Voter*, pp. 3–48. New Haven: Yale University Press.

Rose, Richard, Doh. C. Shin, and Neil Munro. (1999). "Tensions Between the Democratic Ideal and Reality: South Korea." In Pippa Norris (ed.), *Critical Citizens: Global Support for Democratic Government*, pp. 146–168. Oxford: Oxford University Press.

Rule, Wilma. (1994). "Women's Underrepresentation and Electoral Systems." *PS: Political Science and Politics* 27, no. 4: 689–692.

Salamon, Lester M., and S. Wojciech Sokolowski. (2004). "Global Civil Society: An Overview." In Lester M. Salamon, Helmut K. Anheier, Regina List, Stefan Toepler, S. Wojciech Sokolwski, and Associates (eds.), *Global Civil Society: Dimensions of the Nonprofit Sector*, pp. 1–64. Vol. 2. Bloomfield, CT: Kumarian Press.

Sato, Atsushi. (1999). "Bunken shakai: seijuku shakai no shimin sanka." *Toshi mondai* 90, no. 2: 3–14.

Sato, Iwao. (2006). "Kokka shakai kankei: shimin sekutaa no hatten to minkan hieiri housei." In Institute of Social Science, University of Tokyo (ed.), *Ushinawareta 10-nen wokote*. Tokyo: University of Tokyo Press.

Sato, Seizaburo, and Tetsuhisa Matsuzaki. (1986). *Jiminto seiken*. Tokyo: Chuo Koronsha.

Scheiner, Ethan. (1999). "Urban Outfitters: City-based Strategies and Success in Postwar Japanese Politics." *Electoral Studies* 18, no. 2: 179–198.

———. (2005). "Pipelines of Pork: A Model of Local Opposition Party Failure." *Comparative Political Studies* 38: 799–823.

———. (2006). *Democracy Without Competition in Japan: Opposition Failure in a One-Party Dominant State*. New York: Cambridge University Press.

Schoppa, Leonard. (2001). "Locating the LDP and Koizumi in Policy Space: A Party System Ripe for Realignment." *Social Science Japan* 22: 9–15.

Schwartz, Frank J., and Susan Pharr (eds.). (2003). *The State of Civil Society in Japan*. Cambridge: Cambridge University Press.

Seligmann, Albert L. (1997). "Japan's New Electoral System: Has Anything Changed? *Asian Survey* 37, no. 5: 409–428.

Shimizu, Shuji. (1999). *Nimbii shindoromu wo ko: meiwaku shisetsu no seiji to keizai*. Tokyo: Tokyo Shimbun Shuppankyoku.

Shinoda, Tomohito. (2000). *Leading Japan: The Role of the Prime Minister*. Westport, CT: Praeger.

Shugart, Matthew Soberg, and Martin P. Wattenberg. (2001a). "Introduction: The Electoral Reform of the Twenty-first Century?" In Matthew Soberg Shugart and Martin P. Wattenberg (eds.), *Mixed-Member Electoral Systems: The Best of Both Worlds?* pp. 1–6. Oxford: Oxford University Press.

———. (2001b). "Conclusion: Are Mixed-Member Systems the Best of Both Worlds?" In Matthew Soberg Shugart and Martin P. Wattenberg (eds.), *Mixed-Member Electoral Systems: The Best of Both Worlds?* pp. 571–596. Oxford: Oxford University Press.

Shugiin and Sangiin. (1960–1963). *Gikai Seido 70 nen shi.* Tokyo: Okurasho Insatsukyoku.

———. (1990). *Gikai Seido 100 nen shi.* Tokyo: Okurasho Insatsukyoku.

"Shugiin-sen kyu tukaihyu." Chart entitled, "7-tohu no saishûhi no enzetsu no temu betsu jikan haibun." (2005, September 11). *Mainichi Shimbun*, p. 1.

Smith, Sheila A. (2000). *Local Voices, National Issues: The Impact of Local Initiative in Japanese Policy-making.* Ann Arbor: University of Michigan Press.

"Sosenkyo 2005." (2005, September 11). *Mainichi Shimbun.* Online edition. Retrieved January 24, 2008, from www.yomiuri.co.jp/election2005/kaihyou/ya14.htm.

Squire, Peverill. (1989). "Competition and Uncontested Seats in U.S. House Elections." *Legislative Studies Quarterly* 14, no. 2: 281–295.

———. (2000). "Uncontested Seats in State Legislative Elections." *Legislative Studies Quarterly* 25, no. 1: 131–146.

Statistics Bureau and Statistical Research and Training Institute, Ministry of Internal Affairs and Telecommunications. (2004). "Government Employees and Elections." *Historical Statistics of Japan.* Retrieved June 22, 2007, from www.stat.go.jp/english/data/chouki/27.htm.

Steincr, K. (1965). *Local Government in Japan.* Stanford: Stanford University Press.

Strøm, Kaare. (1990). "A Behavioral Theory of Competitive Political Parties." *American Journal of Political Science* 34: 569–598.

Suleiman, Ezra. (2003). *Dismantling Democratic States.* Princeton: Princeton University Press.

Suzuki, Kenji. (1988, July 26). "Amerika no Erabareta Kizokutachi." *The Economist.*

———. (1989, July 3). "Nisei Giin Zoushoku de Tsuyomaru Seiji no Seshuka." *The Economist.*

Takabatake, Michitoshi. (1997). *Chiho no okoku.* Tokyo: Iwanami shoten.

Takabatake, Michitoshi, and Tsuneo Yasuda. (1997). *Mutohaso wo kangaeru: sono seiji ishiki to kodo.* Tokyo: Seori shobo.

Takayose, Shozo. (1999). "Shimin sanka to jichitai seisaku keisei." *Toshi mondai* 90, no. 2: 15–24.

Takenaka, Harukata. (2002). "Introducing Junior Ministers and Reforming the Diet in Japan." *Asian Survey* 42: 928–939.

———. (2003). "Democratic Deepening in Japan in the 1990s: How Can We Make Sense of a Series of Reforms of Political Institutions in the 1990s?" Paper presented at the "Convention on Contemporary Japanese Politics," Tokyo, October.

Tanaka, Aiji. (2001). "Nihon: Kochoku shita Kojinshudo gata Recruitment." In T. Yoshino et al. (eds.), *Dare ga Seijika ni naru no ka.* Tokyo: Waseda Daigaku Shuppanbu.

———. (2003). "Decline of Trust in the Japanese Party System, 1976–2001: Why

Has the LDP Stayed in Power? And What Is the Consequence?" *Waseda Political Studies* 35: 35–51.
Tanaka, Aiji, and Sherry Martin. (2003). "The New Independent Voter and the Evolving Japanese Party System." *Asian Perspective* 27, no. 3: 21–51.
Tanaka, Zenichiro. (1989, July 3). "Jiminto no Senkyo Seiji wo sasaeru Kojin Koen Kai." *The Economist*.
Taniguchi [Onizuka], Naoko. (1997). "Seifu no Hojyokin haibun ni okeru Seijiteki Youso ni tsuite." *Hogaku Seijigaku Ronkyu* 33: 297–318.
———. (2003). "Seshu Kohosha wo sasaeru Shinriteki Keizaiteki Kozo." Paper presented at the annual meeting of the Japan Electoral Studies Association, Kanazawa, May.
Tatebayashi, Masahiko. (2004). *Giin kodo no seiji keizai gaku*. Tokyo: Yuhikaku.
Tatebayashi, Masahiko, and Margaret McKean. (2002). "Vote Division and Policy Differentiation Strategies of LDP Members Under SNTV/MMD in Japan." Paper presented at the "Conference on Citizen-Elite Linkages," Durham, NC, March–April, and at the meeting of the Association of Asian Studies, Washington, DC, April.
Thayer, Nathaniel. (1969). *How the Conservatives Rule Japan*. Princeton: Princeton University Press.
Tokyo Metropolitan Government. (2001). "Shimin katsudou dantai no kyoudou ni kansuru ishiki chousa no gaiyou." Retrieved May 16, 2006, from www.seikatubunka.metro.tokyo.jp/index4file/ishiki-gaiyou.pdf.
———. (2005). "Tokutei hieiri katsudou houjin niizu chousa." Retrieved May 16, 2006, from www.seikatubunka.metro.tokyo.jp/index4files/niizutyousa.pdf.
Tsujinaka, Yutaka (ed.). (2002). *Gendai Nihon no Shiminshakai—Rieki Dantai*. Tokyo: Bokutakusha.
———. (2003). "From Development to Maturity: Japan's Civil Society Organizations in Comparative Perspective." In Frank J. Schwartz and Susan J. Pharr (eds.), *The State of Civil Society in Japan*, pp. 83–115. New York: Cambridge University Press.
"Urban-Rural Vote Disparity Narrows but Still Skewed." (2002, September 3). *Japan Times*. Retrieved from www.japantimes.co.jp/cgi-bin/getarticle.pl5?nn20020903b6.htm.
Vengroff, Richard, Zsolt Nyiri, and Melissa Fugiero. (2003). "Electoral System and Gender Representation in Sub-National Legislatures: Is There a Nation–Sub-National Gender Gap?" *Political Research Quarterly* 56, no. 2: 163–173.
Vogel, Steven K. (1996). *Freer Markets, More Rules: Regulatory Reforms in Advanced Industrial Countries*. Ithaca: Cornell University Press.
Wada, Hassoku, Akio Noro, Izumi Hoshino, and Aoki Muneaki. (1999). *Gendai no Chiho Zaisei*. Tokyo: Yuhikaku.
Watanabe, Noboru. (1997). "Chiho ni okeru 'shimin' no kanosei: Niigata-ken maki machi ni okeru shimin jichi no kokormi kara." *Toshi mondai* 88, no. 2: 3–22.
Watanuki, Joji. (1991). "Social Structure and Voting Behavior." In Scott C. Flanagan et al. (eds.), *The Japanese Voter*, pp. 49–83. New Haven: Yale University Press.
Weiner, Robert James. (2003). "Anti-competition in "Competitive" Party Systems." Ph.D. dissertation, University of California at Berkeley.
———. (2004). "'Mutoha chiji no nami' no shinwa." Paper presented at the annual meeting of the Japan Association for Comparative Politics.
Wildavsky, Aaron. (1959). "A Methodological Critique of Duverger's *Political Parties*." *Journal of Politics* 21, no. 2: 303–318.
Wilson, James Q. (1989). *Bureaucracy: What Government Agencies Do and Why They Do It*. New York: Basic Books.

Woodall, Brian. (1999). "The Politics of Reform in Japan's Lower House Electoral System." In B. Grofman et al. (eds.), *Elections in Japan, Korea, and Taiwan Under the Single Non-transferable Vote: The Comparative Study of an Embedded Institution*, pp. 23–50. Ann Arbor: University of Michigan Press.

Yamada, Masahiro. (1998). "Nukaga Fukushiro: Climbing the Ladder to Influence." In Hideo Otake (ed.), *How Electoral Reform Boomeranged*, pp. 33–58. Tokyo: Japan Center for International Exchange.

Yamauchi, Naoto. (2005). "Shibirusosaetii o sokuteisuru." *Koukyou Seisaku Kenkyuu* 5: 53–67.

Yomiuri Shinbun Seijibu. (2003). *Horitsu ha koshite umareta: documento rippo kokka*. Tokyo: Chuo koron shinsha.

Yoshida, Reiji. (2005, 21 September). "Koizumi to Steer New Lawmakers Clear of Factions." *Japan Times*, online edition. Retrieved January 24, 2008, from search.japantimes.co.jp/cgi-bin/nn20050921a6.html.

Young, Iris Marion. (2002). *Inclusion and Democracy*. Oxford: Oxford University Press.

The Contributors

Dyron Dabney is assistant professor in the Department of Political Science at Albion College, Albion, Michigan. His research interests are in areas of political participation, election campaigns and electioneering, and party politics in Japan and the United States.

Eiji Kawabata is assistant professor of political science at Minnesota State University, Mankato. His research focuses on Japanese politics and political economy, as well as the international relations of East Asia. He is the author of *Contemporary Government Reform in Japan: The Dual State in Flux* (2006). His articles have appeared in *Governance*, *Social Science Japan Journal*, and *International Relations of the Asia-Pacific*.

Yuko Kawato is a Ph.D. candidate in political science at the University of Washington. Her dissertation is on US military bases in Asia and local anti-base protests' impact on base policy. She examines anti-base protests in Japan (Okinawa), South Korea, and the Philippines, with special attention to the state–civil society relationship. Previously, she has worked for Robert Pekkanen as a research assistant dealing with Japan's nonprofit organizations.

Ellis S. Krauss is a professor at the Graduate School of International Relations and Pacific Studies, University of California, San Diego. He has published numerous articles in professional journals and seven books on Japanese politics and US-Japan relations, including *Beyond Bilateralism: U.S.-Japan Relations in the New Asia Pacific* (coedited with T. J. Pempel, 2004) and *Broadcasting Politics in Japan: NHK and Television News* (2000). He is currently writing a book and articles with Robert Pekkanen on the Liberal Democratic Party before and after electoral reform.

Robin M. LeBlanc is associate professor of politics at Washington and Lee University, Lexington, Virginia. She is the author of *Bicycle Citizens: The Political World of the Japanese Housewife* (1999). She is currently working on a book titled *Fraternities of the Gut: Manhood, Power, and Ethics in Japanese Local Politics*.

Sherry L. Martin is assistant professor in the Government Department and the Program in Feminist, Gender, and Sexuality Studies at Cornell University. Her work on gender and political participation has appeared in the *Social Science Japan Journal* and the *Journal of Women, Politics and Policy*. During 2007–2008, she is in residence at the Program on US-Japan Relations at Harvard University.

Robert Pekkanen is assistant professor at the Henry M. Jackson School of International Studies and chair of the Japan Studies Program at the University of Washington. He is the author of *Japan's Dual Civil Society: Members Without Advocates* (2006), which received a prize from the Japan Nonprofit Research Association and was also published in Japanese translation by Bokutakusha Press as *Nihon no shimin shakai no nijyuu kouzou* (2007). His articles have appeared in such professional journals as the *American Political Science Review*, *British Journal of Political Science*, and *Journal of Japanese Studies*.

Gill Steel is assistant professor in the Department of Social Psychology, Graduate School of Humanities and Sociology, University of Tokyo. Previously, she was a COE research fellow at the University of Tokyo Graduate Schools of Law and Politics. She has published articles on Japanese public opinion, voting behavior, and the media and politics.

Naoko Taniguchi is assistant professor in the Department of Sociology, Teikyo University, Tokyo. In 2004 she was a visiting scholar in the Department of Political Science, University of Michigan, and in 2005 was a visiting scholar at the Graduate School of International Relations and Pacific Studies, University of California, San Diego. She has published articles on political behavior, electoral politics, and political methodology in the *American Journal of Political Science* and several leading journals in Japan.

Robert J. Weiner is assistant professor in the National Security Affairs Department of the Naval Postgraduate School, Monterey, California. He was previously assistant professor in the Government Department at Cornell University. His research focuses on Japanese politics and on party, electoral, and legislative politics in established democracies.

Index

Abe Fellowship, 36, 80, 209
Accountability, xii, 2, 3, 4, 8, 15, 40–41, 59, 131, 218, 219; bureaucracy and, 105–107, 108, 116, 119, 121; definition of, 11–12; increased, 34; laws and, 106, 108; of NPOs, 207, 208
Activism, 138; consumer, 131; grassroots, 133, 144–145, 146, 176, 178, 182, 184, 208, 216, 217
Administrative Procedural Law, 2
Administrative reform, xii, 1, 6, 22, 89, 126, 131, 217; NPO Law and, 197
Administrative Reform Committee, 197
Administrative Reform Council (ARC), report, 114, 115
Advocacy: civil society groups and, 194, 208; NPOs and, 204, 205, 207, 208
Akarui Senkyo Suishin Kyokai (Society for the Promotion of Clean Elections) surveys, 83, 84, 90
Akeboshi, Jiro, 180
Alvarez, R. Michael, 94
American Council of Learned Society, 36, 209
Arai, Hiroyuki, 54
ARC. *See* Administrative Reform Council
Asahi Shimbun, 84, 89, 132, 179, 180, 217
Asahi Shimbun Company, 80
Autonomy, 7, 181
Autonomy principle, 179, 180, 185, 189; downside of, 184; referendum association and, 183–184

Baba, Akihito, 179
Balloting, 13, 22
Banaszak, Lee Ann, 183
Basic Law for Gender Equality, 133
Bifurcation, in political system, 215–216
Bribery, 181, 182
Broadbent, Jeffrey, 185
Budgets, 107–108
Bureaucracy, xii, 2, 3, 6, 22, 23; accountability and, 105–107, 108, 116, 119, 121; capability of, 107–108, 116, 119, 121; changes in, 115; controlling aspect of, 101–102; cost-consciousness/entrepreneurship and, 102; economy and, 101, 106; government and, 102; LDP and, 176; MPT/elected officials and, 108–110, 111, 112; NPO Law and, 197–198, 206–207; organizations' independence from, 193; policy and, 14, 105, 106; political insulation of, 194; power balance change between politicians and, 114; power of, 217; referendum association and, 181; reform of, 101, 102–103, 118, 119; responsiveness and, 104–105, 108, 116, 119, 121; scandals and, 113; undemocratic aspects of, 103, 107

Cabinet, 3, 14; expansion of, Cabinet Office, 114, 115, 116, 121; positions for hereditary politicians, 72–73, 74, 76; power of, 22
Campaign(ing): Akio Ito's mayoral,

241

186–190; costs, 188; election, law, xi; ethically questionable/illicit, 40; finance reform bill, 15, 214; LDP, 13, 14; programmatic, 214; rules, 13; rural district, 43, 52–55; suburban district, 48–52; urban district, 43, 45–48. *See also* Electoral campaign behavior

Campaign strategy(ies), 5, 47, 48, 49, 50, 59, 152, 156, 163, 164; candidate-centered, 53, 67; *koenkai*-centered, 52, 53, 54, 55; Momotaro-style, 45–46; name recognition and, 51; organization/association based, 53; of outdoor presentations, 51; of pamphlet distribution, 54. *See also* Direct mobilization strategy; Indirect mobilization strategy

Campbell, John, 103

Candidate(s), xi, xii, 13, 22; advantages of, 160; centered campaign strategy, 53, 67; centered prefectural assembly elections, 166; closeness ratio and sincere voting, 165*fig*; costs and, 165, 166; in DPJ, 156–157; effective numbers of, 171*n2*; electoral strength of, 160, 163; experience of LDP, in 1996 elections, 73*tab*; generational replacement of, 63*n10*; handpicked, 178; image of, 46, 50; incentive of, to run for office, 163; in JCP, 157; in LDP, 157; organizational incentives for, 175; partisan affiliations of, 171*n7*; personal preferences of, 62*n3*; political/electoral maturation of, 40, 41; proportional representation and, 81–82; sincerity of, 167; single-member district electoral system and, 81–82; strategies of weaker, 152, 156, 163, 164; underdogs, 161*fig*, 166; underdogs and expected votes, 162*fig*; voters engaged by, 43. *See also* Political life cycle

Centralization, 11, 129

Certification, of NPOs, 204

Change(s): in bureaucracy, 115; Citizen's Party and political system change, 186; demographic, 126, 180, 183; Junichiro Koizumi instituting LDP, 33; pace of, 218–219; in power balance between politicians/bureaucracy, 114; prime minister instituting, 33, 35

Citizen(s): ability for political control of, 94; centrality, 178; expectations of, 219; ideological beliefs of, 83, 84; leadership, 209*n6*; NPOs and, access to policymaking, 193, 194, 196, 199; participation of, 1, 2, 3, 4, 131, 208, 214, 216; policy preferences of, 83, 90*fig*; political participation of, 132; rise of critical, 176, 192; sovereignty, 179

Citizens' movement(s), 7, 175, 185, 216; for referendums, 178, 180, 182. *See also* Referendum Association

Citizen's Network, 133, 171*n7*

Citizen's Party, 179; Akio Ito supported by, 187–190; critical view of, 190–191; independents supported by, 188, 189; political system change and, 186; service of, 189; skills of, 189; volunteerism and, 187–188

Civil Code, 198

Civil society, 193, 216; advocacy organizations and, 194, 208; breakdown of, organizations' activities, 202*fig*; definition of, 209*n1*; groups, xii, 8; groups' research produced, 205, 206*fig*; NPOs and, 195, 207; political opportunities for, organizations, 193; robustness of, 205; small local groups and, 194; state–, relationship, 194, 208; underprofessionalized, organizations, 205, 208

Class conflict, 189

Closeness ratio, 152, 153, 161, 162, 172*n12*; prefectural assembly elections and, 154*fig*, 166; prefectural assembly elections and, by seat magnitude, 168*fig*; prefectural assembly elections, by district urbanness, 169*fig*; simulated district, 164*fig*; sincere candidate and, 165*fig*. *See also* Strategy(ies)

Coalition, xi, 2, 14, 18, 19

Collective belief, 183

Communication, 5, 219; networking for cooperation and, 202; between NPOs and state officials, 193; between public/politicians, 203

Competitiveness, 3, 4, 7, 21, 40–41, 76,

112, 218; definition of, 12; district magnitude and, 167; increased, 34; measure of, 152–153; prefectural assembly elections, 156, 166, 170; prefectural politics and, 151, 152, 159, 160, 161, 166; uncompetitiveness and, in districts, 155*fig*; urbanness and, 169. *See also* Uncompetitiveness
Consumer activism, 131
Contestedness, 167; urbanness and, 169
Continuity, strength of, 219
Corruption, 2, 12, 15, 81, 102, 177, 186, 191; reduction of, 214
Costa Rica system, 63*n*9
Council for Gender Equality, 137
Council on Economic and Fiscal Policy, 3
Cox, Gary W., 159
Creative conservatism, 214
C's, 203, 204
Culture, 214; institutions and, 218
Curtis, Gerald L., 39, 94

Dabney, Dyron, 5, 24, 215
Dahl, Robert, 130
Decentralization, 6–7, 12, 14, 15, 132, 151, 197; decreased, 34; NPO Law and, 198
Defense, 21, 89, 93
Democratic Party of Japan (DPJ), 19, 21, 25, 29, 34, 46, 50, 53, 77, 85, 86, 87, 152; in 1999 election cycle, 156, 157; candidates in, 156–157; coherent policy and, 214; LDP and, shares of prefectural assemblies after 2007 elections, 157, 158*tab*, 159; LDP similarity to, 94; LDP *vs.*, votes in 2000, 2003, 2005 elections, 32*fig*; as a minor party, 156; NPO Law and, 196, 197; NPOs and, 203; party platform of, 88; policy preferences, 2003, of, 91*fig*, 93; prefectural assembly elections and, 157; privatization and, 122*n*7; strengthening of, 35–36; weakness in prefectural assembly elections of, 157, 170
Democratic Socialist Party (DSP), 16
Demographic change, 126, 180, 183
Demographics, of election mobilization, 185
Deregulation, 21, 197

Diet, 2, 12, 13, 14, 15, 22, 24, 34; hereditary politicians and, 65–67, 68–69, 76; ideological self-placement of, members, 86*fig*, 87*fig*; ideological shift in members of, 89; members writing NPO Law, 197; reform, 3; Revised Diet Law, 3; seats, 19, 20*fig*; seats in 2005 election, 31*fig*
Direct mobilization strategy (DMS), 44, 55, 56*fig*; IMS *vs.*, 57–62, 63*n*12; Koichiro Genba and, 54; means used for, 42–43; Noboru Usami and, 45, 46; scale for, 60–62*fig*; Shigefumi Matsuzawa and, 48, 51
District(s): competitiveness/uncompetitiveness and, 155*fig*; heterogeneity, 160–161; magnitude and competitiveness, 167; rural, campaign, 43, 52–55; simulated, closeness ratio, 164*fig*; suburban, campaign, 48–52; Tokyo, 45, 46; urban, campaign, 43, 45–48; urbanness, 167, 168, 169*fig*. *See also* Single-member district electoral system
DMS. *See* Direct mobilization strategy
Doko, Toshio, 110
Domoto, Akiko, 200, 209*n*6
Downs, Anthony, 83, 88, 94
DPJ. *See* Democratic Party of Japan
Duverger, Maurice, 21
Duverger's law, 159, 160, 166, 167

Economic Planning Agency survey, of NPOs, 207
Economy, 102, 111, 117; bureaucracy and, 101, 106; development of, xi; government intervention in, 120; growth of, 183; independence of, 191; liberalization of, 21; revitalizing local, 132; young, types (*wakai keizaijin*), 178
Education: about grassroots activism, 184; political, for women, 128, 133, 146
Effectiveness, 107, 119
Efficiency, 107, 108, 121
Election 2005, 26–31, 32*fig*, 33
Election Campaigning, Japanese Style (Curtis), 39
Electoral campaign behavior, 39, 42, 55, 56*fig*; factors in, 57; IMS and, 58–59.

See also Koichiro Genba; Noboru Usami; Shigefumi Matsuzawa
Electoral movements, antiestablishment, 177
Electoral reform, xii, 1, 2, 4, 5, 6, 15, 17–22, 24–26, 40, 42, 53, 58, 82, 92, 131, 214, 215; NPOs and, 196; politics affected by, 94; voters, 92; women and, 126, 138–139
Electoral system, xi, 13, 56; prereform, 11–17; rivalry in, 13–14; women and, 138, 139. *See also* Electoral campaign behavior; Electoral reform; Multimember districts; Representation; Single-member district electoral system
Elite(s), 4, 5, 213, 218; choices for national, 176; leaders chosen by unaccountable, 178; seeking votes, 175
EMILY'S List, 133
Emotions, 185
Emperor, 89
Environment, global, 189
Ethics, 40, 181, 182, 217
Experience, value of, 51

Faction(s), 13, 14, 22, 23, 26, 69; Hashimoto, 27; Kamei, 27, 28; Mori, 27, 28; Tanaka, 27; weakening of, 24
Fair Trade Committee, 186
Fairness, 5, 7, 81, 145, 218
50 Net, 128
FILP. *See* Fiscal Investment and Loan Program
Finances: hereditary politicians and local, 75*tab*, 77; hereditary politicians' influence on local, 75*tab*, 77; reform bill for campaign, 15, 214; voters and, 132
Financial support (*kaban*): hereditary politicians and, 65, 68, 74
Fiscal Investment and Loan Program (FILP), 27
Flanagan, Scott C., 130
Foljanty-Jost, Gesine, 132
Freedom, 88; of information statutes, 151, 216
Friends, politics and making, 189, 191
Fukuda, Yasuo, 35

Genba, Koichiro: DMS, 54; IMS *vs.* DMS analysis for, 57–62, 63*n12*; political independence of, 52; running in 1993, 1996, 2000 elections, 42, 44, 52–55, 56*fig*, 62*n7*, 62*n8*, 63*n9*
Government: bonds, 120; bureaucracy and, 102; coalition, xi, 2; failure in providing social services, 200; financial growth of local, 75*tab*; financial transfers from national to local, 74, 77, 78, 130; funding of NPOs, 194–195, 205–206, 207; Hanshin-Awaji earthquake and inadequate, efforts, 196; hereditary politicians and revenue of local, 74*tab*; intervention in economy, 120; local, 151; monitoring process of, 3; NPOs and local, 201; privatization of, corporations, 101; Tokyo Metropolitan, survey, 201, 204, 205; women and local, 125, 126*fig*, 127, 129, 132–133, 134, 135, 136*tab*, 137, 138, 145, 146. *See also* Prefectural assembly elections; Prefectural politics
Grants, special local, 75
Grassroots activism, 146, 176, 178, 182, 208, 216, 217; education about, 184; women's, 133, 144–145
Green Forum, 171*n7*
Guttsman, W. L., 80*n1*

Hadley, Charles D., 139
Hanshin-Awaji earthquake: inadequate government relief efforts after, 196; volunteers after, 128
Hashimoto, Ryutaro, 2, 27, 101, 108, 111, 113–116, 119, 120–121
Hashimoto Reform, 108, 113–116, 120–121
Hatoyama, Yukio, 209*n7*
Hereditary politicians, 5, 25; advantages for, 70–71, 73, 76; Cabinet positions for, 72–73, 74, 76; definition of, 80*n1*; Diet and, 65–67, 68–69, 76; financial support and, 65, 68, 74; forced retirement and, 69; House of Representatives and, 66, 67*fig*; in LDP, 66, 67*fig*, 68–69, 71, 76; local finances and, 75*tab*, 77; measuring impact of, 79*tab*; nonhereditary

politicians *vs.*, victory rates, 70*tab*, 72; revenue of local governments and, 74*tab*; support base of, 65, 72, 73, 77; victory rates for, running first time, 71*fig*, 72, 77
Horie, Takafumi, 29
Horiuchi, Yusaku, 131, 171*n3*
Hosokawa, Morihiro, 23
House of Councilors, 28, 29; opposition parties victories by proportional representation *vs.* multimember districts in House of Councilors, 144*fig*; seats won by opposition parties *vs.* women in, 139, 141*tab*; women elected by proportional representation *vs.* multimember districts in, 142, 143*fig*; women holding seats in, 125
House of Representatives, 17, 28, 105; hereditary politicians and, 66, 67*fig*; percentage of seats gained in, elections 1996, 2000, 2003, 18*fig*; seats won by opposition parties *vs.* women in, 139, 140*tab*; second-generation members of, 66, 67*fig*; women holding seats in, 125
Hsieh, John Fuh-sheng, 152–153

Ichikawa, Taiichi, 68, 74
Ichikawa, Yuuichi, 49, 51
Ichikawa Fusae Kinenkai, 134
Ideology, 5–6, 12, 16, 21, 34, 52, 93; citizens', 83, 84; Diet members', 86*fig*, 87*fig*; Diet members', shifts, 89; of LDP, 86, 87; legislators and, 89; position of voter median and party, 85*fig*; shifts in, 84, 91, 94; structure, 180
Igarashi, Akio, 192
Ikeda, Hayato, 110
Image: of candidate, 46, 50; of prime minister, 22, 23, 35
IMS. *See* Indirect mobilization strategy
Inclusiveness, 3, 5, 7
Incumbency, 50–51, 56, 76, 77, 152
Independence: economic/policy, 191; of Koichiro Genba, 52; of NPOs, 206; organizations', from bureaucracy, 193
Independents: election of, 176, 217; legislator, 171*n7*; supported by Citizen's Party, 188, 189
Indirect mobilization strategy (IMS), 42, 44, 49, 51, 54, 55, 56*fig*; DMS *vs.*, 57–62, 63*n12*; electoral campaign behavior/political life cycle and, 58–59; means used for, 43; Noboru Usami and, 45, 46; scale for, 60–62*fig*
Information Disclosure Law, 3
Inoguchi, Kuniko, 29
Institutional framework, 214
Institutional mechanisms, 3, 4
Institutions: culture and, 218; role of, 1
Insurance: long-term care, 151; work, 196
Ishibashi, Michihiro, 69
Ishida, Takeshi, 214, 215
Ishihara, Shintaro, 45
Ito, Akio, 179; background of, 186–187; Citizen's Party supporting, 187–190; mayoral campaign of, 186–190; network of relationships of, 187
Iwai, Tomoaki, 65
Iwamoto, Misako, 132

Japan Communist Party (JCP), 16, 19, 21, 34, 36*n3*, 46, 94, 156; candidates in, 157; party platform, 88; sincerity/non-strategicness of, 164, 166
Japan Foundation Center for Global Partnership, 36, 209
Japan NPO Center, 203
Japan Self-Defense Forces, 88
Japan Socialist Party (JSP). *See* Social Democratic Party
Japan Society for the Promotion of Science, 192
Japanese Local Autonomy Law, 131, 180, 182, 216
Japanese Local Democracy Project, 171*n4*; database, 171*n3*
Japan-U.S. Security Treaty, 88
JCP. *See* Japan Communist Party
Johns Hopkins Global Civil Society Index, 205
JSP. *See* Japan Socialist Party
Jurisdiction, 116

Kabashima Ikuo Seminar, 70
Kabashima Research Group, 84, 86, 89
Kakuda, Hiroshi, 179, 190; networking of, 189; work of, 188
Kamei, Shizuka, 27, 28
Kanagawa Prefectural Assembly, 48

Kansai Inter-Discipline Studies Inc., 209n9
Kawabata, Eiji, 6, 217
Keiretsu, electoral, 43, 46, 47, 51, 53, 59, 61
Kirksey, Jason R., 139
Kiyomasa, Habara, 80
Kobayashi, Yoshiaki, 69, 88, 99n1
Kodomo Gekijo National Center, 203
Koenkai, 13, 14, 15, 16, 19, 24, 25, 26, 34, 43, 60–61, 68, 215; centered campaign strategy, 52, 53, 54, 55; explanation of, 62n2
Koike, Yuriko, 29
Koizumi, Junichiro, 2, 23–24, 101, 217; general election called by, 28–33; LDP changes instituted by, 33; postal system reform bill of, 26–27, 28, 29; reform by, 117–121; stepping down, 35
Koizumi Reform, 117–121
Krauss, Ellis S., 4, 6, 20, 36, 40, 77, 81, 82, 118, 175, 214, 215, 218

Labor union, 62n6, 179, 203
Law(s): accountability and, 106, 108; Administrative Procedural, 2; Basic, for Gender Equality, 133; Duverger's, 159, 160, 166, 167; election campaign, xi; freedom of information, 132; Information Disclosure, 3; Japanese Local Autonomy, 131, 180, 182, 216; to Promote Decentralization, 3; Public Office Election, 81; Revised Diet, 3; Revised National Administrative, 3; Revised Political Funds Regulation, 3. *See also* Nonprofit Organization (NPO) Law
LDP. *See* Liberal Democratic Party
Leadership, 213; citizens', 209n6; deficit, 15; importance of, 217; inclusive, 218
LeBlanc, Robin M., 5, 7, 40, 138, 147, 216, 217
Legislators: ideological positions of, 89; independent, 171n7; second-generation, in LDP, 66, 67*fig,* 68–69, 71, 76
Leithem, Jessica Louise, 36
Liberal Democratic Party (LDP), xi, 2, 6, 25, 46; in 1999 election cycle, 156, 157; balance within, 34; bureaucracy and, 176; campaigning, 13, 14; candidates' experience in 1996 elections, 73*tab*; candidates in, 157; distribution of posts by, 20, 26; dominance, 7, 18, 19, 129, 130, 175, 214, 218; DPJ and, shares of prefectural assemblies after 2007 elections, 157, 158*tab,* 159; DPJ similarity to, 94; DPJ *vs.,* votes in 2000, 2003, 2005 elections, 32*fig;* hegemony, 177; ideology of, 86, 87; Junichiro Koizumi instituting changes within, 33; NPO Law and, 196, 197; NPOs and, 200, 203; organizational continuity in, 24–26; party platform, 87–88; policy preferences, 2003, of, 91*fig,* 93; prefectural politics and, 151; reforms resisted by, 101, 118; second-generation legislators in, 66, 67*fig,* 68–69, 71, 76; transformation of, 11; victory, 30, 31, 33
Local Assemblies, Handbook of Data on Japanese Women in Political Life (Ichikawa Fusae Kinenkai), 134
Lower House, 2, 22, 29; elections, 41

M + 1 rule, 159, 160, 166, 167, 172n8, 172n15
Madonna Boom, 143
Majority rule, 122n2
Malapportionment, 15, 16, 22, 33
Manin, Bernard, 4
Marginalized groups, expression of, 127
Martin, Sherry L., 5, 7, 15, 40, 216
Massey, Joseph A., 217
Matsuzawa, Shigefumi, 54; DMS and, 48, 51; IMS *vs.* DMS analysis for, 57–62, 63n12; public presentations of, 51; running in 1993, 1996, 2000 elections, 42, 44, 48–52, 56*fig*
McCall, Frances, 36n1
McKean, Margaret A., 20, 36n1, 82
Media: coverage and size of organization, 205; prime minister using, 22–23, 35; voters influenced by, 22–23
Ministry of Finance, 27
Ministry of International Trade and Industry (MITI), 111, 112
Ministry of Posts and Telecommunica-

tions (MPT), 6, 114–115; bureaucracy/elected officials and, 108–110, 111, 112; NTT and, 111–113. *See also* Telecommunications
Ministry of Public Management, Home Affairs, Posts, and Telecommunications (MPHPT),118; definition of, 122*n3*
Minority, 12, 130, 138; right, 122*n2*
MITI. *See* Ministry of International Trade and Industry
Miyazawa, Kiichi, 23
Morals, 185
Mori, Yoshiro, 23, 27, 28, 29
Moriwaki, Toshimasa, 80
MPHPT. *See* Ministry of Public Management, Home Affairs, Posts, and Telecommunications
MPT. *See* Ministry of Posts and Telecommunications
Multimember districts, 40, 139; opposition parties victories by proportional representation *vs.*, 144*fig*; women elected by proportional representation *vs.*, 142, 143*fig*
Multiparty system, 19, 40

Nagai, Eiji, 51
Nagler, Jonathan, 94
Nakasone, Yasuhiro, 2, 22–23, 101, 110–113, 119, 120, 121, 217
Nakasone Reform, 110–113, 120, 121
Name recognition (*kanban*), 65; campaign strategy and, 51
Narita, Ayumi, 80
National Basic Policy Committee, 3
National Tax Agency, 203, 204
Natori, Ryouta, 171*n3*
NCP. *See* New Conservative Party
Nemoto, Kuniaki, 36
Networking, 46, 49, 50, 57, 82, 92, 128, 130, 187, 215; of Akio Ito, 187; for communication/cooperation, 202; of Hiroshi Kakuda, 189. *See also* Citizen's Network
New Conservative Party (NCP), 19
New Frontier Party (NFP), 19, 46, 49, 51, 197
New Komeito Party, 16, 19, 21, 29, 49, 50, 93, 156, 214; party platform of, 88–89; strategy of, 164

New Party Sakigake, 46, 48, 52–53
NFP. *See* New Frontier Party
Niemi, Richard G., 152–153
Nihon Keizai Shinbun, 205
1955 System, xii, 4, 6, 7, 12–17, 22, 84, 110, 120, 214; 2005 system *vs.*, 33–35; conservatism supported during, 216
Nippon Telegraph and Telephone (NTT), 101; MPT and, 111–113; privatization of, 111–113, 120
Nisei, 65
Nobuko Kawashima, 207
Nonprofit Organization (NPO) Law, 3, 8, 182; administrative reform and, 197; bureaucracy and, 197–198, 206–207; decentralization and, 198; Diet members writing, 197; DPJ and, 196, 197; eliminating financial requirements, 198; emergence of, 195–197; impact of, 194; LDP and, 196, 197; number of NPOs after, 199*fig*; number of NPOs increased by, 202; revisions of, 204, 205, 208; scope of groups with legal status expanded by, 193
Nonprofit organizations (NPOs), 8, 132; accountability of, 207, 208; advocacy/monitoring and, 204, 205, 207, 208; certification of, 204; civil society and, 195, 207; communication between state officials and, 193; definition of, 209*n1*; DPJ and, 203; Economic Planning Agency survey of, 207; electoral reform and, 196; Giin Renmei, 204; governance of, 207; government funding of, 194–195, 205–206, 207; increasing citizens' access to policymaking, 193, 194, 196, 199; independence of, 206; LDP and, 200, 203; legal status of, 193, 194, 195–196, 197, 206–207; local government and, 201; NPO Law increasing number of, 202; number of, after NPO Law, 199*fig*; number of, by category, 201*fig*; policymaking and, 194, 199, 200, 204–207, 208, 216; political party access through, 203–204, 208; provision of social services and, 194, 199–200, 207, 208; public interest

and, 197; representation and, 208; social capital created by, 194, 199, 201–202, 207, 208; socially valued purpose of, 198; tax benefits for, 203; tax privileges and, 204; unemployment lowered by, 203; as vote coordination mechanism, 196, 203
North, Christopher T., 80*n3*
NPO Giin Renmei, 204
NPO Support Center, 203
NPOs. *See* Nonprofit organizations
NTT. *See* Nippon Telegraph and Telephone
Nuclear power plant, resistance to, 178–182, 185, 191
Nuclear weapons, 89
Nyblade, Benjamin, 20, 36

Obuchi, Keizo, 23
Ogai, Tokuko, 192
Ogawa, Akihiro, 200
Ogawa, Eiichi, 50
Okada, Katsuya, 29, 37*n6*
Opposition parties: co-opting issues of, 214; seats won by, *vs.* women in House of Councilors, 139, 141*tab*; seats won by, *vs.* women in House of Representatives, 139, 140*tab*; urbanization and, 130; victories by proportional representation *vs.* multimember districts in House of Councilors, 144*fig*; women and, 127, 129, 130–133, 138–139, 142, 143, 145–146, 148*n6*
Organizational support, 50, 51, 57; for candidates, 175; for parties, 175
Organizations: advocacy, and civil society, 194, 208; breakdown of activities of civil society, 202*fig*; campaign strategies and, 53; civil society and large advocacy, 194, 208; independence of, from bureaucracy, 193; limitations of, without legal status, 195–196; media coverage/impact and size of, 205; member participation of, 208; political opportunities for civil society, 193; underprofessionalized civil society, 205, 208. *See also* Nonprofit organizations
Ota, Hiroko, 200
Otake, Hideo, 82

Ozawa, Eichi, 51

PARC. *See* Policy Affairs Research Council
Park, Cheol Hee, 82
Party(ies): convention, 13; dominance of one, 215; endorsement, 52; ideological positions shifting in, 84; NPOs and access to political, 203–204, 208; organizational incentives for, 175; platforms, 21, 40, 82, 87–93; position of voter median and, ideologies, 85*fig*; positions, 5–6; programmatic, 214
Pekkanen, Robert, 4, 6, 8, 20, 36, 40, 77, 81, 82, 118, 132, 138, 175, 205, 214, 218
Pempel, T. J., 214
Philosophy, political, 191
Pluralism, 4, 5, 7, 8, 16; decreased, 34; definition of, 12
Policy: Affairs Research Council (PARC), 14, 15, 16, 25; bureaucracy and, 14, 105, 106; citizens', preferences, 83, 90*fig*; Council on Economic and Fiscal, 3; DPJ and coherent, 214; DPJ, preferences, 2003, 91*fig*, 93; foreign, 89; independence, 191; LDP, preferences, 2003, 91*fig*, 93; National Basic, Committee, 3; preferences, 87–93; related research, 206*fig*; security, 21, 35, 89; voters influenced by, issues, 92, 98*tab*, 99*n6*
Policy Affairs Research Council (PARC), 14, 15, 16, 25
Policymaking, 16, 22, 115; bottom-up, 7, 12; NPOs and, 194, 199, 200, 204–207, 208, 216; NPOs and citizens' access to, 193, 194, 196, 199
Political consciousness, 175–176
Political life cycle, 40–41, 55, 56, 57; IMS and, 58–59
Political News Department, 84
Political system: bifurcation in, 215–216; Citizen's Party and change in, 186; reforms made full use of by, 213
Politics: antiparty, 179, 191; changing of national, 175; clientelist, 2, 215; electoral reform affecting, 94; grass-

roots level, 6, 7; higher faith/higher engagement in, 131; interest group, 188, 189; issue-based, 214; local, 6, 7, 131; local and national, 176; making friends and, 189, 191; money-based, 15, 81, 177, 178, 181, 182, 183, 185; "not in my backyard," 180; patron-client oriented, 177, 191; women participating in, xii, 7, 34, 127, 216. *See also* Prefectural assembly elections; Prefectural politics
Polls, 2
Population density, 148*n14*; women in office and, 133–138
Postal insurance, 27, 117, 119
Postal savings, 27, 109, 117, 119–120
Postal system: Koizumi, reform bill, 26–27, 28, 29; privatization of, 26–27, 30, 33, 115, 117, 118, 119, 120–121; *zoku* and, 27, 109
Postmasters, 115, 122*n4*
Postreform, 22–26, 144, 175
Posts, distribution of, 20, 26
Postwar period, xi, xii, 6, 13
Power: balance, 2; struggle, 6
Predictions, long-term, 218
Prefectural assembly elections, 153, 155; candidate centered, 166; closeness ratio, 154*fig*, 166; closeness ratio by district urbanness, 169*fig*; closeness ratio, by seat magnitude, 168*fig*; competitiveness/noncompetitiveness and, 156, 166, 170; DPJ and, 157, 170; LDP/DPJ shares in 2007, 157, 158*tab*, 159; strategies and, 166
Prefectural politics: competitiveness/ uncompetitiveness and, 151, 152, 159, 160, 161, 166; LDP and, 151
Prime minister, 3, 6, 11, 12, 13; changes instituted by, 33, 35; image of, 22, 23, 35; influence of, 22–24, 33, 116, 119; reform lead by, 101, 102–103; using television, 22–23, 35; weak position of, 14, 15, 16, 217
Privatization: DPJ and, 122*n7*; of government corporations, 101; of NTT, 111–113, 120; of postal system, 26–27, 30, 33, 115, 117, 118, 119, 120–121
Proportional representation, 17–18, 19–21, 22, 25, 30, 39, 41, 53, 55, 134, 139, 196; candidates and, 81–82; opposition parties victories by, *vs*. multimember districts in House of Councilors, 144*fig*; single-member district electoral system *vs*., 31*fig*; women and, 142, 146; women elected by, *vs*. multimember districts in House of Councilors, 142, 143*fig*
Przeworski, Adam, 4
Public Office Election Law, 81
Public opinion, xi

Quality of life, 183

Ramseyer, J. Mark, 36*n1*
Realignment, 154, 156
Recession, 2, 15
Redistricting, 175
Reed, Steven R., 69, 80, 159
Referendum Association, 179; autonomy principle and, 183–184; bureaucracy and, 181; formation of, 182; hierarchy/exclusiveness/secrecy in, 180; women and, 185
Reform(s), 81, 219; 1994 electoral, 39; of bureaucracy, 101, 102–103, 118, 119; campaign finance, 15, 214; Diet, 3; fiscal, xii; fundamental problem with, 120; Hashimoto, 108, 113–116, 120–121; Koizumi, 117–121; LDP resisting, 101, 118; Nakasone, 110–113, 120, 121; officeholding women and, 134, 138, 142, 145, 147; pension, 29; politicians/voters making full use of, 213; postal system, bill, 26–27, 28, 29; prime minister leading, 101, 102–103; success of, 214, 215; women's success increase after, 144. *See also* Administrative reform; Electoral reform
Representation, xii, 3, 15, 145; definition of, 4, 11; descriptive, 5; equality of, 33; NPOs and, 208; substantive, 5. *See also* Electoral system; Proportional representation
Research: civil society groups', produced, 205; Kabashima Research Group, 84, 86, 89; Policy Affairs Research Council (PARC), 14, 15, 16, 25; policy-related, produced by

group, 206*fig*; Social Science Research Council, 36, 209
Responsiveness, xii, 3, 5, 40, 83, 94, 131; bureaucracy and, 104–105, 108, 116, 119, 121
Revised Diet Law, 3
Revised National Administrative Law, 3
Revised Political Funds Regulation Law, 3
Rhetoric, 177, 191; of local veto, 181
Right to say no, 179, 181, 184, 216
Rincho, 110, 112, 113, 114
Rivals, friendly, 53
Rural interest, 2, 5, 7, 13, 15, 16, 22, 32, 35–36, 43, 52–55, 216; women and, 128, 133–138, 139–145

Saito, Jun, 171*n3*
Saito, Yuuki, 51
Sakigake Party, 196
Sato, Iwao, 200, 209*n6*
Scandals, 2, 15, 177; involving bureaucrats, 113
Scheiner, Ethan, 20, 36, 82, 171*n3*, 176
Schmidt, Carmen, 132
SDP. *See* Social Democratic Party
Seat magnitude, prefectural assembly election closeness ratio by, 168*fig*
Second Provisional Administrative Commission. *See* Rincho
Security: Japan-U.S. Security Treaty, 88; policy, 21, 35, 89; United Nations Security Council, 89
Seikatsu Club Consumer Cooperative Union, 146
Self-determination, 7, 177, 191; dignity of, 183
Seniority system, 69
Shingikai, 3
Shinsei Party, 48, 50
Shinzo, Abe, 35, 217
Shokei Arai, 45
Single nontransferable vote (SNTV) system, 13, 21, 24, 25, 67, 68, 70, 138, 139, 142, 148*n17*, 154, 167, 196
Single-member district electoral system, 17–18, 19–20, 25, 30, 35, 39, 40, 41, 53, 55, 59, 71, 77, 134, 142; candidates and, 81–82; proportional representation *vs.,* 31*fig*; two-party system and, 76; voters and, 21–22, 32*fig*

SNTV. *See* Single nontransferable vote system
Social capital: bonding *vs.* bridging and, 202; NPOs creating, 194, 199, 201–202, 207, 208
Social Democratic Party (SDP), 15, 16, 19, 34, 46, 84, 94, 196; party platform, 88
Social Science Research Council, 36, 209
Social services, 216; government failure in providing, 200; NPOs providing, 194, 199–200, 207, 208
Society for the Humanities (Cornell University), 8
Sociodemographic variables, 92
Soka Gakkai, 49–50, 61, 203
Specialization, 14, 24, 36*n1*
Steel, Gill, 5–6, 15, 21, 40, 131, 214
Stokes, Susan C., 4
Strategic entry theory, 163, 170
Strategy(ies): JCP not, oriented, 164, 166; Momotaro-style campaign, 45–46; of New Komeito Party, 164; prefectural assembly elections and, 166; success of, 183; of weaker candidate, 152, 156, 163, 164. *See also* Campaign strategy(ies); Closeness ratio; Direct mobilization strategy; Indirect mobilization strategy
Strøm, Kaare, 26
Subgovernment, 102
Suburban interests, 48–52
Support base (*jiban*), hereditary politicians and, 65, 72, 73, 77
Supporters' list (*meibo*), 187
Suzuki, Zenko, 110

Takahira, Shoji, 203
Takebe, Tsutomu, 28
Takenaka, Heizo, 118
Takeshita, Noboru, 23
Tanaka, Kakuei, 27, 78, 110, 186
Taniguchi, Masaki, 80
Taniguchi, Naoko, 5, 215
Tatebayashi, Masahiko, 36
Tax(es), 6, 75, 80*n4*, 89, 90; benefits for NPOs, 203; consumption, 99*n1*; National Tax Agency, 203, 204; privileges and NPOs, 204
Telecommunications, 109, 111–113. *See*

also Ministry of Posts and Telecommunications
Television, influence of, 22–23, 35
Tokyo, districts, 45, 46
Tokyo Foundation, 171*n3*
Tokyo Metropolitan Government's survey, 201, 204, 205
Trust, 1, 202
Tsujinaka, Yutaka, 209*n1*
Tufte, Edward, 130
Two-party system, 19, 21, 40, 76, 84, 94, 167, 214; single-member district electoral system and, 76

Uncertainty, 163
Uncompetitiveness, 14, 15, 167, 215, 216; competitiveness and, in districts, 155*fig*; prefectural assembly elections, 156, 166, 170; prefectural politics and, 151, 152, 159, 160, 161, 166; prevalence of, 170. *See also* Competitiveness
Uncontestedness, 167; urbanness and, 169
Unemployment, NPOs lowering, 203
United Nations Security Council, 89
United States Congress, 67–68
Urban interests, 16, 22, 29–30, 35, 43, 45–48; factors in, 128; women and, 133–138, 139–145, 146
Urbanization, opposition parties and, 130
Urbanness: competitiveness and, 169; contestedness and, 169; district, 167, 168; district and prefectural closeness ratio, 169*fig*; uncontestedness and, 169
Usami, Noboru, 54; DMS and, 45, 46; IMS and, 45, 46; IMS *vs.* DMS analysis for, 57–62, 63*n12*; running in 1993, 1996, 2000 elections, 42, 44–48, 56*fig*

Veto power, 34
Volunteerism, 128–129, 138, 196; Citizen's Party and, 187–188; after Hanshin-Awaji earthquake, 128
Vote(s), 12; candidate underdogs and, 162*fig*; elite seeking, 175; LDP *vs.* DPJ, in 2000, 2003, 2005 elections, 32*fig*; NPOs and, 196, 203. *See also* Single nontransferable vote (SNTV) system
Voter(s), 2, 59, 218; candidates engaging, 43; contact with, 13, 45–46, 51, 54; decreasing, turnout, 215, 217; electoral reform and, 92; finances and, 132; indifference of, 69, 81, 93; median, 21; mobilization of, 13, 14, 21, 25, 40, 43–44; parties' ideologies and position of, median, 85*fig*; per seat ratios, 173; policy issues' influences on, 92, 98*tab,* 99*n6*; reforms made full use of by, 213; single-member district electoral system and, 21–22, 32*fig*; support from, 43; television influencing, 22–23; turnout of, 131; unaligned, 176; urban, 30, 32

Washida, Koji, 186
Welfare, 90, 93
Wildavsky, Aaron, 167
Winning, 157, 160, 163
WINWIN, 133, 146
Women: centers, 146; elected by proportional representation *vs.* multimember districts in House of Councilors, 142, 143*fig*; election cycle after World War II and, 147*n4*; electoral reform and, 126, 138–139; electoral system and, 138, 139; grassroots activism of, 133, 144–145; House of Councilors seats held by, 125; House of Representatives seats held by, 125; increase in success for, in postreform period, 144; local government and, 125, 126*fig,* 127, 129, 132–133, 134, 135, 136*tab,* 137, 138, 145, 146; opposition parties and, 127, 129, 130–133, 138–139, 142, 143, 145–146, 148*n6*; political challenges for, 129–130; political education for, 128, 133, 146; political participation of, xii, 7, 34, 127, 216; population density and officeholding of, 133–138; proportional representation and, 142, 146; referendum association and, 185; reforms and officeholding, 134, 138, 142, 145, 147; representation on subnational assemblies of, 125, 126*fig,* 127, 129, 133,

135, 136*tab,* 137, 138, 145, 146; rural interests and, 128, 133–138, 139–145; seats won by opposition parties *vs.,* in House of Councilors, 139, 141*tab*; seats won by opposition parties *vs.,* in House of Representatives, 139, 140*tab*; status of, 89; suffrage movements of, 183; urban interests and, 133–138, 139–145, 146

Woodall, Brian, 82

World War II, 101, 103; women and first election cycle after, 147*n4*

Yamada, Masahiro, 82
Yomiuri Shimbun, 2, 84, 86, 171*n7*
Young, Iris Marion, 3

Zoku, 14, 15, 16, 24, 25, 26; politicians, 102, 114, 115, 116, 117; postal, 27, 109

Zōhan, 28

About the Book

WIDESPREAD DISSATISFACTION IN JAPAN IN THE 1990S SET the stage for numerous political reforms aimed at enhancing representation and accountability. But have these reforms in fact improved the quality of Japanese democracy? Through the lens of this question, the authors explore contemporary Japanese politics at the national, local, and grassroots levels. Their systematic analysis of when and how citizens attempt to create and use new opportunities to articulate political interests offers insights not only on the current state of Japanese democracy, but also on the dynamics of political behavior overall.

Sherry L. Martin is assistant professor of government at Cornell University. **Gill Steel** is assistant professor in the Department of Social Psychology at the University of Tokyo.